FINANCING AFRICAN DEVELOPMENT

FINANCING AFRICAN DEVELOPMENT

Edited by Tom J. Farer

THE M. I. T. PRESS
Massachusetts Institute of Technology
Cambridge, Massachusetts

FOREWORD

The authors of the essays collected here, like their colleagues in the M.I.T. Fellows in Africa Program, have experienced a compelling sense of personal identification with the aspirations of the governments and peoples with whom they have worked. To me, this has been one of the most gratifying aspects of the Program. The concern of the Fellows for their host countries is understood by all who know them, and it is well evidenced here in their thoughtful and critical analyses of problems confronting Africa in its determined pursuit of economic development. I want to thank those Fellows who found time over and above their work to write and rewrite these papers so that others might benefit from their experience.

The gratitude of both the authors and myself goes to Tom Farer, who was willing to leave the familiar environs of the law to serve as editor of a collection of papers concerned primarily with economic and financial questions. His assistance to the authors in matters of both form and substance, as they converted their Conference papers into these essays, was invaluable. Both he and the authors have, of course, expressed their private views, not those of the countries in which they have worked, nor those of the M.I.T. Fellows in Africa Program or its supporting organizations.

The editor's, the authors', and my own thanks are due Mrs. Scott

R. Lowden for the many hours she has spent typing the papers and assisting in the preparation of this volume.

Finally, I should like to express my appreciation to all those associated with the Program who participated in the summer Conference and who helped in many ways to make it a meaningful experience.

CARROLL L. WILSON

Cambridge, Massachusetts
February 1965

CONTENTS

vii

FINANCING AFRICAN DEVELOPMENT

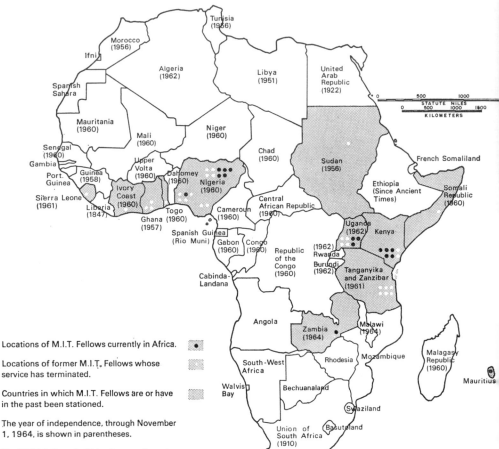

Tunisia
(1956)

Morocco
(1956)

Ifni

Spanish
Sahara

Algeria
(1962)

Libya
(1951)

United
Arab
Republic
(1922)

Mauritania
(1960)

Mali
(1960)

Niger
(1960)

Chad
(1960)

Sudan
(1956)

French Somaliland

Senegal
(1960)

Gambia

Port.
Guinea

Guinea
(1958)

Upper
Volta
(1960)

Dahomey
(1960)

Nigeria
(1960)

Ethiopia
(Since Ancient
Times)

Somali
Republic
(1960)

Sierra Leone
(1961)

Ivory
Coast
(1960)

Liberia
(1847)

Togo (1960)

Ghana
(1957)

Cameroun
(1960)

Central
African Republic
(1960)

Uganda
(1962)

Kenya

Spanish Guinea
(Rio Muni)

Gabon
(1960)

Congo
(1960)

Republic
of the
Congo
(1960)

(1962)
Rwanda

Burundi
(1962)

Tanganyika
and Zanzibar
(1961)

Cabinda-
Landana

Angola

Zambia
(1964)

Malawi
(1964)

South-West
Africa

Rhodesia

Mozambique

Malagasy
Republic
(1960)

Mauritius

Walvis
Bay

Bechuanaland

Swaziland

Union of
South Africa
(1910)

Basutoland

STATUTE MILES
0   500   1000
0   500   1000   1500
KILOMETERS

Locations of M.I.T. Fellows currently in Africa.

Locations of former M.I.T. Fellows whose
service has terminated.

Countries in which M.I.T. Fellows are or have
in the past been stationed.

The year of independence, through November
1, 1964, is shown in parentheses.

The M.I.T. Fellows in Africa Program is made
possible through a grant of the Ford Foundation.

INTRODUCTION:
THE M.I.T. FELLOWS IN AFRICA PROGRAM

The authors of the essays collected here have all been members of the M.I.T. Fellows in Africa Program. This Program was conceived in January 1960 as a means for bringing well-trained, working-level assistance to African development institutions at a time of acute need. The aim is to help a few African governments by recruiting to their service exceptionally able young men whose education is directly relevant to problems facing these governments. A corollary objective is to expose young Americans of exceptional promise to line operating experience within such African institutions in the belief that (a) such men and their wives will present a favorable image of young Americans today, (b) they will mature rapidly through responsible action in the actual business of economic or institutional planning and development, and (c) upon completing a two-year tour in Africa they will form an unusual pool of talent for meeting the manifold needs of the United States in its role toward emerging Africa.

An observer of the M.I.T. Fellows working in Africa recently remarked: "I think the aspect of the program which impressed me most was that the Fellows, rather than being in a sheltered advisory or consulting relationship, are working in positions of operational responsibility as subordinates, obliged to produce and be evaluated on their production." It is this direct employment relationship of the Fellows to a ministry or development corporation in Africa that distinguishes the Program.

The M.I.T. Management Fellows are selected from among men who have completed the two-year program of graduate study leading to the Master's degree at the M.I.T. Sloan School of Management or at other schools such as the Harvard Graduate School of Business Administration. Typically, their education includes a first degree in science, engineering, or economics, followed by intensive graduate study in economics, statistics, accounting, finance, production, marketing, and organization. Since 1960, thirty-three Management Fellows have served or are now serving two-year tours in twelve different governments.

The M.I.T. Law Fellows have rendered useful service in situations in which new and changing problems confront African governments in the revision of laws, the preparation of legal reports, and the development of policies and negotiating positions on a wide range of issues from trade agreements to investment guarantees. Law Fellows are chosen from among leading graduates of the three-year LL.B. programs at the Harvard or Yale Law School. Most of them have also served as assistants to judges of high United States courts or have done equivalent work subsequent to receiving their LL.B.

Management Fellows are identified in the list that follows by (M) for M.I.T. men and (HM) for those from Harvard. The Law Fellows are designated by (HL) from Harvard Law School and (YL) from Yale Law School. The places and institutions in which M.I.T. Fellows have served are listed below the men's names. An asterisk marks those who have completed their tours and have returned to the United States as of February 1965.

Ghana

Robert W. Norris* (M)
National Investment Bank
Accra

Douglas A. Scott* (HM)
Office of the Planning Commission
Accra

Scott M. Spangler* (HM)
National Investment Bank
Accra

Ivory Coast

Archibald S. Alexander, Jr.*
  (HL)
Présidence Cour Suprême
Abidjan

Kenya

Michael W. Christian (HL)
Office of the Legal Secretary
East African Common Services
  Organization
Nairobi

Michael G. Dixon (HM)
The Treasury
Nairobi

Mark Hoffman, Jr. (HM)
East African Common Services
  Organization
Nairobi

John N. Knapp (HM)
Ministry of Commerce and Industry
Nairobi

John R. Lyman (M)
East African Railways and Harbours
Nairobi

John R. Rockart* (HM)
Finance Division
East African Posts and Telecommunications Administration
Nairobi

Michael Roemer* (M)
Development Division
The Treasury
Nairobi

Mauritius

Robert W. Norris (M)
Development Bank of Mauritius
Port Louis

Nigeria

Christopher J. Armstrong* (YL)
Office of the Director of Public
  Prosecutions
Government of Eastern Nigeria
Enugu

D. Nicholas Carter*(M)
Rockefeller Brothers Fund
Lagos

William R. Cotter* (HL)
Office of the Attorney General
Government of Northern Nigeria
Kaduna

Kurt B. Eckrich (HM)
Nigerian Industrial Development Bank
Lagos

C. Davis Fogg* (M)
Ministry of Economic Planning
Government of Eastern Nigeria
Enugu

John S. Glass* (M)
Ministry of Economic Planning
Government of Northern Nigeria
Kaduna

Douglas R. Gustafson* (M)
Investment Company of Nigeria
Lagos

William L. Hooper* (M)
The Treasury
Government of Western Nigeria
Ibadan

William P. Mott* (M)
Finance Division
Ministry of Finance
Government of Northern Nigeria
Kaduna

Robert C. Musser (M)
Ministry of Animal and Forest Resources
Government of Northern Nigeria
Kaduna

Walter L. Ness (M)
Ministry of Finance
Government of Northern Nigeria
Kaduna

Charles H. Olmstead* (M)
Investment Company of Nigeria
Lagos

Russell A. Phillips (YL)
Ministry of Finance
Government of Northern Nigeria
Kaduna

David M. Schroedl (M)
Ministry of Economic Planning
Government of Northern Nigeria
Kaduna

Frederick A. O. Schwarz, Jr.*
(HL)
Office of the Attorney General
Government of Northern Nigeria
Kaduna

John B. Sloat (M)
Revenue Division
Ministry of Finance
Government of Northern Nigeria
Kaduna

Sierra Leone

Philip E. Beach, Jr.* (M)
Industries Branch
Ministry of Trade and Industry
Freetown

Somalia

Tom J. Farer* (HL)
Office of the Commanding General
Police Forces of Somalia
Mogadiscio

Sudan

Carroll W. Brewster* (YL)
Office of the Chief Justice
The Judiciary
Khartoum

Tanganyika (Tanzania)

Stephen F. Hall* (M)
Tanganyika Development Corporation
Dar es Salaam

Warren J. Keegan* (HM)
Ministry of Development Planning
Dar es Salaam

Frederick E. Mangelsdorf* (M)
The Treasury
Dar es Salaam

Donald H. Shaw* (M)
The Treasury
Dar es Salaam

James A. F. Stoner* (M)
Ministry of Commerce and Industry
Dar es Salaam

Gilbert P. Verbit* (YL)
Ministry of External Affairs and Defense
Dar es Salaam

Togo

Michael H. Payson* (M)
Bureau de Développement Economique
La Présidence
Lome

Uganda

Mitchell Alland (HM)
Ministry of Commerce and Industry
Kampala

Bruce A. Blomstrom* (M)
Commerce and Industry Division
Ministry of Economic Affairs
Kampala

Jonathan Mallamud* (HL)
Ministry of Justice
Entebbe

Gary A. S. Owen (M)
Ministry of Commerce and Industry
Kampala

Douglas A. Scott* (HM)
Economic Planning and Statistics
    Division
Ministry of Economic Affairs
Entebbe

Scott M. Spangler (HM)
Ministry of Finance
Entebbe

Henry B. Thomas* (M)
Uganda Development Corporation
Kampala

Zambia

Dennis A. Cross (HM)
Planning Division
Ministry of Finance
Lusaka

The M.I.T. Fellows in Africa Program, in which these men have served, is made possible by a grant from the Ford Foundation.

The Summer Conference

Final nominees for Fellowships are chosen from January through March of the year in which they take up their duties in Africa in September. There is little time for special preparation for the conditions of newly independent Africa. While such special preparation as can be obtained is important, candidates for degrees already have a heavy work load in completing their studies by June. Law candidates who are clerking for judges often have a full-time schedule of duties until July. We have concluded that the experience gained by those actually serving in such posts in Africa provides the best teaching material for those about to take up such duties for the first time. In addition, the exchange of experience among those already in active service adds much to their ability to perform.

Such considerations have led to our making a summer Conference a central feature of the Fellows in Africa Program. The first Fellows in 1960 went to their posts without the benefit of such orientation. But at Entebbe, Uganda, in August 1961, the first summer Conference brought together the 1960 men with the 1961 Fellows and wives who were en route to their posts in Africa. The second Conference at Evian-les-Bains, France, in August 1962, included three groups: the new 1962 Fellows, the 1961 group, and the 1960 Fellows who were en route to the United States. The same pattern prevailed for the third Conference, held at Athens in August 1963, and for the most recent ingathering of the M.I.T. Fellows at Palma de Mallorca last August.

The essays collected here are based on selected papers presented at last summer's Conference and subsequently revised on the basis of Conference discussion. The Conference theme was "Financing

Economic Development in Africa." As the essays suggest, discussion ranged widely, embracing, in addition to economic and managerial questions, such fertile sources of controversy as the appropriate political context for and the human cost of forced-march development.

As was true of our previous Conferences, the dialogues were enriched and given sharper focus by the distinguished discussion leaders. Professor James S. Coleman, Director of the African Studies Center, University of California at Los Angeles, spearheaded the session on political problems, focusing particularly on the insistent trend toward single-party states. Dr. Dragoslav Avramovic, a leading economist of the International Bank for Reconstruction and Development, explored the parameters of fiscal strategy for a developing state. He pointed up and elaborated on the major conclusions of the Conference, namely, that viable project identification and implementation often pose greater obstacles to development than inadequate access to financial resources. Dr. Wolfgang Friedmann, Professor of International Law at Columbia University, examined the labyrinthine relationship between law and economic development, with special emphasis on modifications of the structure of international law which are attributable to the effort to channel funds to the developing nations. Mr. Duncan Ndegwa, Permanent Secretary to the Prime Minister of Kenya, and Mr. Peider Könz, Secretary of the Council and Head of the Legal Service, Organization for Economic Cooperation and Development, led a general debate on the value, as investment incentives, of investment-protection agreements between investors and governments and between and among governments. Dr. Jo W. Saxe, Economic Adviser to the Secretary-General, Organization for Economic Cooperation and Development, gave a valuable report, well salted with his insights and observations, on the 1964 United Nations Conference on Trade and Development. Elting Morison, Professor of Industrial Management at M.I.T., drew the Fellows toward an examination of their own experiences — their problems, achievements, and reactions. He served, indeed, as the "conscience of the Conference." Dean Howard W. Johnson of M.I.T.'s Sloan School of Management, in addition to participating in Conference sessions with accustomed vigor, described M.I.T.'s continuing effort to identify areas where it can enlarge its contribution, particularly in terms of manpower resources, to the development process.

The Honorable J. Wayne Fredericks, Deputy Assistant Secretary of State for African Affairs, joined us for the second week of the Conference. While outlining United States policy toward Africa, he provocatively illustrated some of the dilemmas which stubbornly confront the organizers of our foreign policy.

The Essays

The essays collected in this volume do not and could not span the massive and protean subject of the financing of economic development in Africa. They do record the insights (we hope) and, without doubt, the opinions and perspectives of a group of young men possessing somewhat unusual qualifications as observers of the African scene. Although it is uncommon for Americans to serve, in effect, as expatriate civil servants, there are today, as in the past, a very substantial number of Europeans assisting in this capacity.

What perhaps distinguishes the M.I.T. Fellow from most of his European colleagues is the nature of his graduate academic training, which has strongly emphasized business-oriented decision making. This kind of training has proved readily applicable to development problems. It provides the M.I.T. Fellow with a rather distinctive and elaborate methodology, which is yet a flexible instrument because of the powerful *ad hoc* and inductive bias of the case-method pedagogy of his graduate education. Moreover, despite the similar cultural and political environment of Americans and Britons, there are inevitable differences in perspective — or shall we call it predisposition? — which reflect differing national traditions and myths. It has seemed to us likely, therefore, that the American who has worked in an operational capacity for an African government should be able to make a useful contribution to the rapidly expanding corpus of materials designed to illuminate the problems, the opportunities, and the vast hope of contemporary Africa.

CARROLL L. WILSON

PART I

THE FINANCIAL PLANNING OF
ECONOMIC DEVELOPMENT

The first three essays in this section are concerned in varying degrees with specific national development plans. Warren Keegan, an Assistant Secretary in Tanganyika's Ministry of Development Planning from 1962 to 1964, subjects Tanganyika's Five-Year Plan to a critical analysis. His concern is the over-all realism of the financial projections.

Although pursuing a somewhat different objective — an assessment of the realism of debt-servicing projections over the planning period — Douglas Scott's approach is quite similar. He examines the principal assumptions and projections of Ghana's ambitious Seven-Year Plan, noting where optimism in a number of sectors has serious implications for planned debt servicing. While his theme is the evident casualness of the world-wide planning community to the seemingly elemental question of whether a proposed loan structure can really be afforded, he points, along the way, to certain special facets of the Ghanaian situation, including that country's unusually heavy reliance on supplier credits. *Sub silentio*, Mr. Scott assumes, of course, that the funds required for African development will continue to be provided, for the most part, on a loan rather than grant basis. Yet his paper inevitably raises the question of whether, over the long run, what appears to be a loan structure will prove more illusion than reality, if present lending rates and terms are maintained. The author spent two years in Uganda as an Assistant Secretary in the Ministry of Economic Affairs with responsibilities in the area of foreign technical and financial assistance, before going to Ghana to serve as an Economic Officer with the State Planning Commission.

Douglas Gustafson worked in Lagos from 1961 to 1963 for the Investment Company of Nigeria. His essay on the monetary and fiscal background of Nigeria's Six-Year-Plan is more descriptive and historical than analytic; however, it does suggest how, in view of the contemporary monetary environment, the Plan could affect the economy's private sector. But its main objective is to chart the relationship between financial planning and the monetary and fiscal context in which it occurs. Originally, this essay was simply the first part, or background, of a larger piece on the evolution and functioning of Nigeria's securities market. On reflection, it seemed more appropriate to divide the article and place its first section here. The remainder appears among the Part II essays in the area of private investment.

The injection of foreign capital into a developing country's economy places more money into people's pockets, but — at least in the short run — it may have little positive effect on the stock of available consumer goods. Financial planning must confront this potential for inflation. Ghana has both repatriated most of its once large external reserves and borrowed heavily abroad. Moreover, it has emphasized investment in massive projects like the Volta River complex and in other activities which offer little or no immediate return in terms of additional goods and services. The resulting inflation has been aggravated by the relative inelasticity of the food supply and by certain fiscal policies. Robert Norris, formerly with the National Investment Bank in Accra and presently serving as an officer of the Development Bank of Mauritius, analyzes the inflation, with particular emphasis on governmental monetary and fiscal policy, in his essay, which concludes Part I.

1

TANGANYIKA'S¹ FIVE-YEAR (1964–1969) DEVELOPMENT PLAN: SOBER REALISM OR BUOYANT OPTIMISM?

Warren J. Keegan

The Tanganyika Government's Five-Year Development Plan is the first step toward long-term objectives to be reached by 1980. The Plan, which was prepared under the direction of J. Faudon, a French engineer trained in the School of Pierre Masse, is unique in East Africa. It is the first comprehensive plan covering both the public and the private sectors, and the first perspective plan looking well into the future. The income objectives of the Plan are based on target sectoral growth rates and, for the agricultural sector, target levels of physical production. Analysis of world supply and demand was undertaken to support assumptions of average agricultural export prices during the 1964–1970 period.

The Plan has three main long-term (1980) objectives. The first and most important is to raise real per capita income from the present £24 per head to £45. The second goal is to achieve "manpower self-sufficiency." The third is to increase life expectancy from between thirty-five and forty years to fifty years.

The goal of an average life expectancy of fifty years by 1980 is thought by most observers to be not only feasible but likely. The

1 This essay was completed before Tanganyika's name was changed to Tanzania. The old name has been retained here because the Plan was conceived for Tanganyika alone and there is as yet no indication of how, if at all, it will be modified as a consequence of the union with Zanzibar.

11

Population Branch of the United Nations Department of Economic and Social Affairs has suggested, on the basis of mortality trends in Asia and Latin America, that population projections for underdeveloped countries should assume a reduction in mortality sufficient to bring about an annual gain in life expectancy of 0.5 years. If we assume, as did the authors of the 1957 Tanganyika African Census Report, that the average life expectancy of the Tanganyika African population at that time was between thirty-five and forty years, the adoption of the United Nations' benchmark implies that it will be between forty-seven and fifty-two years by 1980.

The goal of manpower self-sufficiency is clearly a long-term objective, as President Nyerere was careful to explain in his speech presenting the Plan to Parliament. He pointed out that during the first Five-Year Plan, the Government Service alone would have to recruit about 500 skilled people from abroad, not including the 1,200 graduate teachers[2] required to fill the Plan's educational objectives.

The most pressing goal, and the one which has captured the imagination of the people, is the objective of doubling real per capita income by 1980. How is this to be achieved? Is it feasible and realistic or, as many observers feel, unrealistic and overly ambitious?[3]

Target Growth and Past Economic Performance

Target Growth

Tables 1 and 2 show the evolution of Tanganyika's economy from 1954 to 1960/62[4] and target rates of growth for the period

---

[2] In May of 1964, there were only twenty African graduates teaching in the country's secondary schools.

[3] Even though most people, including President Nyerere, feel the Tanganyika Plan is ambitious, Sheikh Abeid Karume, the first Vice-President of the Republic of Tanganyika and Zanzibar, on June 6, 1964, promised the 320,000 people of Zanzibar that they "would all be earning £450 by 1966," an income £25 greater than the 1962 U.K. average. This remarkable objective is to be achieved by a three-year Zanzibar development plan prepared by the revolutionary government of Zanzibar. When I questioned an important figure in the revolutionary government about the feasibility of this promise, he replied, "If the Government says it will happen, it will," and eagerly dropped the subject. The Chinese People's Republic has already promised Zanzibar an interest-free loan of £5 million, but this is, unfortunately, only about 1 per cent of the investment required to reach the promised per capita income level.

[4] The Plan adopts the convention of averaging gross domestic product data for

1960/62 to 1980. The Plan, which is based on the premise that Tanganyika's poverty is the result of structural deficiencies, seeks to achieve the over-all target, 6.7 per cent average real growth of gross domestic product, by continuing at a somewhat increased rate the expansion of the marketed output of primary production (6 per cent), while at the same time expanding the industrial and commercial sectors at substantially higher rates (14.8 per cent and 8 per cent respectively) in order to achieve the more balanced economic structure shown in Table 3.

Past Economic Performance

A starting point in evaluating the feasibility of these goals is an examination of Tanganyika's past economic performance and present economic structure. The basic structure of the economy (communications network, people, institutions, etc.) is inherited from the past and will inevitably limit and influence future possibilities. It is true that the Plan calls for a shift in the structure of the economy, and a rapidly increasing development expenditure; but policies take time to become effective, and investment, particularly infrastructure investment (one half of the Plan's target gross investment), frequently requires many years to become productive. As Dr. A. Waterston, World Bank economist and leading authority on development planning, has observed, unrealistic assumptions that substantial improvements in public administration, taxation, and agrarian conditions can be made in a few years are an almost universal characteristic of development plans.[5]

Over 95 per cent of Tanganyika's population of ten million are rural peasant families whose average annual cash income is under £10 per capita. Although an increasing number of these families are participating in the production of cash crops such as cotton, coffee, cashew nuts, tea, and tobacco, the vast majority are subsistence farmers using primitive and backward methods. There are

the period 1960/62 to obtain a fictitious "1961." All target rates of growth are for "1961" to 1970, a nine-year period. The averaging of three years' data does, of course, produce a more representative base year. Unfortunately, however, the convention is misleading, not only to the public, but to the planners themselves. The introduction to the Plan, for example, states that industrial production "will by 1970 be thrice its present level." In fact, the planned increase in industrial production is just short of twofold its present (1964) level.

[5] See A. Waterston, "Planning the Planning under the Alliance for Progress," in *Development Administration: Concepts and Problems*, Irving Swerdlow, ed. (Syracuse: Syracuse University Press, 1963), p. 141.

Table 1
The Evolution of the Gross Domestic Product
(£ Million)

Sectors	Actual 1954 Mone-tary	Sub-sistence	Total	Actual Average 1960/62† Mone-tary	Sub-sistence	Total	Target 1970 Mone-tary	Sub-sistence	Total	Target 1980 Mone-tary	Sub-sistence	Total
Crop Husbandry*	29.6	40.0	69.6	37.7	45.7	83.4	72.2	54.6	126.8	123.4	65.4	188.8
Livestock*	5.9	8.4	14.3	5.9	12.3	18.2	10.6	15.1	25.7	20.9	18.8	39.7
Fishing*	1.3	0.4	1.7	1.3	0.4	1.7	2.1	0.6	2.7	3.3	0.8	4.1
Forest Products*	0.7	1.4	2.1	1.1	1.5	2.6	1.6	1.8	3.4	2.6	2.3	4.9
Mining, Quarrying	3.0	—	3.0	5.2	—	5.2	7.5	—	7.5	10.3	—	10.3
Processing and Manufacturing	5.0	—	5.0	7.4	—	7.4	25.0	—	25.0	84.9	—	84.9
Public Utilities	0.4	—	0.4	1.3	—	1.3	3.7	—	3.7	9.0	—	9.0
Construction	5.6	—	5.6	6.3	—	6.3	18.5	—	18.5	40.0	—	40.0
Transport and Communications	5.7	—	5.7	8.7	—	8.7	17.2	—	17.2	35.8	—	35.8
Distribution	13.1	—	13.1	22.1	—	22.1	44.2	—	44.2	93.5	—	93.5
Rents and Royalties	3.5	—	3.5	8.0	—	8.0	17.0	—	17.0	33.5	—	33.5
Public Administration and Defense	7.5	—	7.5	12.6	—	12.6	25.2	—	25.2	54.4	—	54.4
Other Services	3.9	—	3.9	6.9	—	6.9	15.0	—	15.0	37.2	—	37.2
Total Gross Domestic Product	85.2	50.2	135.4	124.5	59.9	184.4	259.8	72.1	331.9	548.8	87.3	636.1
Population (million)			(8.3)			(9.4)			(11.3)			(14.1)
Per Capita Gross Domestic Product (£)			£16.3			£19.6			£29.3			£45.1

† Primary rural product for the years 1960/62 valued in 1960 prices. Other sectors' product in current prices.
* Not strictly comparable with pre-1960 data because of different sector coverage and valuation conventions.
SOURCE: *Tanganyika Five-Year Development Plan (1964–1969)*.

Table 2
Target Sector Rates of Growth
(Percentage, Compounded)

	1954–1961*			1960/62–1970			1970–1980		
	Mone-tary	Sub-sist-ence	Total	Mone-tary	Sub-sist-ence	Total	Mone-tary	Sub-sist-ence	Total
Crop Husbandry	3.5	1.9	2.7	7.5	2.0	4.8	5.5	1.8	4.1
Livestock	0.0	5.6	3.5	6.8	2.3	3.9	6.9	2.2	4.4
Forest Products	6.7	1.0	3.1	4.3	2.2	3.2	5.0	2.2	3.7
Fishing	0.0	0.0	0.0	5.5	4.6	5.3	4.6	2.9	4.3
Mining and Quarrying			8.2			4.7			3.2
Processing and Manufacturing			5.8			14.8			13.0
Public Utilities			18.0			12.3			9.3
Construction			1.7			12.7			8.0
Transport and Communications			6.2			7.8			7.6
Distribution			7.7			8.0			7.0
Rents and Royalties			12.6			8.7			7.0
Public Administration and Defense			7.6			7.9			8.0
Other Services			8.5			9.0			9.5
Total Gross Domestic Product	5.6	2.6	4.5	8.5	2.1	6.7	7.7	2.0	6.7
Population			1.8			2.1			2.3
Per Capita Product			2.7†			4.6			4.3

* Not strictly comparable because of different sector coverage and valuation conventions introduced after 1960.

† Less about 1 per cent for annual price changes.

SOURCE: *Tanganyika Five-Year Development Plan (1964–1969).*

less than a thousand African-owned tractors in the country, and over half of these have been provided in the past year by a government-subsidized credit scheme. One can travel thousands of miles in Tanganyika and not see a single African farmer using even draft animals.

Agricultural and livestock products account for over half of the gross product and about 80 per cent of export earnings. Industrial activities, including transport, communications, and public utilities have been growing rapidly, yet they still account for under 10 per cent of the country's gross domestic product. Moreover, most industrial activities are controlled by aliens (mainly Asian) whose future in the country is by no means certain, although some of them are becoming citizens.

Table 3
Comparative Structure of Gross Domestic Product
(Percentage)

	Tanganyika Average 1960/62	Typical for Underdeveloped Economies*	Tanganyika Target 1970	Tanganyika Target 1980	Typical for High-Income Economies†
I. *Primary Production*					
All Rural and Mining Activities	60.0	47	50.0	39.0	13
II. *All Industrial Activities*	13.0	20	19.4	26.7	49
Manufacturing and Processing	(4.0)	(11)	(7.5)	(13.3)	(32)
Basic Facilities‡	(5.6)	(5)	(6.3)	(7.1)	(11)
Construction	(3.4)	(4)	(5.6)	(6.3)	(6)
III. *Tertiary Activities*					
Services, Distribution, Rents, and Administration	27.0	33	30.6	34.3	38
Total Gross Domestic Product	100	100	100	100	100

* With per capita income under £44.
† Industrialized countries with per capita income above £280.
‡ Transport, Storage, Communication, and Public Utilities.
SOURCE: *Tanganyika Five-Year Development Plan (1964–1969)*.

Estimates of gross domestic product for the 1954 to 1961 period indicate an annual rise in real per capita income of 1.7 per cent. The basis of this growth was primarily an increase in exports of the main agricultural products. Over a quarter of the gross domestic product during this period was derived from exports which declined 13 per cent in value; thus the physical increase in production was even greater than that reflected by monetary valuation. Fortunately, import prices also declined, so that the over-all terms of trade declined by only 3 per cent as compared to 28 per cent for East Africa as a whole. Owing to the diversity of her exports and the increasing prices for sisal, the main export crop, Tanganyika's terms of trade were reasonably favorable.

Because of the predominance in the economy of agriculture and exports of primary commodities, the gross national product fluctuates with the weather and export prices. Recent economic performance, summarized in Tables 4 and 5, indicates this very clearly.

The growth of the agricultural sector between 1960 and 1963 at current prices was 7.2 per cent. Under the stimulus of the buoyant agricultural sector, manufacturing, construction, and services each exceeded a 10 per cent growth rate. Only the smaller rent and transport sectors grew at less than 8 per cent (see Table 4). Yet agricultural output, the cornerstone of this impressive over-all performance, grew at an average rate of only 1.2 per cent in constant 1960 prices (see Table 5). In fact, the economic growth at current prices over this period was the result of price inflation, and not production increases. Fortunately, the greatest price increases were for primary products sold overseas, and the real wealth of Tanganyika did in fact grow at about 5 per cent per annum during this period.

In detail, what actually happened between 1960 and 1963? Adverse weather conditions in 1961 resulted in a 10 per cent decline in agricultural production. Export prices also declined so that both volume and value of exports fell. Shortages caused internal agricultural prices to rise, so that over-all agricultural output increased at current prices. On the whole, national income showed little gain. In 1962 good weather and rising export prices resulted in a full monetary recovery from the 1961 setbacks. Real agricultural production, however, was still below 1960 levels.

Table 4
Gross Domestic Product at Factor Cost
(at Current Prices)

Industry	1960 (£ Thousand)	1961 (£ Thousand)	1962 (£ Thousand)	1963 (£ Thousand)	% Change 1962–1963	% Average Annual Growth 1960–1963
Agriculture	112,809	114,087	125,096	139,082	+ 12.5	7.2
Mining and Quarrying	5,194	5,476	5,128	4,414	− 13.9	(5.0)
Manufacturing	5,469	6,958	7,853	8,442	+ 7.5	15.6
Construction	4,565	5,840	6,213	6,640	+ 6.9	13.3
Electricity and Water	1,231	1,360	1,485	1,558	+ 4.9	8.2
Commerce	20,931	22,062	25,221	27,599	+ 9.4	9.7
Rent	8,026	8,377	8,782	9,214	+ 4.9	4.7
Transport	8,734	8,585	9,539	9,781	+ 2.5	3.7
Services	18,094	20,759	22,924	24,566	+ 7.2	10.7
Total	185,053	193,504	212,241	231,296	+ 9.0	7.7
Index (1960 = 100.0)	100.0	104.6	114.7	125.0		

SOURCE: 1960–1963 data and percentage change 1962–1963 from *Budget Survey 1964/65* (Dar es Salaam: Tanganyika Government Printer, 1964). Average growth calculated by author.

Table 5
Net Output of Agriculture
(at Constant 1960 Prices)

Sector	1960 Total (£ Thousand)	1961 Total (£ Thousand)	1962 Total (£ Thousand)	1963 Subsistence (£ Thousand)	1963 Monetary Peasant (£ Thousand)	1963 Monetary Estate (£ Thousand)	1963 Total (£ Thousand)	Total % Average Annual Growth 1960–1963
Crop Husbandry	89,083	77,435	85,942	47,262	24,968	19,538	91,768	1.0
Livestock	17,690	18,453	18,384	12,266	5,059	586	17,911	0.4
Forestry	2,636	2,678	2,569	1,563	786	345	2,694	0.7
Fishing	1,599	1,659	1,889	504	1,776	—	2,280	12.6
Total	110,958	100,225	108,784	61,595	32,589	20,469	114,653	1.1
Public Sector	1,851	1,946	2,076				2,205	6.0
Grand Total	112,809	102,171	110,860				116,858	1.2

SOURCE: 1960–1963 data from *Budget Survey 1964/65* (Dar es Salaam: Tanganyika Government Printer, 1964). Average annual growth calculated by author.

The year 1963 saw a major economic advance. The weather was good, and export prices continued to rise (sisal's price increased by almost 50 per cent). Real output in agriculture was up over 5 per cent and exceeded the 1960 record for the first time. Over the three-year period manufacturing increased at an average rate of 7.5 per cent at constant prices, as compared with over 15 per cent at current prices. Constant price data for other sectors are not available.

Table 6 shows gross capital formation by sector since 1960 and the Plan's target gross capital formation. The rise of private sector investment in 1963 is encouraging, and provides some indication of a revival of confidence by private investors. Nevertheless, considering the over-all growth of the economy and savings in recent years and the excellent investment opportunities in many fields such as building construction, the growth of private sector investment has been very disappointing.

Public sector capital formation fluctuated over the 1960–1963 period and has not yet returned to the peak expenditure level of 1961, largely owing to completion of a major project by East African Railways and Harbors. This sector was almost entirely dependent upon external finance, which came mainly from the United Kingdom, the United States, and West Germany. The Central Government spent about 85 per cent of its planned development expenditure of £24 million.

Comparison of Planned Investment and Growth with Past Tanganyika Performance and with Other Countries

Table 7 compares Tanganyika's past growth with the target growth rates of the Five-Year Plan. If the export element of agricultural production is valued at current prices, the over-all and sectoral target growth rates for the Plan are a reasonable extension of the economy's performance over the past three years. However, the current level of export prices is unusually high. Actually, export prices are expected to decline about 15 per cent during the next five years. Planned growth has therefore been based on increases in production. Because of the relative size of the agricultural sector, success in achieving targeted growth for it is essential

Table 6
Total Gross Capital Formation by Sector
(£ Thousand)

Sector	1960	1961	1962	1963	1964–1969 Five-Year Plan Average	Five-Year Plan Total
A. Private:						
Building and Construction	7,022	7,433	7,443	8,325		
Machinery and Equipment	8,027	8,027	7,409	8,371		
Total Private	15,357	15,460	14,852	16,696	23,000	116,000
B. Public:						
Building and Construction	6,725	9,595	8,015	7,883		
Machinery and Equipment	1,099	1,366	1,534	562		
Total Public	7,824	11,061	9,549	8,445	27,000*	133,000*
Grand Total	23,181	26,521	24,401	25,141	50,000	249,000

* Excluding £4 million public sector "self-help" investment; including £7 million central government investment carried forward from the Three-Year (1961–1964) Plan.

SOURCES: 1960–1963 data from Budget Survey 1964/65 (Dar es Salaam: Tanganyika Government Printer, 1964). 1964–1969 data derived from Tanganyika Five-Year Plan (1964–1969).

Table 7
Percentage Rates of Growth in Tanganyika

	1954–1961 (Estimated)	1960–1963 (Estimated)	1960/62–1970 (Planned)
Gross Domestic Product*	3.5%	5.0%	6.7%
Population Growth	1.8	1.9	2.1
Per Capita Product	1.7	3.1	4.6
Key Sectors:			
Agriculture*		5.0	4.5
Manufacturing*		7.5	14.8
Construction*		12.0	12.7
Distribution*		9.7	8.0
Agricultural Production		1.2	4.5

* Internal transactions at constant prices and export transactions at current prices.
Sources: The 1954–1963 percentages derived from data published by the Tanganyika Central Statistical Division and annual Treasury Budget Surveys. The 1960/62–1970 percentages from the Five-Year Development Plan.

to the Plan's over-all income objective. The 6 per cent increase in agricultural production in 1963 is very encouraging, but it will be difficult to maintain, even if prices do not decline. A significant decline in export prices, particularly in the sisal industry, would virtually wreck the Plan's targets. Fortunately, this is not expected, but the disastrous effect a large price drop would have on the Plan underlines the vital importance of stable export prices to a developing country such as Tanganyika.

In evaluating the realism of Tanganyika's Plan, it is useful to compare the targets of 6.7 per cent over-all and 8.5 per cent monetary real-income growth with performance in the rest of the world. Of the sixty-two countries reporting national income statistics to the U.N. for the period 1952–1960,[6] only fifteen achieved an average growth in real income greater than 6.7 per cent. Ten countries — China (Taiwan), the Federal Republic of Germany, Japan, Bulgaria, China (mainland), Czechoslovakia, Poland, Rumania, the U.S.S.R., and Yugoslavia — were recovering from the devastation of World War II, and they exhibit rates of growth that reflect an abnormally low base (in many cases lower than prewar levels), plentiful supplies of skilled manpower, and in most cases large quantities of external aid. Four of the countries received excep-

[6] See *United Nations Yearbook of National Accounts and Statistics, 1962*, p. 311. Some countries reported for the period 1952–1959, others for 1954–1960.

tional supplies of capital and skilled manpower: Algeria from France, and Israel, Jamaica, and Trinidad from Europe and the United States. Venezuelan growth was a result of the enormous postwar oil strike in that country.

A comparison can also be made between Tanganyika's target of 11.1 per cent growth for the processing, manufacturing, and mining sector, and U.N. statistics. Of the forty countries reporting statistics between 1952 and 1960 for this sector, only five — Burma, Jamaica, Korea, Rumania, and Yugoslavia — exceeded the Tanganyika Plan's target growth rate. The Burmese figure can probably be attributed to statistical error, and the Korean, Rumanian, Jamaican, and Yugoslav performances to the postwar conditions already referred to.

Present economic conditions in Tanganyika and postwar conditions in those countries reporting high rates of growth to the United Nations are in some respects similar. Like the high-growth countries in the decade of the 1950's, Tanganyika starts from a low base and receives large amounts of external aid. But the third and probably key factor in the postwar growth countries — skilled manpower — although growing rapidly, is still in very short supply. In May 1964, for example, half of the 1,200 top-level administrative and professional posts in government were held by expatriates. In the private sector, the vast majority of administrative, professional, and skilled jobs are still held by noncitizens and expatriates. The success of the Plan, as President Nyerere emphasized in a recent speech to Parliament, will depend to a very large extent upon how successfully Tanganyika can utilize the skills of noncitizens and expatriates.

Planned Investment Expenditure

Sectoral Allocation of Planned Investment

Table 8 shows that of the total planned investment of £246 million, 53 per cent is to be undertaken by the public sector. Almost half (48 per cent) of the total planned capital formation is to be spent on social (29 per cent), economic (16 per cent), and administrative (3 per cent) infrastructure. Of planned infrastructure investment, 35 per cent (£42 million) is allocated to housing

Table 8
Target Gross Capital Formation in Public and Private Sectors, July 1964–June 1969 (£ Million)

Sector	Central Govern- ment	Local Govern- ment	E.A.C. S.O.*	Private Sector	Total	Percentage of Total
Social Infrastructure	29.0	7.2		33.7	69.9	29.0%
Industry	14.6			44.4	59.0	24.0
Economic Infrastructure	19.6	1.7	18.0		39.3	16.0
Agriculture	27.6	0.9		8.4	36.9	15.0
Commerce	3.6			29.5	33.1	13.0
Administrative Infrastructure	7.6	0.2			7.8	3.0
Total	102.0	10.0	18.0	116.0	246.0	100.0

* East African Common Services Organization (Railways and Harbors, Posts and Telecommunications, Customs and Excise, East African Airways, and a number of small research organizations).

SOURCE: Derived from a table in Volume I of the *Five-Year Development Plan.*

and township development, a surprisingly large amount. The second most important investment sector is industry, where the majority of funds (£36 million) will be spent on manufacturing and construction equipment. Economic infrastructure is third, with most of the funds going into roads (£13.4 million), and railways and harbors (£15.5 million). Agriculture, the economy's most important sector, is a poor fourth with only 15 per cent of planned investment. Commerce and administrative infrastructure receive 13 per cent and 3 per cent, respectively, of investment funds.

The allocation of investment is questionable when measured against the Plan's objectives. If the Plan is to bring about a structural transformation of the economy, why does social infrastructure receive a higher priority than industry and economic infrastructure? The low priority given agriculture (it is to receive only £4 million more than commerce) ignores the vital role which must be played by this sector for many years to come, if Tanganyika is to achieve her aim of rapidly rising incomes.

Sources of Finance

If past levels of capital formation were any guide, the prospects of achieving the Plan's gross capital formation target of £246 million would be very dim indeed. The average gross capital formation required by the Plan is double the 1963 total and will require an annual compound growth of 18.5 per cent in gross capital formation.

The private sector. Private sector confidence is essential if the Plan's private investment objectives are to be achieved. An indication of Government policy toward foreign private investment was provided by the passage in 1963 of the Foreign Investments (Protection) Act, which provides certain guarantees for approved foreign investments in the event of nationalization. This is a step in the right direction, but investors will examine the over-all attitude of the Government and not just a single act. As of June 1964, of over seventy applications for protection under the Act, none has been approved, a phenomenon hardly calculated to inspire investor confidence. Recent attacks against the United States and the United Kingdom in a Government-supported newspaper have not improved the prospects of obtaining private investment from these countries. The confidence of local private investors is extremely important in view of the fact that they are asked to provide three quarters of planned private investment. A local private investment protection act or a clear statement of Government policy on the protection of domestic private investment would encourage confidence. It is a sign of the times that the expression and implementation of such a policy would take a great deal of courage on the part of the Government. The jobs and rising incomes that result from private investment are popular, but the profits which make such investment possible are not.

If the Government succeeds in convincing private investors that their funds are welcome and that they will be allowed to export reasonable profits if they wish to, the private sector investment target of £116 million is realistic, perhaps even slightly conservative.

The public sector. If export prices do not decline significantly and the Government maintains reasonable financial discipline on the growth of recurrent expenditure, the indicated budget surplus (see Table 9) for development expenditure could be realized and perhaps even exceeded. But the indicated local borrowing of £14 million for development is open to serious question. In the whole history of the country, only a few million pounds have been borrowed locally. It is unlikely that the Government will be able to establish the necessary institutions and to encourage the requisite savings in the short period of five years. It is likely, therefore, that about £100 million of external finance will be required to achieve the Central Government development-expenditure target.

The extent to which such funds will be spent during the Plan depends upon both the willingness of external sources to pledge financial support and the capacity of government to take advantage of this support by producing acceptable development projects.

Table 9

*Possible Sources of Central Government Development Finance
as Indicated in the Plan 1964–1969*
(£ Thousand)

Domestic		External		Total
Budget Surplus	Local Borrowing	Loans	Grants	
8,500	14,000	78,911*	8,000	109,411

*Includes £7,411 thousand carried forward from the Three-Year Plan.

The volatility of international politics conceivably may permit Tanganyika to secure adequate financial promises from external sources.

Promises of finance are one thing; actual expenditure is another. Between promise and actuality lies lengthy project preparation and negotiation requiring from one to three years. It is the difficulty of developing viable projects and the time required to negotiate the precise terms of their financing, much more than the feasibility of obtaining external financial commitments, which cast doubt on the realism of planned Central Government developed expenditure. The 1964/65 development estimates, for example, call for the expenditure of £22 million; yet financing for only £8 million of this expenditure has been secured and committed to actual projects. Most of this £8 million will be spent. Perhaps another £5 to £10 million will be negotiated and financed during the coming year, but it is unlikely that anything more than £2 million of this additional amount will actually be spent. Thus, expenditure for 1964/65 will probably result in a shortfall of 50 per cent on the development estimates. Even if the amount of planned five-year Central Government development expenditure is largely pledged by external sources, a shortfall of 25 per cent on planned expenditure would not be surprising in view of programming difficulties.

Table 10
Planned Phasing of Central Government Development Expenditure, 1964–1969*
(£ Thousand)

Estimated Expenditure 1963/64	1964/65	1965/66	1966/67	1967/68	1968/69	Total 1964–1969
7,300	22,089†	16,542	19,712	23,954	27,114	109,411

* Includes ministries and parastatal organizations.

† Includes £14,687 thousand from the Five-Year Development Plan and £7,411 thousand carried forward from the Three-Year Plan.

The Productivity of Capital

The Capital/Output Ratio

In evaluating the feasibility of a development plan, it is necessary to go beyond the question of the feasibility of investment targets to an evaluation of whether planned investment rates will be sufficient to bring about desired increases in income. The answer to this question depends upon the productivity of the capital invested, which can be evaluated in terms of the so-called capital/output ratio. W. W. Rostow, in *The Stages of Economic Growth*,[7] offers the following description of this analytic tool:

Capital/output ratio is the amount by which a given increase in investment increases the volume of output: a rough — very rough — measure of the productivity of capital investment; but since the arithmetic of economic growth requires some such concept, implicitly or explicitly, we had better refine the tool rather than abandon it. In the early stages of economic development, two contrary forces operate on the capital/output ratio. On the one hand, there is a vast requirement of basic overhead capital in transport, power, education, etc. Here, due mainly to the long period over which investment yields its return, the apparent (short-run) capital/output ratio is high. On the other hand, there are generally large unexploited back-logs of known techniques and available natural resources to be put to work; and these back-logs make for a low

[7] W. W. Rostow, *The Stages of Economic Growth* (Cambridge, England: Cambridge University Press, 1960), p. 37.

capital/output ratio. We can assume formally a low capital/output ratio for the take-off period because we are assuming that the pre-conditions have been created, including a good deal of social overhead capital. In fact, the aggregate marginal capital/output ratio is likely to be kept up during the take-off by the requirement of continuing large outlays for overhead items which yield their returns only over long periods. Nevertheless, a ratio of 3:1 or 3.5:1 for the incremental capital/output ratio seems realistic as a rough benchmark until we have learned more about capital/output ratios on a sectoral basis.

The Productivity of Capital in Tanganyika

Limited evidence indicates that the capital/output ratio in Tanganyika over the 1957–1961 period when export prices were relatively stable was in the region of 2.25:1 (see Table 11). This com-

Table 11
The Capital/Output Ratio of Tanganyika, 1957–1961
(£ Thousand)

Year	Monetary Gross Domestic Product†	Estimated Capital Replacement*	Gross Monetary Capital Formation†	Estimated Net Capital Formation
1957	92,941	9,300	24,136	14,836
1958	97,945	9,800	22,720	12,920
1959	106,231	10,600	21,826	11,226
1960	114,447	11,400	25,227	13,827
1961	115,448	11,500	26,080	14,580
1962	123,297	12,300	26,797	14,497

* Represents 10% of monetary gross domestic product.
† Source for these figures is Tanganyika Government Central Statistical Bureau.

Note: Allowing a lapse of one year for investment to become productive, the capital/output ratio for the 1957–1962 period is 2.25:1.

Net Capital Formation, 1957–1961 = £67,389,000
Increase in Monetary Gross Domestic Product, 1957–1962 = £30,356,000

$$\frac{\text{Net Capital Formation}}{\text{Increase in Income}} = \text{Capital/Output Ratio} \qquad \frac{£67,389,000}{£30,356,000} = 2.25$$

pares with ratios of 2.3:1 for India and Malaya, 2.6:1 for Ceylon, and a recent estimate of 2.8:1 for Kenya.

Although the estimated Tanganyika capital/output ratio of 2.3:1 (that is, for every £2.3 of net investment, output increased by £1) is very rough indeed, it is likely that the actual figure is somewhere in the range of 2:1 to 3:1. Empirical sectoral studies in countries where better data exist indicate that the capital/output ratio is low for agriculture, often around 1:1; high, 7:1 to 10:1, for housing; and intermediate, 3:1 to 4.5:1, for manufacturing and processing. One would expect the Tanganyika ratio to be low for the years 1957–1961 because over 60 per cent of the country's gross domestic product during that period was derived from agriculture.

The productive sector receiving the highest investment priority in the new Plan is industry, where target gross capital formation of £60 million is expected to increase production from the present £16.5 to £32.5 million in 1970. Table 12 shows capital/output

Table 12
Industrial Sector Capital/Output Ratio with Gross Sectoral Capital Formation of £60 Million

Assumed Proportion of Net Capital Formation in Planned Gross Capital Formation	Net Capital Formation	Target Increase in Production	Capital/ Output Ratio
%	£ Thousand	£ Thousand	£ Thousand
40	24,000	16,000	1.5 : 1
45	28,000	16,000	1.7 : 1
50	30,000	16,000	1.9 : 1
75	45,000	16,000	2.8 : 1

ratios for the industrial sector based on various assumptions regarding the proportion of net capital formation in the indicated gross capital formation of £60 million. The industrial sector projection, like that for the over-all economy, is based on very optimistic assumptions regarding the productivity of capital. It is likely that the rapid increase in the indicated rate of investment, if achieved, will result in a higher proportion of net to gross capital formation than the average 45:55 ratio found in underdeveloped countries where data exist. Yet, even if the proportion of net to gross capital formation is assumed to be 75:25, and if no allowance is made for a time lag to allow invested capital to become productive, the industrial sector capital/output ratio would be 2.8:1, still a low estimate.

There is no mention of capital/output ratios in the Plan. Analysis indicates (see Table 13), however, that the Plan's implicit ratio

Table 13
The Implicit Capital/Output Ratio of the Tanganyika Five-Year Development Plan

	£ Thousand
Target Gross Investment 1964–1969	246,000
Estimated Capital Replacement Required during the Plan (10% of Average Target Gross Monetary Product) = £18 million × 5 Years =	90,000
Net Capital Formation 1964–1969	156,000
Target 1970 Monetary Gross Domestic Product	260,000
Estimated June 1964 Monetary Gross Domestic Product	140,000
Target Increase of Monetary Gross Domestic Product	120,000

Note: If a six-month lapse to allow investment to become productive is assumed (one year is more likely), the Plan's implicit marginal capital/output ratio is 1.3 : 1.

$$\frac{\text{Net Capital Formation 1964–1969}}{\text{Target Monetary Gross Domestic Product Increase}} \frac{£156,000}{£120,000} = 1.3 : 1$$

Alternative Assumption Regarding Capital Replacement Requirements

Annual Capital Replacement Requirements during the Plan Do Not Increase over 1962 Estimated Level

	£ Million
Capital Replacement £12 Million × 5 Years =	60
Net Capital Formation 1964–1969	186

$$\text{Capital/Output Ratio} \frac{£186,000}{£120,000} = 1.55 : 1$$

is a surprisingly low, 1.3:1 to 1.55:1, depending upon assumptions regarding capital replacement requirements during the Plan. Target monetary gross domestic income of £260 million by 1970, an increase of £120 million over the June 1964 income level, is to result from a net investment of from £156 to £186 million (depending upon replacement-requirement assumptions) between July 1964 and June 1969 (£156/£120 = 1.3, £186/£120 = 1.55). It is difficult to reconcile the Plan's extremely low implicit capital/

output ratio with the planned shift in the structure of the economy (an increase in the relative importance of industrial activity), with the Plan's heavy emphasis on infrastructure investment, with evidence of past productivity of capital in Tanganyika, or with evidence of the productivity of capital in other countries.

Any allowance made for production increases in the sisal industry which will result from pre-Plan investment is more than offset by the large proportion of investment to be spent on infrastructure, a sector with a high, short-run capital/output ratio. The Government is guided by the prospect of high, long-run pay-off to invest heavily in infrastructure such as education and communications, and by political and social considerations in infrastructure with a low, short- and long-run pay-off such as housing. However, having made its decision on investment allocation, it must be prepared to live with the consequences. The Plan, in promising high medium-term returns for indicated investment, does not face up to the realities of capital productivity and is therefore misleading to Government policy-makers.

Main Economic Features of the Plan

The stated main economic features of the Plan are an emphasis on agricultural production and development of the industrial sector (processing, manufacturing, and mining). Physical production targets have been established for the main crops, livestock products (meat, hides, milk, etc.), fishing, and primary forest products. Achievement of these targets will result in a 7 per cent annual growth in the agricultural sector. The Plan's physical production "targets" for manufacturing and processing industries, if achieved, will result in a 13 per cent annual growth for this sector.

Agriculture

Agricultural production will be stimulated by two approaches. One, termed the improvement approach, will seek to increase production by encouraging farmers to employ improved methods of crop husbandry, to rationalize the use of their land, and to spend more time in their fields. It is known, for example, that by using traditional tools and tested techniques, cotton yields in Tanganyika could be almost doubled. The technical staff of community development and extension services will be more than doubled in order to carry the improvement approach to the people.

The second program for increasing agricultural production, called the transformation approach, is concentrated on a massive village settlement scheme, which is to absorb £10,350,000 during the Plan, almost 30 per cent of indicated Central Government investment in agriculture, water, and irrigation. The typical village will cost £150,000, cover 3,000 acres, and contain about 250 families. The scheme is, of course, untested, and the planners quite wisely have indicated that the bulk of investment in the program should come toward the end of the Plan, when it will be possible to evaluate the success of the initial settlements.

The village settlement program has been inspired by social as much as economic considerations. The impelling social idea behind the settlements is that they will bring people together where they will be able to enjoy the benefits of schools, wells, community centers, and health services. This admirable social philosophy may prove to be economically unfeasible. It is noteworthy that the only financially successful settlement scheme in Tanganyika, the Tanganyika Agricultural Corporation tobacco settlement at Urambo, is diametrically opposed to the proposed village settlement scheme in every important aspect of policy and philosophy. The organization of the Urambo scheme has been guided solely by the economics of the crop. At Urambo, instead of concentrating settlers in villages, they live next to their fields, which require constant attention during the growing season. This makes it difficult to provide community services, but ensures that the crop is cared for with a minimum of wasted effort in getting to and from the fields. To ensure the profitability of the scheme and also because only small financial subsidies have been available, settlers build their own houses, dig their own wells, and clear their own land. The only assistance they receive is a liberal credit advance based on the expected value of their crop, and training and advice on how to grow tobacco. The Corporation also manages a tobacco sales floor and keeps individual accounts for each farmer. Urambo policies were developed on the basis of trial and error and have been so successful that this year 300 new settlers joined the 400 already participating in the scheme. The new settlers came because the scheme is a proved opportunity to engage in profitable cash-crop farming. It is wise to experiment with new approaches to agricultural development, but, in the process of doing so, the proved success of existing schemes should not be overlooked.

Industry

The target of £60 million gross capital formation in the industrial sector (manufacturing, processing, and mining) represents a major effort to shift the structure of the economy toward import substitution and further processing of exports and away from primary product exports and the concomitant vulnerability to the fluctuations of world market prices. It is to be achieved by the private sector with assistance from the parastatal Tanganyika Development Corporation, which will receive a subsidy of £7 million to encourage industrial development. Although the Tanganyika Development Finance Company Limited (under the joint sponsorship of the Tanganyika Government, the Commonwealth Development Corporation, and the Federal Republic of Germany) and the Mwananchi Development Company Limited (sponsored by T.A.N.U., the ruling political party in Tanganyika) are not mentioned, it is hoped that the operations of both of these organizations will be fully coordinated with the Plan.

A list of output "targets" for 56 manufacturing and processing industries has been included in the Plan. These "targets" are estimates of the potential market in 1970, and include the industries allocated to Tanganyika by the recent special meeting of an East African industrial allocation working party. The market estimates are interesting (they would be more interesting if present production levels were included in the table), but their practical value to potential investors will be realized only if the full analysis and basis of estimates are made available. It will be very useful, therefore, if the planning secretariat publishes a full report on the findings of its market analysis.

Economic Policy

The Plan contains many policy statements — on agriculture, power, education, health, defense, industrial and commercial development, transportation, investment, cooperatives, the Common Market, and African socialism. Through no fault of the planners, some of these policies are contradictory. For example, there is virtually unanimous agreement among Tanganyikans that African socialism, defined by one observer as a concern with both the creation and distribution of wealth, is desirable. But which is more important, creation or distribution? The objectives of maximum growth and an "equitable" distribution of wealth are unfortunately not entirely complementary. Already some people are contending that the Plan is not sufficiently "socialistic," and it is reported that the President has arranged a series of meetings with top government and political figures to explain in common language that it is.

In the end, however, the people will support the Plan only if it results in the full involvement of the black African majority in economic development. As Edward Tenenbaum puts it in his A.I.D.-financed report on a Tanganyika Five-Year Industrial Plan:

The Tanganyika Government has adopted a policy of multi-racialism, promising equality to all Tanganyikan citizens, and hospitality for all desirable foreign investors, regardless of race. Sooner or later, however, that policy must show political and economic results that are acceptable to the Negro majority.

As regards our specific topic of industrial development, the matter may be put very baldly: Unless *some* Negro industrialists develop soon, there will soon not be a satisfactory climate for *any* Indo-Pakistani or white industrialists. Unless industrial development begins to include the majority of the population at all levels from boss to lowest unskilled laborer, it will fail politically and probably will become impossible economically.

In saying this, we recognize that Negroes do not have the capital resources or training to take major responsibility for industrial progress, immediately or for some years to come. No miracle, private or governmental, will create rich, industrially experienced Negroes in large numbers overnight. Therefore, the pace of industrial development will be set largely by Indo-Pakistani and foreign investors during the period covered by this [Five-Year] Plan.

But Negroes must begin to be able to accumulate industrial experience and capital now, or they will not tolerate continued non-Negro predominance for long. They must begin to demonstrate to themselves that they have won equal opportunity. They must begin to learn through their own experience the joys and pains of industrial development. To industrialize sensibly, Tanganyika must open the door of industrial opportunity for all races, and not least widely for the Negro majority.[8]

Education

The Plan envisages that Tanganyika's formal education program will be reconstructed in such a way that by 1980 the country will need to rely on external assistance only for people with exceptional qualifications. Thus, the greatest emphasis in the planned educational program will be on teacher training, secondary, and higher education. This is a continuation of a policy, initiated during the Three-Year Plan, of giving the highest priority to secondary education. This policy has, in turn, made it possible to develop university education in Tanganyika on an unprecedented scale.

The Plan recognizes that the obstacle to educational development in Tanganyika is the recurrent cost of running the schools and universities after they have been built, not the capital cost of construction. The rate of growth in secondary classes, therefore, will be the same as during the Three-Year Plan (forty-eight new classes in five years as compared with thirty-two classes in three years). This program will require about 20 per cent of planned recurrent expenditure.

In 1964, an estimated 13,000 students will complete Standard VIII (eight years of primary education). There is no target for Standard VIII output in 1969, but the Ministry of Education will continue to subsidize over half of the cost of primary education, which is, nevertheless, to remain the responsibility of local education authorities. With regard to the great desire for education in Tanganyika, an estimated average Standard VIII output during the Plan of 15,000 is probably conservative. An average of only 6,000 of these Standard VIII graduates will be selected to enter secondary schools. Most of the remaining 9,000 will look for wage employment.

The number of Tanganyika's students in degree courses in the University of East Africa[9] is to increase from 435 in 1964/65 to 1,496 in 1968/69. The cost of educating students in East Africa

8 *Tanganyika Five Year Industrial Plan,* Volume I: *The Industrial Climate,* a report under A.I.D. contract submitted in April 1964 to A.I.D., Washington, D.C.

9 Formed by Makerere University College in Uganda, the Royal College in Kenya, and the University College in Tanganyika.

is much higher (25 per cent) than the cost of sending students overseas and is likely to remain so. Because of this, the Ministry of Education proposes to restrict the annual allocation of Tanganyikan students to the University of East Africa unless the cost can be brought down to the level required to send students overseas. The desire to reduce the average cost per student of East African education is admirable, but surely the Ministry of Education misses the point of the University of East Africa if its policy of allocating students to universities is based largely on cost. It is cheaper to send students abroad because the cost of overseas education is subsidized by overseas countries either directly through grants, or indirectly through tuition and fees which represent only a fraction of the actual cost of education to a student. The University of East Africa therefore will never "compete" with the apparent cost of sending students abroad. It will, however, not only make indirect contributions to the intellectual life of East Africa, but will educate East Africans in the environment in which they will spend their working lives. The argument that students educated in East Africa will be better prepared to make a contribution to East Africa should be fully considered in formulating a university student allocation policy.

Manpower

The manpower proposals of the Plan relate almost entirely to programs to overcome the present shortage of skilled personnel faced by the country. The total high-level requirements of Government (staff-grade, administrative, and professional posts, but not including teachers, police, and nurses) are estimated at 1,000. Estimated private sector requirements increase this estimate to 1,300. Against this requirement, it is estimated that 558 Tanganyikans[10] will be coming forward from various educational and training programs to fill government posts, leaving an additional government requirement of 440 to be met by expatriate recruitment.

The Plan emphasizes that high-level manpower is in short supply and notes that there is an abundant supply of unskilled labor

[10] A recent and very encouraging report by the Ministry of Education indicates that of the 1,954 Tanganyika students studying abroad in early 1964 (523 of whom are not citizens), 1,179 will return with degrees by 1969.

waiting for employment opportunities. It is assumed that indicated increases in income will bring about increases in productive employment for this underutilized labor force. If one considers that the only problem in manpower planning is the supply of skilled labor, this attitude is justified. However, the ranks of unskilled and semiskilled people seeking wage employment are increasing rapidly as the lure of the towns becomes irresistible. In Tanganyika, African urban population increased more than 80 per cent between 1948 and 1957. Recent studies in Kenya indicate that the growth of African population of the country's ten largest urban centers is almost 7 per cent per annum. Providing urban employment opportunities for a very substantial number of these people appears essential to the avoidance of civil strife.

An examination of recent employment trends is not reassuring. Table 14 shows the decline of estimated African employment in

Table 14
African Employment in Tanganyika

Year	African Employment*
1951	423,000
1962	397,000
1963 (June)	340,000

* Excluding household servants, estimated at 20,000 to 30,000.

Tanganyika since 1951. Between 1962 and June 1963 African employment declined 14 per cent. During the same period average cash earnings of African employees increased 35 per cent, and the annual wage bill increased 10 per cent. The sharp decline in employment in 1963 can be attributed to minimum-wage legislation. This legislation, which became effective in December 1962, intensified a long-term trend toward the more productive utilization of labor and more capital-intensive production in many fields, particularly estate sisal production.[11]

The Plan calls for an increase in the productivity of the public service. This is an admirable objective, but under present condi-

[11] Between 1958 and 1963, a large sisal estate near Dar es Salaam reduced its labor force from 1,400 to 700 largely by investment in capital equipment. Oddly enough, there were about 500 unfilled jobs available in the sisal industry in early 1964. Numerous appeals were made to urban unemployed to go to the estates, but the work is not popular and many of the unemployed prefer to take their chances of obtaining employment in the towns.

tions very difficult to achieve. The critical gap in the present public service of Tanganyika is the lack of experienced middle and top managers. This lack, particularly of experienced middle management, has a damaging short-term effect on the efficiency and capacity of the entire government service. This also makes it very difficult for younger officers to develop administrative and technical skills on the job. Thus the present management gap has a tendency toward self-perpetuation.[12] A good education, which most newly appointed government officers have, is a great advantage; but it is not, unfortunately, a substitute for on-the-job development.

In sum, the manpower picture in Tanganyika is one of feast and famine. There are virtually unlimited opportunities for people with high-level skills. For those with a primary education or less, however, the prospects do not appear bright. The past years have seen decreasing employment during times of rising incomes and wage bills, a surplus of semieducated Standard VIII graduates, and a rapidly increasing urban population anxious to find work. The people are being told about the nation's objective of raising average per capita income. An ever-growing number will wish to share in the nation's growing wealth by obtaining wage employment. The recent disturbances caused by the unemployed in Kenya are an indication of the problems that may arise. Employment is soon likely to become a vital issue in national economic policy, and should therefore be the object of careful study in the program of continuous planning promised by the President.

Implementation of Development Programs

An important feature of Tanganyika's Plan is the sectoral economic targets which are supported by public sector projects and programs. These targets will be enormously useful in stimulating and guiding effort if they are realistic and feasible, and if the people and organizations responsible for their achievement know what is expected of them. The first step, therefore, in the organization of an effective program of implementation is assigning re-

12 Lack of middle and top management results in poor training and development of low-ranking officers. When these officers are promoted, they tend to be poor managers and do not develop their subordinates, and so on.

sponsibility for sector programs and projects. The Implementation and Control Division of the Planning Secretariat should assist responsible organizations in disaggregating continuously revised sector programs and production targets prepared by the planners. For example, over-all crop targets should be disaggregated to regions and districts, production and investment targets by industrial branch, and so on. (A strong feature of the Plan is that much of this disaggregation has already been carried out.) The continuously revised disaggregated targets must be understood by the people and organizations responsible for their achievement—farmers, civil servants, industrialists, investors, bankers, cooperatives, workers, educators, Ministries, and Chambers of Commerce — and these implementing agents must indicate whether the targets are feasible, pessimistic, or overly ambitious. The Implementation Division of the Planning Secretariat should ensure a continuous flow of information between the planners and implementing agents. This flow of information is an enduring *raison d'être* for the planning process, since it is only through a continuing dialogue among all those involved in the process of economic development that a country can approach the goal of optimizing resource allocation and promoting the maximum effort of its people.

Conclusion

As President Nyerere has emphasized, the Plan is not a blueprint or even a large-scale map of the future. Many of the factors that had to be taken into account are outside the Government's control — export prices and overseas financial assistance, to mention only two. Some assumptions may be proved incorrect by experience, and certain of its objectives appear inconsistent. The productivity of capital, for example, is unlikely to be nearly as high as the planners have assumed. The heavy government investment in housing is inconsistent with the objective of maximum income growth. The village settlement scheme is of doubtful viability. If the Plan were regarded as the ultimate, optimum matrix of economic and social forces, conceptual errors, mistaken assumptions, and changes in external factors could cause a national disaster.

Thus, useful planning must be a continuous process. If the

present Plan is regarded as a starting point for a series of successive approximations of complex, dynamic, and interrelated technical, social, and financial forces, and not a static program, it will make a vital contribution to the achievement of national goals. In the final analysis, the value of the Plan should be judged by the contribution of the planning process toward the achievement of these goals.

2

EXTERNAL DEBT-MANAGEMENT POLICY IN A DEVELOPING COUNTRY

Douglas A. Scott

The literature of development and individual development plans too seldom make more than passing reference to the question of whether a country can actually afford to commit resources on the scale envisaged, particularly when a large proportion of total resources must be borrowed from overseas and repaid in hard currencies. For this reason I shall examine, in the light of the experience of Ghana, some aspects of the seldom-asked question, "How much should be borrowed?" I have drawn very extensively on a paper prepared by the International Bank for Reconstruction and Development[1] for an analytical framework and wish at the outset to acknowledge my indebtedness.

Much of the analytical portion of this paper is devoted to projections of Ghana's balance of payments. This is tedious, but fundamental. Too often the question of how much external capital should be borrowed for development financing is approached as a problem of sums. The difference after adding foreign exchange earnings and subtracting uses is a residual called "net foreign borrowings." Altogether too infrequently is this residual then reconsidered for reasonableness in terms of annual export earnings,

[1] I.B.R.D., Economic Department, *Economic Growth and External Debt*, Volume I: *An Analytical Framework*, 1964 (to be published).

41

marginal savings, or rates of economic growth, whether historic or projected. My purpose here is really to test the reasonableness of the "residual," which is another way to approach the problem of formulating a debt-management policy.

The economic variables which affect a country's debt-service capacity are the major variables included in the balance of payments, including the debt-service burden. However, as with a corporation, debt service is a fixed obligation, and therefore special consideration must be given to the degree of uncertainty associated with major payments variables.

As noted in the I.B.R.D. study on debt-service capacity and economic growth, "the factors which affect the balance of payments and hence a country's capacity to service debt in the short and medium term can be classified as

1. Fluctuating Variables
   a. Exports
   b. Capital flows
   c. Emergency- and inflation-induced imports
2. Offsetting Variables
   a. Reserves
   b. Compensatory finance
   c. Compressible imports
3. Rigid Variables
   a. Minimum tolerable imports
   b. Debt-service — interest
   c. Debt-service — amortization"[2]

It has not been possible to give adequate attention to each of these variables in preparing this study. However, those variables which seem of most importance — exports and inflation-induced imports; reserves and compressibility of imports; and the aggregate debt-service burden — have been considered. Unfortunately, information about capital flows is not readily available; but some projections can be made about the new private foreign capital that Ghana wishes to attract and the private outflows associated with foreign capital.

2 I.B.R.D., *op. cit.* p. 9.

The Plan: Background

General Provisions

On March 16, 1964, the Parliament of Ghana approved a new Seven-Year Development Plan. The Plan covers seven budget years from October 1, 1963, through September 30, 1970. It sets forth a target for gross investment of £1,016.5 million over the seven years and an estimated net investment of £876 million.[3] New foreign loans and grants, public and private, are expected to provide £239[4] million, or just over 33 per cent of total investment resources. This includes £239 million on public account and £100 million of new private capital.[5] However, the contribution of foreign resources rises to 36 per cent of total *monetary* resources. The difference represents an adjustment for the imputed value of direct labor in the private sector.[6] This is one measure of the relative importance of foreign borrowings to Ghana's Seven-Year Plan.

Another measure is to be found in the relationship between foreign borrowings and total foreign exchange requirements during the same period. From the summary of balance of payments during the Plan, it is apparent that new foreign capital is expected to account for £327 million of foreign exchange out of a total foreign exchange requirement of £1,417 million.[7] There is considerable doubt, though, whether the £327 million estimated for foreign capital is a gross or net figure, with a higher level of borrowings offset by an unspecified level of debt-service charges on new commitments. The foreign exchange projections do allow £100 million for debt-service charges; but that figure appears to be based on the level of Ghana's debt, both public and private, at the outset of the Plan[8] excluding obligations in respect to the

---

3 *Seven-Year Development Plan* (Accra, 1962), Table 13.8 (p. 271).

4 *Ibid.*, p. 277.

5 *Ibid.*, p. 278.

6 *Ibid.*, pp. 278, 279.

7 *Ibid.*, p. 235. The difference between this figure and 339 lies in two different estimates of foreign private investment.

8 Debt-service obligations on existing *public* debt can be estimated from "The Financial Statement 1963/64." A rough estimate would be about £72 million including interest but not principal payments due on the International Monetary Fund and Joint Consolidated Fund loans. An amount equal to 15 per cent of payments due on other loans has been subtracted in order to make allowance for payments due in local currency. These estimates do not make any provision for private debts, including the Tema Oil Refinery.

Volta River Project. In apparent reference to this anomaly between net and gross borrowing the Plan points out:

> Besides, it seems clear that unless the amortization of the loans received during this plan period is mostly postponed to later plan periods the projected levels of consumption and investment and the imports to support these cannot be attained.[9]

The implication seems to be that gross borrowings have been equated to net borrowings by assuming that new obligations will not bear significant debt-service costs until after 1970. Indeed, it appears that new obligations have been assumed to require no amortization or interest payments (or remittance of earnings in private capital) during the Plan period.

External Debt at the Outset of the Plan

Appendices I and II (pp. 61–62) show the foreign debt, including service charges, according to sector of investment and creditor countries. The data are based upon the schedule of foreign credits published with "The Financial Statement, 1963/64" and make no allowance for contracts negotiated since July 1, 1963. The principal amount of the International Monetary Fund (I.M.F.) drawing and Joint Consolidated Fund credit have been omitted.

About 51 per cent of Ghana's debt is due in the period from 1963/64 through 1967/68. The corresponding figures for several other developing countries can be found in Column 1, Appendix VI (pp. 70–71). By this measure, the percentage of foreign debt payments due within five years, it is clear that very few other countries have as unfavorable a debt structure as Ghana. If the Volta loans are excluded, then 77 per cent of the debt is due in the next five years. This is one of the most adverse characteristics of a debt based upon medium-term export credits from more industrialized countries. The debt structure according to maturities is not an inherent indication of a liquidity problem, but rather an indication of the extent to which loans with terms of insufficient length are used for foreign borrowings.

An inspection of Appendix I (p. 61) will indicate something of the distribution of debt payments according to the sector of investment. Of total debt payments, some 72 per cent pertain to

---

[9] *Seven-Year Development Plan, op. cit.,* p. 235.

investments in basic economic overheads, including the Volta River Project. This compares with 3 per cent for agriculture, 16 per cent for industry, and nothing for education.

During the Seven-Year Plan period, through 1969/70, about 59 per cent of foreign debt payments on present liabilities will be related to economic overheads. The significance of these figures can be measured best in terms of the stated economic policy to increase substantially investments in agriculture and industry during the course of the Plan. The combined public investment in agriculture and industry is projected to increase from 38 per cent of public investment in recent years to over 48 per cent.[10] The present debt structure is weighted heavily against achieving this target.

Appendix II shows the distribution of foreign debt payments according to creditor nations. No effort has been made to allocate either the International Monetary Fund drawing or the Volta loans to individual countries. It may be noted, however, that in addition to the World Bank, Britain and the United States have agreed to lend £5 million and £13.215 million, respectively, for the Volta Project. The foreign capital for the Valco Aluminum smelter is regarded as private lending and has been excluded from the tables.

It should be noted that the typical loans which the Ghana Government has thus far negotiated are primarily medium-term export guarantee credits. This is particularly true of borrowings from Britain and West Germany, which represent 45 per cent and 20 per cent, respectively, of all debt, excluding the International Monetary Fund and Volta loans. The loans for the Volta Project, and the recently negotiated West German loan for the Tefle Bridge are the only foreign credits thus far obtained with repayment periods in excess of twelve years.

External Liquidity and Reserves at the Outset of the Seven-Year Plan

Like many other developing countries, Ghana's exports reflect a heavy dependence upon a single primary commodity — in this case, cocoa. And with the commodity slump since 1956, Ghana's

10 *Ibid.*, Table 2.3 (p. 33).

terms of trade have deteriorated markedly. As a consequence of
that slump and of a drawdown of reserves for investment purposes,
there has been a steep decline in external reserves, as shown in
Table 1.

Table 1

End of Year	Total Overseas Assets* (£ Million)
1957	171.5
1958	181.2
1959	169.6
1960	148.6
1961	73.7
1962	72.4
1963	43.5

* *Bank of Ghana Annual Report for the Year Ending June 30, 1963*, Table 9
(p. 84). The 1963 figure is from the *Quarterly Digest of Statistics*, March 1964
(Central Bureau of Statistics, Accra, Ghana).

Declining reserves are not inherently a sign of economic problems. It is more relevant to consider the purposes to which the
foreign exchange was applied. In Ghana's case most recent data
indicate that rates of real economic growth have been declining
during and after the drawdown of the reserves. Although it may
be too early for sound conclusions, preliminary indications are
that most of the foreign reserves have been utilized for nonpro-
ductive purposes including luxury consumption and prestige investments.

In the wake of 1961's 50 per cent decline in reserves, Ghana
borrowed £5 million from the International Monetary Fund in
August 1962. This drawing is still outstanding, and, because it
carried above the gold *tranche* (the point beyond which drawings
can no longer be made at will), Ghana's *unconditional* liquidity
with the I.M.F. must be regarded as nonexistent; that is, access to
additional resources of the Fund presumably will be conditioned
upon some measure of I.M.F. control.

Thus, at the outset of the Seven-Year Plan, Ghana is faced with
the lowest level of external reserves in its recent history and a
trend of continuing decline. Borrowings from the I.M.F. already
have been made up to the level where such credit is virtually
automatic. Consequently, foreign exchange resources are likely to
present a much more serious constraint for development policy

than at any time in the recent past. This constraint has important implications, not only for plans to increase investment, but also for Ghana's ability to maintain domestic price stability.

Foreign Exchange Requirements of the Seven-Year Plan

As previously indicated, the Seven-Year Plan will require an estimated £339 million of new foreign loans and grants. This represents 36 per cent of total investment in the monetized sector and 23 per cent of total foreign exchange requirements during the seven years. It seems probable that the amount of foreign loans and grants necessary to achieve the Plan's investment targets may be more nearly £450 million. But, regardless of which figure proves more accurate, borrowings will play a very significant role in Ghana's efforts to stimulate investment and economic growth.

With this introduction, it is necessary to turn now to a more detailed analysis of the Seven-Year Plan. I have chosen to deal first with the estimates as presented in the Plan and subsequently to examine several of the most important assumptions and projections which underlie the Plan's foreign exchange projections. Next there follow the projections of Ghana's external debt and debt-service charges and an examination of Ghana's capacity to service additional external debt. This includes a brief analysis of trends of major exports and the debt-service ratio based upon export projections through 1970. Thereafter, I shall consider fluctuations in capital flows and briefly examine future import requirements.

The Plan: Implications for Servicing of External Debt

Projections of External Debt through the Seven-Year Plan

Appendices III A and III B (pp. 63–66) show projections year by year of the debt structure and annual service charges through 1969/70. Appendix III A is based upon an assumed total foreign borrowing of £219 million during the Plan, while Appendix III B assumes net borrowings of £119 million. Both tables are derived from current debt position, and both assume that on the average new foreign borrowings will be obtained on the terms as detailed in Appendix IV, that is, interest at 6 per cent with 10 per cent payable upon signing of agreements, 15 per cent more during the period of investment, which is assumed to average two years, and the balance payable over seven and one-half years following completion of the project. Twenty per cent of principal payments are assumed to be in Ghanaian currency on two thirds of all borrowings. Obviously, whatever assumptions are made about the average terms of new borrowings will be of overriding importance in projecting the debt. The terms used in Appendix IV are characteristic of supplier credits being obtained by Ghana and make allowance for the portion of new credits that may be repaid in Ghanaian currency. The debt projections also assume that new credits of £70 million will be negotiated in the period from July 1963 through September 1964. This assumption is based upon projects currently under negotiation, as shown in Appendix V (pp. 68–69), which total nearly £68 million. A small allowance is made for additional contracts that could conceivably be negotiated by the end of the financial year.

An important consideration in selecting this particular pattern of borrowing terms is that they are likely to correspond quite closely with the terms actually negotiated on contracts this year. Furthermore, in the absence of immediate prospects for negotiating long-term public development credits, it seems likely that additional borrowings through 1964/65 will also be obtained on similar terms.

The assumption underlying Appendix III A is that Ghana must obtain additional foreign loans totaling £219 million during the Seven-Year Plan. This figure is taken from the aggregate foreign exchange balance on page 234 of the *Seven-Year Development Plan,* and appears again in Table 13.9 (page 277) of the *Plan.* In the exchange balance it has been estimated that £100 million will be required for debt service, and this is shown as an "import." However, from Appendix III A it appears likely that something like £186 million of foreign exchange will actually be required for debt service if loans totaling £219 million are to be obtained. This would imply an annual reduction of some £12 million in imports, that is, the difference between 186 and 100 spread over seven years. Alternatively, additional loans must be negotiated so that net foreign borrowings during the Plan total £119 million

(£219 million less the £100 million allowed for debt-service payments).

Appendix III B has been constructed as a projection of the debt on the basis of additional *net* foreign borrowing equal to £119 million through 1969/70.

Before considering whether either or both of these projections represent a reasonable level of debt-service burden for Ghana, several general comments about the figures in the appendices are in order. First and most important, the rate of increase of new foreign liabilities, since July 1, 1963, is about £6.7 million per month. This is equivalent to new contracts valued at £7.5 million being signed each month. One implication in both appendices is that 1964/65 must see a very substantial decline in the value of new supplier credits negotiated. Appendix III B assumes a maximum of £30 million, while Appendix III A sets a limit of £25 million. If these figures are substantially exceeded, as they obviously have been this year, Ghana's short-term foreign debt will rise more rapidly than shown in these projections, unless, of course, much of next year's borrowing is to be on substantially more favorable terms. The immediate prospects for softer loans do not seem bright, in view of the time usually required to conclude negotiations and receive capital from the major sources of long-term development assistance.

An additional comment is in order in regard to the feasibility of raising the level of foreign borrowings significantly above the planned level of £219 million. Generally, development assistance is available to finance specific capital requirements as opposed to credits for general balance-of-payments support. The distinction in Ghana's case is extremely important. Unless general balance-of-payments credits are obtained, external borrowings in excess of £219 million will necessarily mean an over-all increase in capital spending. The consequences of substantial "overinvestment" are twofold. First, the import levels of the Plan will be exceeded in respect to industrial raw material and consumer goods and services, the demand for which will increase as an indirect consequence of additional investment. Second, to the extent that increased investment will require either more working capital or fixed capital from local sources, the demand for domestic resources has been understated in the Plan. This raises the question of what additional domestic resources can be mobilized and how. As the Plan presently envisages some deficit financing, and with inflationary pressures already in evidence, if the additional demand for domestic resources required to augment "excess" investment is not met by real savings, further inflationary pressures will result.

Thus, it is reasonable to doubt whether gross foreign borrowings in excess of £219 million can be absorbed, unless the excess is in the form of direct balance-of-payments support, including various forms of surplus agricultural commodity programs.

Debt-Service Capacity

Ultimately, the question of what constitutes a reasonable level of foreign indebtedness depends upon a country's ability to earn and save foreign exchange over and above the immediate requirements for consumption. Unfortunately, little work has been done on this subject in Ghana, except as contained in the foreign exchange projections of the Seven-Year Plan.

The debt-service ratio. One commonly used measure of debt-servicing capacity is the debt-service ratio (DSR). This is defined as annual external debt-service charges divided by total foreign exchange earnings on current account. Unfortunately, this concept is of a static nature and is not really an adequate indicator of the long-term aspect of servicing debt. In particular, it does not adequately take into account the rate of growth of foreign exchange earnings and savings which are, in turn, functions of real rates of economic growth in the export- and import-substituting sectors. Notwithstanding the limited usefulness of the debt-service ratio as a long-run measure of debt limits, it may serve as a useful indicator in the short run.

Projections of export earnings are given on page 234 of the *Seven-Year Development Plan* and are reproduced in Table 2 for convenience.

Since 1955, foreign exchange earnings on current account and cocoa exports have been as shown in Table 3. Several observations are in order with regard to the past and projected foreign exchange earnings. The projections to 1969/70 imply a compound rate of growth of 7 per cent per annum over the period. This is further divided into a 5½ per cent growth through 1966/67 and an 8¾

Table 2

Item	Yearly Average 1960–1962 (£ Million)	Projections 1966/1967 (£ Million)	1969/70 (£ Million)
Cocoa Products	70	86	100
Wood Products	15	21	32
Gold	11	13	14
Manganese	5	5	7
Diamonds	8	10	11
Aluminum	—	—	14
Re-exports	2.5	4	5
Services and Other Items	11	12	12
	122.5	151	195

Table 3*

	1955	1956	1957	1958	1959	1960	1961	1962	1963†
Current Account Earnings, £ Million	110	95	103	118	126	128	129	125	122
Cocoa Exports (beans), £ Million, F.O.B. Accra	64.7	50.3	50.4	61.2	68.0	65.4	69.3	67.0	68.1
Cocoa as *Percentage* of Total	59	53	48	52	54	51	54	54	55
Average Price (£) Realized per Ton of Cocoa (F.O.B.)	267	216	194	316	270	220	171	158	168

* *Economic Survey, 1962,* Central Bureau of Statistics, Accra, Ghana.
† Preliminary estimate by author.

per cent annual growth thereafter; the rapid rate of growth over the last three years is attributed mainly to wood products and aluminum.

Since 1955, the highest rate of growth was experienced during the three years from 1957 to 1959, and this was equivalent to $9\frac{1}{2}$ per cent annually. However, this was not sustained, and the five-year growth rate through 1961 was only $6\frac{1}{2}$ per cent. The years since 1961 have seen a decline of earnings to an estimated low in 1963 of £122 million, and preliminary projections for 1964 indicate current account earnings may reach £126 million, about the same level achieved in 1962 and 1959.

Without a great deal of further study it is difficult to comment more fully on export projections through 1969/70. The cocoa projections allow for an annual growth of 5½ per cent over current exports. This rate is somewhat above the current rate of growth of cocoa consumption (about 4 per cent per annum). The difference may be justified by Ghana's plans to export more finished and semifinished cocoa products. Whatever the validity of the cocoa projections, the estimates for wood products and aluminum seem beyond all reasonable expectation. In fact, for the former commodity the estimate produces an internal inconsistency.

In its sector analysis, the Plan projects exports of wood products at £17.1 million. Even if separate computation of the export of logs at the current level of £5–6 million is assumed, the resulting figure falls well short of the £32 million total envisioned by the Plan. In other words, foreign earnings from the wood industry do not seem to be related to the level of planned activity in that industry.

The estimates for aluminum are somewhat more complicated. Although exports are projected at £16.7 million by 1969/70,[11] imports of aluminum raw materials are shown at £15.6 million, which is equivalent to net export of £1.1 million. Yet the aggregate scheme of imports for the Plan does not seem to make full allowance for aluminum raw material imports, since the *total* planned increase in producer goods imports (excluding fuels) from 1967/68 through 1969/70 is only £15.0 million.[12] This increase is only sufficient for aluminum raw materials, and even that sufficiency is grounded on the assumption that the level of these imports in 1966/67 does not exceed £0.6 million. To compensate for this possible omission really requires an increase in the net foreign borrowings by an amount to offset the demand for aluminum raw materials. Instead, aluminum export earnings have been adjusted and shown as a net export of £2 million in 1969/70.

After making the appropriate adjustments suggested by the preceding analysis, projected export figures for 1969/70 will be reduced to about £174.0 million. The increase from £126 million to £174 million over a six-year period corresponds to an annual growth rate of 5.5 per cent, and this will be used as a basis for calculations of debt-service ratios in this paper. If the assumptions on export projections prove to be excessively conservative, there

---

[11] *Seven-Year Development Plan, op. cit.,* Table 5.2 (p. 103).
[12] *Ibid.,* Table 13.5 (p. 263).

will be a favorable margin of error; but this result seems unlikely in view of the fact that a sustained annual growth rate of 4.5 per cent for exports has not been maintained for any six-year period in the past decade.

Based upon the 5.5 per cent annual growth in export earnings, Table 4 shows exports and debt-service ratios corresponding to the

Table 4

	1963/64	1964/65	1965/66	1966/67	1967/68	1968/69	1969/70
Export Earnings (£ Million)	126.0	132.9	140.2	147.9	156.1	164.7	173.7
DSR, III A	15.3	15.3	16.5	19.1	19.6	19.0	18.9
DSR, III B	15.3	16.0	17.7	24.8	25.9	27.8	27.8

projected debt burden in Appendices III A and III B. In considering the difference between the ratios derived from Appendices III A and III B, it is worth recalling that in order for Appendix III A to represent a *possible* borrowing pattern, it is necessary to reduce projected imports by some £85 million during the Plan, in addition to the adjustments already made in regard to aluminum.

Under the most optimistic estimates, the DSR for the years 1964/65 through 1967/68 is already committed to reach or exceed 15 per cent except for the years 1965/66 and 1967/68, when it could fall to 14.3 and 13.7 per cent respectively. This rapid rise in external credits precludes the possibility of establishing a debt-management policy to keep the debt-service ratio in the 10–15 per cent range. Although a debt-service ratio above this level is not of itself an index of danger, a combination of debt-service costs at this level, stagnating exports, and low unconditional liquidity could produce serious economic dislocations in the short run.

Variables that affect ability to service foreign debt. This section will mention only briefly selected economic variables that may have an important bearing on a country's ability to service foreign debt. This is not intended to be an exhaustive study of any or all of the variables. Rather, by calling attention to these additional aspects of the debt-service problem, it is possible to show that the determinants of a debt-management policy include some of the most important variables of economic growth.

The variables that ultimately affect the capacity to service foreign debt are essentially the important variables in a country's balance of payments. Those of most immediate concern to Ghana are fluctuations of exports, capital flows, and the possibility of limiting imports in the face of inflationary leakages.

The fluctuations in Ghana's exports due to a heavy reliance on cocoa are a well-known story. Tables 2 and 3 give a brief history of export earnings since 1955. From 1956 through 1963 the annual rate of growth in earnings has been only slightly in excess of 4 per cent. Yet during this time Ghana's output of cocoa has risen from 233,000 tons to 404,000 tons (export quantities only). Prices, however, have declined from a historical high of £584 per ton in 1955 to £160 per ton in the early 1960's and have since risen to about £175 per ton in 1964.

It may be noted that by 1970, even if the targets of the Seven-Year Plan are met, more than 50 per cent of Ghana's export earnings are expected to come from cocoa, although a larger portion may be attributed to finished and semifinished products. It could be argued that cocoa prices over the past two to three years represent a "rock bottom" level and that further sharp declines are unlikely. That, however, would seem to be a somewhat precarious basis for estimating Ghana's vulnerability to further export price fluctuations.

The problem of fluctuating capital flows is largely beyond Ghana's direct control. The availability of funds from abroad will be determined ultimately by prospective creditors. Capital outflows, however, are more directly controllable locally with exchange-control regulations.

The importance of the availability of new foreign borrowings cannot be overemphasized. It is estimated that between £20 million and £25 million of current imports are being financed on credit. This provides some measure of relief on the balance of payments. However, if, in the future, new capital inflows should be reduced substantially for a period of one or more years, then Ghana's current foreign earnings would be forced to pay for all imports, as well as debt-service charges due from previous years. Such a situation would almost certainly give rise to serious economic dislocations, even if only temporary in nature.

Because this factor may sometimes be overlooked, it is worth while to emphasize that the continued availability of foreign credits will be determined largely by potential creditors and their evaluation of Ghana's ability to service additional debt. In the case of supplier credits the continued availability seems primarily to be a function of domestic export promotion efforts in the creditor countries. However, it may be expected that the supply of even these aggressively pushed credits is not unrelated to Ghana's apparent ability to service an expanded level of external debt.

Indeed, one of the more unfortunate aspects of Ghana's debt problems arises out of the "hard sell" efforts of capital exporting countries, West and East, to increase their own export earnings regardless of the economic implications for the borrower. It is difficult not to question motives for the sale of three (not just one) expensive jet aircrafts to the hopelessly unprofitable Ghana Airways. For practically the same price Ghana has been sold a massive shipyard (how Ghana can provide credits to finance the sale of ships is a mystery) by a contractor from one of the several countries where the shipbuilding industry is notably "depressed." Perhaps this is one explanation for the contract?

Situations that might give rise to sudden increases of imports because of inflationary pressures are almost entirely within the control of the Ghanaian authorities. Judicious use of import restrictions is now essential in order further to reduce imports in the face of increasing evidence of inflationary pressures.[13] If it were not for stringent controls on imports, the balance of payments would undoubtedly deteriorate rapidly. Until such time as domestic productive capacity is sufficiently expanded and the rate of domestic savings increased, the pressures for a sharp rise in imports are likely to remain. In the years immediately prior to introduction of import controls in 1961, Ghana's marginal propensity to import was about 0.35. Controls, either quantitative or through near-prohibitive duties, are apt to be required for some time in order to avoid a sudden rise in imports.

---

[13] "Over the past eighteen months, Government borrowing [internal] has proceeded at a pace that cannot be expected to continue much longer without serious consequences in the form of inflationary pressures in the economy. Some restraint in fiscal policy will have to be exercised in order to ease the present strains on the economy." *Bank of Ghana Annual Report for Year Ending June 1963*, Accra.

There are factors that may operate to offset any sudden deterioration in the balance of payments of a country, and as such these factors may be regarded as a form of insurance against the prospects of a foreign exchange crisis or default on fixed obligations. The availability of foreign reserves and access to balance-of-payments credits are the most important insurance factors. Ghana's unconditional liquidity, including gold, convertible foreign exchange reserves, and the gold *tranche* position with the International Monetary Fund, is presently equivalent to £42 million. The International Monetary Fund drawing of £5.0 million carried over into the first credit *tranche*; hence there is little or no unconditional liquidity left with the Fund. Expressed as a percentage of imports on current account in 1963, the unconditional liquidity is equivalent to 34 per cent. This ratio is expected to improve somewhat in 1964 as a result of further measures to reduce imports. From Appendix VI it may be seen that this ratio is in the middle range of those countries listed.

In the discussion of reserves and unconditional liquidity, no mention was made of current liabilities that are a claim on the reserves. Currency cover requires 60 per cent backing for currency in circulation. This is equivalent to £25–30 million. At the discretion of the Minister of Finance, and after consultations with the Bank of Ghana, the cover requirement can be reduced to 40 per cent, or £16–20 million. The £5.1 million drawing from the International Monetary Fund and £4.3 million overdraft facility, the Joint Consolidated Fund borrowing, are additional liabilities which are a potential claim on reserves, at least to the extent that they have not been included in the general debt-service calculations.

Another factor that should be considered in ascertaining Ghana's capacity to service external debt is the degree to which imports can be reduced readily. This is often described as the compressibility of imports. Fixed obligations, such as debt-service charges, are usually regarded as relatively incompressible. Unfortunately, this factor has not been analyzed during the preparation of this study. However, there is evidence that in 1964 Ghana is trying to restrict imports to the level of £110–115 million, a reduction on current account of about 15 per cent. This may allow for some increase in reserves. However, because the debt-service costs for 1964/65 will rise nearly £10 million above the estimate for 1964, it is expected that similar restraint must be exercised in 1965 in order to keep reserves from falling further. Experience during the period through 1965 should give reasonable indication of the degree of compressibility with respect to import levels in 1963. Further reductions may be most difficult to effect and sustain.

Service transactions. At this point it is necessary to question the validity of one important import estimate in balance-of-payments projections in the Seven-Year Plan. The most important item in doubt, and indeed a major item, is service transactions.

Service payments have been projected from a 1960–1962 base of £21.0 million.[14] Even though imports have been valued on a C.I.F. basis in the Plan, a comparison for 1962 with actual balance-of-payments figures as reported by the Bank of Ghana[15] indicates a discrepancy of £11 million. Service payments, excluding all freight and insurance payments, were actually £26.3 million. Freight and insurance payments were an additional £12 million, but allowing for C.I.F. valuation of imports in the Seven-Year Plan, about one half of this charge should go into the "service" item (this assumes that exports were valued on the conventional F.O.B. basis). Thus, a more realistic estimate of payments for services (excluding freight and insurance on imports) would be £32 million, £11 million above base-year estimates. The implication is that total service payments are probably underestimated by £75 million.

Remittance requirements for new foreign private investment. Having thus far discussed a number of variables that may cause sudden changes in the balance of payments, we must return to the specific variable of servicing foreign debt. So far we have considered only the burdens imposed by a growing public debt. However, if the Seven-Year Plan is to succeed, new foreign private investment of at least £85 million is required. In order to attract such capital it will be necessary to allow remittances for debt service and profits.

The Plan calls for foreign private loans equivalent to £12 million annually. If we assume that investors may wish to remit annually

14 *Seven-Year Development Plan, op. cit.,* Table 13.5 (p. 263).
15 *Bank of Ghana Annual Report for Year Ending June 1963,* Accra.

up to 6 per cent of their total capital investment, this would mean an additional allowance of £5.1 million annually by 1969/70 as a charge against foreign exchange. This is only a guess at remittances, but it should serve to illustrate the need to estimate the added foreign exchange servicing costs associated with private capital.

Present Debt-Management Policy

There is little written evidence that the Ghanaian Government has given serious consideration to the policy problems of a rising external debt. One of the few statements of policy is contained in a letter written to the World Bank on February 8, 1962, at the time agreements were concluded for the Volta River Dam. The relevant passage on debt-management policy is as follows:[16]

> The Government has no intention of borrowing from overseas sources in excess of her capacity to service all loans in accordance with the terms of any loan agreements concluded, and we would be pleased to exchange views with the Bank from time to time regarding the level of Ghana's external debt in relation to her prospective capacity to service such debt.

This was written two years ago when the external public debt was about £33 million. One and one-half years later, by July 1963, external liabilities had increased to £134 million, excluding drawings from the International Monetary Fund and the Joint Consolidated Fund. One half of this increase is associated with the Volta scheme. Since July 1963, net additional external liabilities are estimated to exceed £40 million.

The most important issue raised in this paper concerns the need to relate debt-service costs to some parameter that would reflect Ghana's capacity to service external debt. As suggested in an earlier section, the debt-service ratio is a suitable indicator for short-run correlation, but lacks the capacity to reflect long-term savings and growth trends in an economy.

From an inspection of Appendix VI it is apparent that Ghana's projected debt-service ratio of 15–16 per cent for 1964/65 is substantially above that of many other less developed countries. If one recalls also that more than 50 per cent of Ghana's debt

---

16 *Volta River Project Agreements,* I.B.R.D., Washington.

burden is payable within five years, a debt-service ratio at present levels appears to be somewhat high, at least until a significant growth trend for exports can be established or some increase in unconditional liquidity is effected.

It is evident that Ghana must seek substantially more favorable terms on future loans. It is necessary to recognize that there are limits both to the ability and to the willingness of some countries to liberalize the terms of export-credit loans. Because these credits, usually of five- to eight-year limit, increase the debt-service costs in the short term, it may be advisable for Ghana to set an annual limit on such credits. Such a limit could readily be set within an agreed policy in respect to the debt-service ratio.

Consideration also must be given to the probable impact on foreign exchange earnings of new investments. After a look at Appendix V, it seems questionable whether some of the projects already agreed on or currently under negotiation will make a significant contribution toward improving Ghana's balance of payments.

Summary

Three parameters have been used to compare Ghana's external debt-service burden with several other countries. In the current year, Ghana's debt-service ratio exceeds 15 per cent and is likely to exceed 16 per cent in 1964/65. Fifty-one per cent of the external debt is payable within five years. Continued reliance upon supplier credits will raise this ratio, which is already one of the most unfavorable among the nations listed in Appendix VI. Finally, Ghana's unconditional liquidity, foreign exchange, and gold reserves plus the gold credit *tranche* with the International Monetary Fund are equivalent to only 32 per cent of imports on current account. This ratio may improve if the import program for 1964 is effective. However, even if reserves are increased by £10 million this year, the ratio of unconditional liquidity to debt-service costs will deteriorate further because of the sharp rise of the latter that must be expected in 1964/65.

The immediate prospects indicate that the external debt will continue to rise sharply unless an effective debt-management policy is put in operation soon. In the absence of an effective policy, Ghana may rapidly approach a situation where potential foreign creditors are reluctant to extend further credits, except at very high insurance premiums, which today are equivalent to nearly 5 per cent of borrowed capital.

Finally, perhaps the most important point of this brief study of Ghana's external debt and balance-of-payments forecasts is that much more attention must be given to the problem of a realistic appraisal of the impact of foreign borrowing on the balance of payments. I have suggested earlier that Ghana's Seven-Year Plan may be substantially overestimating exports and underestimating imports. The combined effect is a potential shortage of foreign exchange of about £125 million in addition to the sums already earmarked to be met by external resources. If this combined sum, perhaps as much as £452 million, were given explicit consideration as the net addition to external debt, public and private, through 1969/70, the magnitude of annual fixed obligations would be more readily apparent. As it stands though, borrowing seems to be regarded primarily as a residual, the difference between the foreign exchange required and the amount of exchange generated by the economy. Unless explicit consideration is given to the question of whether the residual is reasonable, foreign borrowing may continue to be regarded more as a problem of subtraction than as a problem of government policy.

Appendix I

Foreign Debt by Sector (July 1, 1963)

(£ Million)

Sector	1963/64	1964/65	1965/66	1966/67	1967/68	1968/69	1969/70	1970/71	1971/72	Other	Total	%
Infrastructure	3.190	3.146	3.046	2.889	2.571	1.438	0.802	0.434	0.169	1.513	19.198	14.3
Transportation Equipment	3.852	4.850	4.379	3.662	3.108	2.962	2.102	1.360	0.678	1.310	28.263	21.0
Industry	3.828	4.719	3.969	3.520	2.687	1.300	0.661	0.336	0.099	0.281	21.390	15.9
Agriculture	0.770	0.689	0.603	0.508	0.336	0.325	0.295	0.185	0.100	0.316	4.077	3.0
Miscellaneous	1.242	0.981	1.063	0.870	0.904	0.718	0.664	0.185	0.100	0.388	7.595	5.6
Communications	0.540	0.818	0.764	0.521	0.397	0.185	0.036	—	—	—	3.261	2.4
Volta River Projects*	0.221	0.254	0.438	0.890	2.010	2.220	2.210	2.199	2.189	37.540	50.171	37.2
I.M.F. Drawing (Interest Only)	0.112	0.162	0.212	0.250	—	—	—	—	—	—	0.736	0.6
Total Debt	13.755	15.569	14.474	13.110	12.013	9.148	6.770	4.905	3.606	41.348	134.641	100.0

* The Volta River Project debt assumes that the three loans with lowest interest rate will be fully utilized (i.e, £30 million) and the fourth loan will not be drawn at all. In fact, about £400,000 has been drawn against the U.K. loan. Interest allocated during first six years is based upon best information available.

Appendix II
Ghana Foreign Debt (July 1, 1963) by Country of Creditor

Country	Schedule of Payments (£ Million)										Total	Total %
	1963/64	1964/65	1965/66	1966/67	1967/68	1968/69	1969/70	1970/71	1971/72	Other	Total	
United Kingdom	6.137	6.706	6.446	5.611	4.814	3.402	2.470	1.329	0.452	0.838	38.205	28.3
Federal Republic of Germany	3.460	3.539	2.775	2.109	1.357	0.402	0.171	0.167	0.163	1.500	15.643	11.6
Netherlands	1.171	1.390	1.339	1.037	0.882	0.644	0.307	0.052	—	—	6.822	5.1
Soviet Union	0.765	0.844	0.864	0.873	0.751	0.732	0.399	0.278	0.191	0.628	6.325	4.7
Yugoslavia	0.515	0.528	0.541	0.433	0.485	0.473	0.460	0.438	0.371	0.360	4.604	3.4
France	0.172	0.632	0.515	0.664	0.636	0.607	0.293	—	—	—	3.519	2.6
Japan	—	0.225	0.291	0.280	0.269	0.259	0.248	0.237	0.227	0.471	2.507	1.9
Czechoslovakia	0.217	0.406	0.383	0.376	0.360	0.225	0.142	0.139	—	—	2.248	1.7
Italy	0.203	0.231	0.255	0.255	0.127	—	—	—	—	—	1.075	0.8
Belgium	0.226	0.122	0.117	0.111	0.106	0.100	—	—	—	—	0.782	0.6
German Democratic Republic	0.130	0.127	0.132	0.133	0.130	—	—	—	—	—	0.652	0.5
Hungary	0.072	0.088	0.086	0.084	0.083	0.081	0.079	0.064	0.014	—	0.651	0.5
Canada	0.328	0.310	0.075	—	—	—	—	—	—	—	0.713	0.5
United States	0.023	0.010	—	—	—	—	—	—	—	—	0.033	—
Volta River Project	0.221	0.254	0.438	0.890	2.010	2.220	2.210	2.799	2.189	37.540	50.171	37.2
I.M.F. Drawing (Interest Only)	0.112	0.162	0.212	0.250	—	—	—	—	—	—	0.736	0.6
Total	13.756	15.574	14.469	13.106	12.010	9.145	6.779	4.903	3.607	41.337	134.686	100.0

Appendix III A

Projections of Foreign Indebtedness through 1969/70: Gross Borrowing £219 Million (£ Million)

Down Payment	63/64	64/65	65/66	66/67	67/68	68/69	69/70	70/71	71/72	72/73	73/74	74/75	Gross borrowings	Foreign borrowings
Debt Structure as of Oct. 1, 1963														
5.53	13.76	15.57	14.47	13.11	12.01	9.15	6.78	4.90	3.61				70.0	60.67
Debt Structure as of Oct. 1, 1964														
2.00		18.37	20.07	22.95	21.43	18.15	15.36	13.06	11.35	10.81			25.3	22.0
Debt Structure as of Oct. 1, 1965														
2.09			21.08	24.97	24.83	21.40	18.46	16.01	14.30	13.61	4.85		26.5	23.0
Debt Structure as of Oct. 1, 1966														
2.28				26.03	26.95	25.10	22.02	19.42	17.55	16.70	7.78	4.93	28.8	25.0

(Continued)

Appendix III A (continued)

Debt Structure as of Oct. 1, 1967

Down Payment: 2.46

67/68	68/69	69/70	70/71	71/72	72/73	73/74	74/75	75/76
28.10	27.40	26.07	23.29	21.25	20.23	11.14	8.11	5.15

Gross borrowings 31.1
Foreign borrowings 27.0

Debt Structure as of Oct. 1, 1968

Down Payment: 2.64

68/69	69/70	70/71	71/72	72/73	73/74	74/75	75/76	76/77
28.64	28.56	27.66	25.43	24.23	14.95	11.73	8.59	5.38

Gross borrowings 33.4
Foreign borrowings 29.0

Debt Structure as of Oct. 1, 1969

Down Payment: 2.92

69/70	70/71	71/72	72/73	73/74	74/75	75/76	76/77	77/78
29.90	30.33	30.12	28.72	19.04	15.82	12.48	9.07	5.62

Gross borrowings 36.9
Foreign borrowings 32.0

Debt Structure as of Oct. 1, 1970

70/71	71/72	72/73	73/74	74/75	75/76	76/77	77/78	78/79
31.80	33.07	33.90	24.00	20.56	17.00	13.37	9.70	5.97

Gross borrowings 252.0
Foreign borrowings 218.7
Foreign Debt Service 185.8

Notes: 1. The projections assume that gross *foreign* borrowings will total £219 million during the Seven-Year Plan as indicated in Table 13.9 of the *Plan*. This sum has been divided annually as follows:

63/64	64/65	65/66	66/67	67/68	68/69	69/70
60.7	22.0	23.0	25.0	27.0	29.0	32.0

2. The estimate of £60.7 million for 1963/64 is based upon known additional contracts already signed plus an allowance of £2.5 million for further contracts through Sept. 30, 1964. This is expected to be net of probable cancellations of existing contracts.

3. The gross borrowings for each year are 1.154 times the annual foreign exchange borrowings.

4. Annual debt-service projections are based upon the distribution of the foreign exchange component only and are derived fully in Appendix IV.

5. The down-payment column represents the additional foreign exchange liability of contracts negotiated each year.

Appendix III B

Projections of Foreign Indebtedness through 1969/70: Net Borrowing £120 Million (£ Million)

Debt Structure	63/64	64/65	65/66	66/67	67/68	68/69	69/70	70/71	71/72	72/73	73/74	74/75	75/76	76/77	Annual Gross Borrowing	Down Payment
July 1, 1963	13.76	15.57	14.47	13.11	13.01	9.15	6.78	4.90	3.61							5.53
Oct. 1, 1964		18.37	20.07	22.95	21.43	18.15	15.36	13.06	11.35	10.81					70.1	2.94
Oct. 1, 1965			21.56	25.93	26.66	23.15	20.14	17.62	15.68	14.92	6.05				37.2	3.27
Oct. 1, 1966				27.59	29.97	28.97	25.71	22.94	20.75	19.74	10.62	6.48			41.4	4.07
Oct. 1, 1967					32.03	33.09	32.95	29.87	27.37	26.05	16.62	12.17	7.53		51.5	4.16
Oct. 1, 1968						35.43	37.62	38.08	35.22	33.55	23.77	18.97	13.98	8.24	58.4	5.06

(Continued)

Appendix III B (continued)

Down Payment									Annual Gross Borrowing
Debt Structure Oct. 1, 1969									
69/70	70/71	71/72	72/73	73/74	74/75	75/76	76/77	77/78	
40.18	43.21	44.23	42.17	32.01	26.82	21.45	15.32	8.82	64.1
5.54									
Debt Structure Oct. 1, 1970									
70/71	71/72	72/73	73/74	74/75	75/76	76/77	77/78	78/79	
46.01	49.84	52.02	41.44	35.83	30.04	23.49	16.57	9.44	70.1

Notes: 1. This table is based upon projected *net* foreign borrowings of £119 million during the Seven-Year Plan. The distribution is as follows:

63/64	64/65	65/66	66/67	67/68	68/69	69/70
41.4	11.0	11.0	13.0	14.0	15.0	15.0

2. The figure for 1963/64 is derived from the expectation that contracts valued at £70.0 million will be negotiated in the current year.

3. The table shows only the estimated foreign component of debt.

4. The down-payment column shows the additional foreign exchange liability of contracts negotiated each year.

Gross Borrowings	392.7
Foreign Borrowing	340.4
Foreign Debt Service	None
Payments	220.4
	———
Net Foreign Borrowing	120.0

Appendix IV

Distribution of Payments over Life of Typical Loan

(Principal: 1,000,000; interest: 6%; payments: 10% down, 15% during first two years, balance of 75% spread over 7½ years)

Date	Balance of Principal Owing before Payments	Principal Payments	Interest Charged Half-Yearly in Arrear	Total Payments	Payments by Year	Annual Payments as % of Principal	Annual Foreign Exchange Payments as % of Principal*
	£	£	£		£	%	%
Jan. 1, 1964	—	100,000	—	100,000	—	—	—
July 1, 1964	—	37,500	—	37,500	137,500	13.75	7.9
Jan. 1, 1965	—	37,500	15,000	52,500	—	—	—
July 1, 1965	—	37,500	—	37,500	90,000	9.0	4.0
Jan. 1, 1966	—	37,500	45,000	82,500	—	—	—
July 1, 1966	750,000	50,000	22,500	72,500	155,000	15.5	8.0
Jan. 1, 1967	703,000	50,000	21,000	71,000	—	—	—
July 1, 1967	653,000	50,000	19,500	69,500	140,500	14.05	14.05
Jan. 1, 1968	600,000	50,000	18,000	68,000	—	—	—
July 1, 1968	550,000	50,000	16,000	66,500	134,500	13.45	13.45
Jan. 1, 1969	500,000	50,000	15,000	65,000	—	—	—
July 1, 1969	450,000	50,000	13,500	63,500	128,500	12.85	12.85
Jan. 1, 1970	400,000	50,000	12,000	62,000	—	—	—
July 1, 1970	350,000	50,000	10,000	60,500	122,500	12.25	12.25
Jan. 1, 1971	300,000	50,000	9,000	59,000	—	—	—
July 1, 1971	250,000	50,000	7,500	57,500	116,500	11.65	11.65
Jan. 1, 1972	200,000	50,000	6,000	56,000	—	—	—
July 1, 1972	150,000	50,000	4,500	54,500	110,500	11.05	11.05
Jan. 1, 1973	100,000	50,000	3,000	53,000	—	—	—
July 1, 1973	50,000	50,000	1,500	51,500	104,500	10.45	10.45

* This estimate assumes that one third of all borrowings require full repayment in foreign exchange and on two thirds of all borrowings local currency will be accepted for one half of initial payment and for 100% of principal payments during first two years; i.e., 20% of principal will be paid in local currency.

Appendix V

External Commitments under Negotiation
or Agreed since July 1963

I. Commitments Agreed

		£ Million
A.	Infrastructure	
	1. Accra-Tema Water Supply	9.45
	2. Morno and Yapei Bridges	0.61
	3. Kumasi-Bibiani road	1.81
	4. Eastern trunk road	2.10
	5. Yeji ferry craft	0.19
	6. Tamale Airport	7.0
		21.16
B.	Transportation Equipment	2.1
C.	Industry	
	1. Extension to Tema cocoa factory	7.6
	2. Tema shipyard and drydock	7.3
	3. Sodefra contracts for Tema hotel, airport hotel, pharmaceutical factory, and three fruit-processing factories	3.90
	4. Brick and tile factory	0.25
	5. Gold refinery	0.50
	6. Taylor-Woodraw contracts for shoe, rubber tire, and tannery factories	1.90
		21.45
D.	Agriculture	
	1. Fishing trawlers	14.40
	2. Akuse Sugar Project	3.44
		17.84
E.	Communications	
	1. Phillips, Telecommunications Projects	0.64
	2. Underground telephone cables	1.10
	3. Purchase of wireless company	0.20
		1.94
F.	Miscellaneous	
	1. Accra sport complex	4.3
	2. Abuakwa College	0.3
	3. Ghana Supply Commission Purchases	0.42
		5.02
		69.51

Appendix V *(continued)*

II. Projects Currently under Negotiation

A.	Infrastructure		
	1. Ankobra mouth bridge	0.31	
	2. Water supplies, Kumasi and Sekondi/Takoradi	3.68	
			3.99
B.	Transportation equipment		2.1
C.	Industry		
	1. Cement factory	1.5	
	2. Commercial explosives factory	1.05	
	3. Pencil factory	0.29	
	4. Oil-processing equipment	0.37	
	5. Tobacco factory	0.07	
	6. Solar salt processing	1.40	
			4.68
D.	Agriculture		
	1. Fish-marketing cold-storage facilities	5.42	
			5.42
E.	Communications		
	1. Automatic telephone exchange equipment	0.09	
	2. ILS, Accra airport	0.03	
			0.12
F.	Miscellaneous		
	1. Hospital Project	12.42	
			12.42
	Total		28.73

Appendix VI

Debt Structure, Public-Debt-Service Ratios, Exchange Reserve Ratios, and Export Growth Rates

Country	Scheduled Amortization over the Next Five Years as Percentage of Outstanding Debt as of 1962	Public Debt Service as Percentage of Exports of Goods and Services, 1962	Foreign Exchange Reserves as Percentage of Imports, 1962 (Unconditional Liquidity)	Annual Rate of Growth in Export Volume, Recent Years or 1950's
Brazil	n.a. (extremely high)	20	11	4.2
Argentina	n.a. (very high)	22	12	3.9
Philippines	50	3	13	3.1
Israel	51	29	86	19.0
Spain	50	2	66	9.1
Mexico	49	16	39	3.0
Turkey	48	17	30	1.6
Taiwan	47	5	61	10.6
El Salvador	45	3	38	9.9
Chile	44	25	15	4.1
Nicaragua	44	5	37	1.5
Ethiopia	42	4	72	2.6
Costa Rica	41	9	17	7.9
Burma	40	n.a.	77	0.4
Colombia	40	11	20	3.1
Peru	40	7	21	6.8
Iran	38	9	36	n.a.
Thailand	36	3	100	6.4
Ecuador	35	8	34	6.1
Korea	33	n.a.	27	n.a.
Sudan	33	9	64	5.2
Nigeria	30	2	60	4.3
Bolivia	25	n.a.	8	n.a.

Appendix VI (*continued*)

Country	Scheduled Amortization over the Next Five Years as Percentage of Outstanding Debt as of 1962	Public Debt Service as Percentage of Exports of Goods and Services, 1962	Foreign Exchange Reserves as Percentage of Imports, 1962 (Unconditional Liquidity)	Annual Rate of Growth in Export Volume, Recent Years or 1950's
India	25	9	26	1.4
Pakistan	23	7	45	0.4
Ceylon	22	1	29	1.5
Honduras	17	3	20	3.0
Malaya	16	1	94	5.0

Note: Countries are ranked according to how unfavorable their debt structure is (Column 1). This is not necessarily a ranking which indicates the gravity of the liquidity problem.

SOURCES: I.B.R.D. study, *Economic Growth, Foreign Capital and Debt Servicing Problems of the Developing Countries*, December 1963.

3

THE MONETARY AND FISCAL BACKGROUND OF NIGERIA'S SIX-YEAR DEVELOPMENT PLAN

Douglas Gustafson

Historical Background

Monetary and Fiscal Developments in the Colonial Era

In general. As a result of the nature of the colonial relationship, Nigeria was developed to a considerable extent as a branch of the parent economy. The entire colonial purpose centered on trade considerations. The colony was a source of raw materials and a market for finished goods. All the economic and financial institutions created to service this system were oriented around external trade, and assets not required in Nigeria for this purpose were exported. In 1950, commercial bank assets totaling £17.75 million were held as deposits overseas.[1] The banking system was actually withdrawing capital from the Nigerian economy for use in other Commonwealth countries. Official Government reserves were all held overseas as were the substantial investments of the marketing boards and the Post Office Savings Bank. In December 1958, these deposits totaled £133 million.[2] Other savings of the community, in the form of life insurance payments and pension fund contributions, were also invested abroad.

[1] Federation of Nigeria, *Quarterly Digest of Statistics,* Vol. 12, No. 3 (July 1963), p. 15.
[2] Federation of Nigeria, *Quarterly Digest of Statistics,* Vol. 11, No. 4 (October 1962), p. 16.

In addition, the currency system itself was externally controlled. The West African Currency Board was created in 1912 by the Colonial Office to manage the system. A common currency was issued for Gambia, Sierra Leone, Gold Coast, and Nigeria. This currency was backed 100 per cent by sterling securities of the United Kingdom Government and the governments of other developed Commonwealth countries. West African securities were not eligible investments until 1954, and then only to a very limited extent. In addition to the complete sterling backing, accumulated profits up to 10 per cent of the Currency Board's assets were also invested in sterling securities as a reserve to cover the Board's obligations in the event of a capital loss in its portfolio. Profits exceeding this 10 per cent level were remitted to the governments of the territories.[3] The purpose of this currency arrangement was to make the West African pound completely and freely convertible to the pound sterling, an arrangement well tailored for the trade economy in the colonial period. Under the West African Currency Board, there was no possibility of an exchange problem between West African and British currencies. The system was manifestly stable, and for its limited objectives this was the pre-eminent requisite.

In the decade of the 1950's, a more dynamic and diversified economy and a strong indigenous political consciousness began to emerge in Nigeria. These forces fused to create a compelling drive for social, political, and economic development and independence. With economic and political objectives changing, modifications of the monetary system itself were desirable and inevitable.

Commercial banking. In 1949 there were two major British banks in Nigeria operating forty-four branch banking offices.[4] During the 1950's approximately 150 additional offices were established by these and other banks, and total deposits (demand, time, and savings) increased from £13.7 million to £65.3 million.

The orientation of commercial banking activities was also changing. Although the available statistics do not give enough detail to compute accurately the net external assets of the system,

[3] David E. Carney, *Government and Economy in British West Africa* (New York: Bookman Associates, 1961), pp. 63–64.
[4] Central Bank of Nigeria, *Annual Report and Statement of Accounts,* December 31, 1960 (Lagos), p. 5.

Table 2 indicates that the system began responding to local credit requirements.

Table 1
Liabilities of Principal Banks (£ Million)

Date		Demand Deposits	Time Deposits	Savings Banks	Balance Due to Other Banks		Other Liabilities	Total
					Nigeria	Abroad		
1950	Dec.	13.19	1.76	1.45	0.22	0.74	0.40	17.75
1951	Dec.	18.43	2.36	1.63	0.35	0.98	2.36	26.11
1952	Dec.	22.23	3.33	2.29	0.64	2.44	5.12	36.04
1953	Dec.	24.47	3.85	2.92	1.40	1.76	4.46	38.86
1954	Dec.	32.87	4.29	3.45	1.92	2.84	6.76	52.12
1955	Dec.	31.64	4.73	5.86	1.82	5.27	8.43	57.74
1956	Dec.	35.35	4.13	6.53	3.39	7.24	11.01	67.65
1957	Dec.	37.33	5.65	8.92	2.36	8.16	10.50	72.91
1958	Dec.	40.27	6.65	11.15	3.89	5.60	12.15	79.70
1959	June	39.09	14.25	12.61	4.05	2.78	12.45	85.21
1959	Dec.	40.17	10.85	14.28	3.66	12.69	18.89	100.53
1960	June	44.70	9.28	16.78	1.82	8.78	16.96	101.18
1960	Dec.	41.12	8.95	18.44	2.50	18.37	25.57	117.92
1961	June	42.58	8.20	20.07	1.12	17.77	20.75	116.67
1961	Dec.	41.66	14.07	21.19	1.17	21.98	37.06	147.33
1962	June	39.43	14.67	23.38	1.13	30.50	33.81	154.91
1962	Dec.	45.30	17.42	24.22	0.44	8.65	33.52	142.62
1963	June	42.14	18.28	26.09	1.24	14.65	22.19	143.00

Assets of Principal Banks (£ Million)

			Balance Due by Other Banks		Loans, Advances		Investments		Other Assets	Total
		Cash	Nigeria	Abroad	1 Year or Less	More than 1 Year	Nigeria	Abroad		
1950	Dec.	2.04	0.14	10.39	4.35		0.02	0.03	0.78	17.75
1951	Dec.	3.36	0.60	13.50	5.52		0.05	0.03	3.06	26.11
1952	Dec.	3.86	0.68	15.96	9.15		0.32	0.03	6.04	36.04
1953	Dec.	5.38	1.17	16.07	10.03	0.18	0.28	0.03	5.73	38.86
1954	Dec.	5.31	1.41	24.83	11.40	0.49	0.16	0.04	8.48	52.12
1955	Dec.	7.45	1.61	20.47	18.90	0.18	0.38	0.03	8.73	57.74
1956	Dec.	6.81	1.82	21.77	23.34	2.17	0.39	0.06	11.30	67.65
1957	Dec.	7.02	2.11	16.90	34.07	0.39	0.39	0.03	11.99	72.91
1958	Dec.	6.65	3.51	15.89	36.94	1.35	0.26	0.34	14.75	79.70
1959	June	6.41	4.20	25.27	29.48	0.87	0.65	4.43	13.91	85.21
1959	Dec.	8.45	6.10	23.67	39.10	1.79	0.70	0.62	20.11	100.53
1960	June	5.40	2.99	28.44	35.97	1.74	5.41	0.73	20.49	101.18
1960	Dec.	7.97	4.65	21.25	54.64	2.37	2.68	0.18	24.19	117.92
1961	June	5.76	4.63	24.35	45.68	2.64	7.88	0.03	25.70	116.67
1961	Dec.	7.62	4.65	36.45	57.09	2.91	4.30	0.03	34.29	147.33
1962	June	5.98	4.50	35.83	57.46	3.63	10.87	0.03	35.71	154.91
1962	Dec.	7.55	4.27	21.51	75.37	5.04	4.97	0.03	23.88	142.62
1963	June	9.14	3.51	20.06	78.85		6.84	0.03	24.57	143.00

SOURCE: Federation of Nigeria, *Quarterly Digest of Statistics.*

Table 2
Commercial Bank Orientation

	Total Assets or Liabilities (£ Million)	Balance Due to Other Banks as % of Total Liabilities		Balance Due by Other Banks as % of Total Assets		Loans, Advances as % of Total Assets
		Nigeria	Abroad	Nigeria	Abroad	
1946	14.37	10%	—	3.7%	77.6%	6.7%
1947	15.08	7	1%	2.6	72.7	11.2
1948	16.67	10	1	2.5	63.9	21.2
1949	14.19	1	1	1.0	54.0	25.9
1950	17.75	1	4	0.8	58.5	24.5
1951	26.11	1	4	2.3	51.8	21.1
1952	36.04	2	7	1.9	44.2	25.4
1953	38.86	4	5	3.0	41.2	26.3
1954	52.12	4	5	2.7	47.6	22.8
1955	57.74	3	9	2.8	35.4	33.0
1956	67.65	5	11	2.7	32.1	37.6
1957	72.91	3	11	2.9	23.2	47.2
1958	79.70	5	7	4.4	20.0	48.0

SOURCE: Computed from Table 1.

Balances due to banks abroad increased from 0 per cent of total assets in 1946 to 11 per cent in 1957, while balances due from banks abroad fell from 77 per cent of total assets to 23 per cent in the same period. Further, the percentages of total assets absorbed in local loan activities shifted markedly from 6.7 per cent in 1946 to 48 per cent in 1958.

The reorientation of banking activities during the 1950's was motivated by the increasing local demand for commercial bank loans (and an awareness of the possibility of profiting from this demand), particularly in trade and agriculture. Although specific data on commercial bank lending are not available for this period, the rapid growth of trade from an import-export total of £150 million in 1950 to £339 million in 1959 suggests the magnitude of the increase in demand for credit to finance trade.[5]

External orientation of financial institutions. Although commercial banks had begun to reorient their operations in the direction of serving local credit requirements, other organizations of substantial financial importance were still externally oriented. During this period the currency circulation grew rapidly, increasing from

[5] Federation of Nigeria, *Annual Trade Report,* 1954 and 1960.

£23 million in 1946 to £58 million in 1958. All the assets backing this currency were invested in sterling securities. Moreover, Government and quasi-Government organizations held the bulk of their reserves overseas, and the assets under the control of insurance companies, pension and provident funds, and superannuation schemes were all invested overseas. Table 3 shows the external assets of official and semiofficial Nigerian authorities at the end of 1958.

Table 3

Overseas Assets of Governments, Semiofficial and Other Organizations, December 31, 1958

	£ Million
Federal Government	47.2
Regional Governments	31.5
Local Governments	3.5
Regional Development Corporation	6.3
Marketing Boards	31.7
Other Semiofficial Agencies	9.4
West African Currency Board	70.0
Post Office Savings Bank	3.4
Net Balances of Banks	10.6
Total	213.6

SOURCE: Federation of Nigeria, *Quarterly Digest of Statistics,* October 1962, p. 16.

Government revenue and expenditure. Another important factor leading to the reorientation of credit activity was the rapidly expanding demand for funds by the Federal and Regional Governments. Tables 4, 5, and 6 show the pattern of revenue and expenditure for the Federation during the decade of the fifties. Three points are apparent from these tables: (*a*) there has been a very rapid expansion in the size of the current portion of the Governments' budgets; (*b*) the revenue to finance these budgets has been generated primarily from custom and excise duties; and (*c*) the budgets have gone from substantial surpluses to substantial deficits.

The supply of revenue has not kept up with requirements. Direct taxes to the Federal Government increased only from approximately £5.3 million to £6.3 million in the 1950–1960 period. This minimal growth was due to a very slowly expanding personal income tax base in the Federal Territory and the administrative

Table 4
Federal Government Finance (£ Million)

		Current Revenue			Current Spending				Current Surplus	Capital Revenue			Capital Spending			
		Tax	Other	Total	Federal	Re-gions	Devel-opment	Total		Loans	Other	Total	Loans, Grants	Works	Total	Deficit
Year	Custom								(4−8)							(15−12)
	1	2	3	4	5	6	7	8	9	10	11	12	13	14	15	16
1951	18.2	5.3	9.3	32.8	18.5	9.3	2.6	30.4	2.4	—	—	—	—	—	—	—
1952	32.1	6.8	11.4	50.3	29.9	10.0	3.8	43.7	6.7	—	—	—	—	—	—	—
1953	33.9	6.8	10.1	50.9	25.9	13.8	4.3	44.1	6.8	—	—	—	—	—	—	—
1954	42.1	5.7	11.5	59.3	36.9	13.3	4.8	55.0	4.3	—	—	—	—	—	—	—
1955	43.9	6.7	11.8	62.5	31.2	27.4	2.1	60.7	1.8	—	—	—	—	—	—	—
1956	44.8	6.8	8.4	60.0	29.2	25.8	0.4	55.4	4.6	2.0	—	2.0	—	—	—	—
1957	50.8	6.6	13.2	70.6	26.0	28.4	8.6	62.9	7.6	9.3	—	9.3	2.2	10.6	12.7	3.4
1958	51.7	6.7	12.6	70.9	30.5	29.0	6.1	65.7	5.3	—	1.2	1.2	1.6	15.5	17.1	15.9
1959	55.9	6.7	14.7	77.3	35.0	31.1	9.3	75.4	1.9	3.8	0.8	4.6	5.8	22.3	28.1	23.5
1960	63.1	6.3	19.5	88.8	40.3	38.5	3.0	81.7	7.1	6.7	1.0	7.7	6.3	29.5	35.8	28.1
1961	75.2	7.7	28.9	111.9	40.7	46.8	7.1	84.6	17.3	21.1	3.5	24.6	9.9	38.2	48.1	23.5
1962	76.7	8.7	29.0	114.5	54.2	46.6	8.4	109.2	5.2	16.2	5.8	22.0	9.9	22.1	32.0	10.0

Table 5
Regional Budgets (£ Million)

Year	Federal Sources	Current Budget Region, Other	Total	Current Spending	Capital Budget Grants	Loans	Total	Capital Expend- itures
	17	18	19 (17+18)	20	21	22	23 (21+22)	24
1951	—	—	8.5	7.8	—	—	—	—
1952	—	—	9.8	9.4	—	—	—	—
1953	16.9	2.1	18.9	14.0	—	—	—	—
1954	14.8	4.2	19.0	17.3	—	—	—	—
1955	26.9	9.3	36.2	26.8	—	—	—	—
1956	24.6	13.5	38.2	34.6	—	—	—	—
1957	26.8	16.5	43.3	40.6	23.6	13.5	37.1	15.8
1958	27.8	16.6	44.5	40.1	3.5	2.5	6.0	10.5
1959	29.9	17.4	47.3	39.6	2.4	2.0	4.4	12.6
1960	27.2	26.1	53.3	51.6	5.0	3.4	8.4	21.8
1961	30.5	24.6	55.1	54.8	14.2	9.6	23.8	25.0
1962	35.4	28.3	63.7	62.8	0.3	5.8	5.8	31.0

SOURCE: Federation of Nigeria, *Quarterly Digest of Statistics.*

Table 6
Total Surplus or Deficit on Current and Capital Accounts
(£ Million)

Year	Federal	Regions	Total	Cumulative from 1957
	25 (9—16)	26 (19+23—20—24)	27 (25+26)	
1951	+ 2.4	+ 0.7	+ 3.1	+ 3.1
1952	+ 6.7	+ 0.4	+ 7.1	+10.2
1953	+ 6.8	+ 4.9	+11.7	+21.9
1954	+ 4.3	+ 1.7	+ 6.0	+27.9
1955	+ 1.8	+ 5.4	+ 7.2	+35.1
1956	+ 4.6	+ 3.6	+ 8.2	+43.3
1957	+ 4.2	+14.0	+18.2	+61.5
1958	−10.6	− 0.1	−10.7	+50.8
1959	−21.6	− 0.5	−21.6	+29.2
1960	−21.0	−11.7	−32.7	− 3.5
1961	− 6.2	− 0.9	− 7.1	−10.6
1962	− 4.8	−24.3	−29.1	−39.7

SOURCE: Federation of Nigeria, *Quarterly Digest of Statistics.*

difficulties encountered in the taxation of a large, diffuse commercial sector.

In summary, the rapid growth of financial institutions in the postwar period, the rapid increase in Government expeditures which outpaced revenues, the widening responsibility of Government to assume an important role in capital expenditures, the prospect of political independence, and the aspiration for economic autonomy all contributed to the desire and need to reorient the monetary system toward internal requirements. The first step was the mobilization of overseas reserves, and the initial targets were currency reserves, commercial bank balances, and the funds held abroad by various Government or quasi-Government organizations and some private financial institutions.[6]

Formation of the Central Bank

In 1959 the Central Bank of Nigeria was established as an instrument whereby Nigeria would be able to influence the internal monetary environment. The Bank's first major tasks were to assume control of the West African Currency Board's sterling securities which were backing the Nigerian currency and to issue and manage Nigerian notes and coin. Currency Board notes and coins were gradually withdrawn; by July 1962, the transfer was completed.[7]

Under its initial governing legislation, the Central Bank was required to maintain external reserves equal to 60 per cent of the currency in circulation and 35 per cent of other demand liabilities.[8] Despite the latitude provided by the new legislation, within the Government there was a distinct emphasis on the need to maintain confidence in the new currency by following a conservative course in the repatriation of currency reserves. The Minister of Finance stated in his address at the opening of the Central Bank: "Initially the currency will be backed one hundred per cent by sterling reserves. . . . We firmly believe that for at least the first two or three years this fiduciary element should be kept well within the permitted margin."[9] Furthermore, the Central Bank was required to exchange Nigerian pounds for sterling free

[6] For a complete discussion of the need to create internal monetary mechanisms in such situations see: Edward Nevin, *Capital Funds in Underdeveloped Countries* (London: Macmillan and Co., Ltd., 1961).

[7] Central Bank of Nigeria, *Annual Report and Statement of Accounts,* December 1962, p. 20.

[8] Laws of Nigeria 37 of 1959, Central Bank of Nigeria Ordinance, May 15, 1958.

[9] Address by the Federal Minister of Finance when opening the Central Bank Building, July 1, 1963. Reprinted in Central Bank's *Annual Report and Statement of Accounts,* March 31, 1960.

from exchange control; for all practical purposes, the currency was still freely convertible.

In addition to its function of issuing currency, the new Central Bank began to support and administer local issues of Government securities. In Nigeria, the demand for funds to finance agricultural exports is very seasonal, with a high demand in December and low demand in June. Because of this fluctuating demand, the growth of commercial bank assets, and the fact that banks had voluntarily begun to shift their loaning operations to the home market, it became clear that a Nigerian short-term security with high liquidity and a competitive yield would be salable. Thus, there was an opportunity to market a security comparable to the ninety-day treasury bills of the developed countries. In March 1960, the Central Bank began monthly issues of ninety-one-day Nigerian Treasury Bills. During the first three years of the Central Bank's existence, Treasury Bills outstanding reached £24 million. Also during this period, the Federal Government had issued £19.3 million long-dated development loans in the local market.

An important point to note in respect to the large increase in domestically held Nigerian Government debt is that it was accomplished without a major repatriation of sterling assets backing the currency, even though the use of these assets for domestic capital expenditure programs is one of the major motivations for an internally managed currency. The initial minimum requirement for external reserves of 60 per cent was reduced to 40 per cent in 1962,[10] but, as indicated in Table 7, repatriation of these assets has not approached this minimum level. At the end of 1962 the ratio was 0.87, and by October 1963, it was still 0.79.

Financial Developments, 1959–1962

The large increase in domestic debt with minimal support from the Central Bank was accomplished by the mobilization of other external reserves. At the same time other important developments took place which had, and will continue to have, significant effects on the development of Nigeria's capital market. These other developments included a continued shift in commercial banking

10 Central Bank Amendment Act, 1962, Clause 4.

Table 7
Central Bank: External Backing of Nigerian Currency (£ Million)

	Nigerian Currency	External Reserves	Reserve Ratio	Federal Government Security Holdings
Dec. 1960	77.1	77.6	1.01	1.6
Dec. 1961	80.1	68.5	0.85	5.0
Dec. 1962	87.3	76.6	0.87	1.5
June 1963	71.9	58.5	0.81	8.1
Oct. 1963	75.6	60.0	0.79	11.9

Source: *Return of Assets and Liabilities of Central Bank of Nigeria,* published monthly by the Central Bank.

Table 8
Bank Loans by Sector
(December 31)

	1959	1960	1961	1962
Government, Utility, Mining	1.8%	3.8%	2.4%	1.8%
Financial Institutions	8.4	5.2	4.1	1.1
Agriculture	23.2	21.2	21.0	22.5
Manufacture	4.1	4.3	5.5	7.3
Construction	7.7	6.4	9.2	6.5
Commercial	33.8	37.2	32.4	34.5
Miscellaneous	21.0	21.9	25.4	26.3

Source: *Central Bank Annual Reports* and *Monthly Returns of Commercial Banks,* published by the Central Bank.

orientation, some rather severe balance-of-payments deficits, and the formulation of an ambitious Six-Year Development Plan.

Purchases of Government securities: banks, marketing boards, and pension funds. The shift from budget surpluses to deficits in 1958 and the prospects for even larger deficits after 1958 were major factors leading to the marketing of short- and long-term Government securities. The original issues of these securities were directed to the repatriation of accumulated savings of the economy which were held abroad by Nigerian-based private and official organizations. During the 1959–1962 period the Federation issued its first three development loan stocks. The maturities on these stocks range from four to sixteen years, and the stocks yield 5 to 6 per cent. The stocks are:

May 1959	£400,000	5%	Federation of Nigeria First Development Stock 1964
	£600,000	5½%	Federation of Nigeria First Development Stock 1969
	£1,355,000	6%	Federation of Nigeria First Development Stock 1979
March 1961	£2,000,000	5%	Federation of Nigeria Second Development Stock 1967
	£4,000,000	5½%	Federation of Nigeria Second Development Stock 1977
	£4,000,000	6%	Federation of Nigeria Second Development Stock 1985
Feb. 1962	£2,000,000	5%	Federation of Nigeria Third Development Stock 1966
	£5,000,000	6%	Federation of Nigeria Third Development Stock 1986

The first of these three loans was oversubscribed. Initially, the Central Bank was called upon to purchase about 35 per cent of the second and third; but during the course of 1961 and 1962, buyers came forward and purchased all of the Central Bank's holdings of these two securities. The Government has pegged the price of its stocks at par by agreeing to buy or sell upon demand. Moreover, transfers of Government stock are made at par plus or minus accrued interest to the date of purchase; consequently, these securities have the characteristics of a short-term bill. Because of the nature of the market, the Central Bank has not had to repurchase any of the Government stock to maintain the price and seemingly will not be required to do so in the future.

As had been anticipated, the stock issues generated a substantial repatriation of externally held reserves. The subscribers (see Table 9) were all institutions holding large assets abroad.

PURCHASES BY BANKS. Banks made initial subscriptions for £3.3 million of the £19.355 million total. Since commercial banks have concentrated their investments in treasury bills and the demand for commercial bank credit will clearly remain at a high level, it is unlikely that they will be able to purchase significant amounts of Government stock in the future. Nor is the Post Office Savings Bank a likely future market of significant capacity for Government securities. In the first place, although at the end of 1958 this

Table 9
Development Loan Applicants (£ Thousand)

Purchaser	First Development Loan		Second Development Loan		Third Development Loan	
	Amount	Percent-age of Total	Amount	Percent-age of Total	Amount	Percent-age of Total
Banks (and Post Office Savings Bank)	353	15%	1,225	12.3%	1,720	24.6%
Marketing Boards	332	14	3,505	35.0	—	—
Pension Provident Funds	730	31	1,226	12.3	1,734	24.8
Insurance Companies	165	7	70	0.7	40	0.6
Statutory Corporations	634	27	86	0.8	54	0.8
Cooperative Societies	49	2	43	0.4	35	0.5
Other (Firms, Schools, Individuals)	92	4	158	1.6	976	13.9
Central Bank	—	—	3,687	36.9	2,441	34.8
Total	2,355	100%	10,000	100.0%	7,000	100.0%

SOURCE: *Central Bank Annual Reports.*

organization held assets overseas totaling £3.4 million, by March 1962, the entire amount had been repatriated.[11] Moreover, the total deposits of this organization have been falling steadily since 1956. The accumulated balance per account has dropped to about £10.[12] In any event, given the cost of servicing the system, the savings mobilized through it are expensive and of marginal benefit.

PURCHASES BY MARKETING BOARDS. The Marketing Boards purchased £332,000 of the First Development Loan, £3,505,000 of the Second Loan, and none of the Third. Their purchases were linked to the repatriation of their overseas assets, which fell from £35 million to £4 million during this three-year period. However, only a small portion of these funds has been invested in Federal Government long-term debt. These are Regional organizations, and as the Regional Governments have been running deficits, Marketing Board reserves have been used to help fill the gap. Moreover, the Marketing Boards would only want to commit their hard-core reserves to long-dated stocks; therefore, they have concentrated their investments in Treasury Bills. The prospect of financing future Federal Government development expenditures out of

[11] Federation of Nigeria, *Quarterly Digest of Statistics,* Vol. 11, No. 4, p. 16.
[12] *Ibid.,* p. 17.

Marketing Board reserves is not hopeful. The major crops involved are palm oil and kernels, cocoa, and groundnuts. The world market for these crops is not buoyant. Only nominal growth is expected in their consumption. Producer prices on all crops but groundnuts have already been cut back substantially from their peak year prices. For both political and economic reasons, the increment between producer price and world-market price cannot be increased substantially by a continued lowering of the former.

PURCHASES BY PENSION-PROVIDENT FUNDS. The other major source of funds for the purchase of Government stock has been the pension and provident funds. The organizations operating such funds purchased upon application £730,000, £1,226,000, and £1,734,000, respectively, of the first three Government stock issues amounting to about 20 per cent of the £19.355 million total. In addition, during the period between issues they purchased a large proportion of the £6.1 million of stock taken up by the Central Bank. It is possible that these organizations now hold between 40 and 50 per cent of the first three issues.

Through 1961, the major pension and provident funds were operated by the large statutory corporations (Electricity Corporation, Ports Authority, Coal Corporation, and the Railway Corporation) and by the large private employers such as the United Africa Company. The proceeds of these funds and many other smaller funds were invested outside Nigeria. Hence, in this case also, purchase of Development Loan Stock reflected the return of assets held abroad.

In October 1961, the Government initiated the National Provident Fund (N.P.F.), which is basically a nonvoluntary savings program covering about 300,000 employees. Contributions are at the rate of 5 per cent of the employee's salary and are matched by the employer. The scheme now covers public and private agencies employing ten or more people. The intake of the N.P.F. is about £300,000 per month, or £3.5 million per annum. All of the proceeds are invested in Government development stock. Monthly purchases of development stock are approaching £500,000. Thus about 60 per cent of total subscriptions are accounted for by N.P.F. purchases and probably another 20–25 per cent by other pension and provident funds. It is evident that these financial institutions have become the most important instrument for mobilizing domestic savings in Nigeria.

Commercial banking activity. Assets of commercial banks continued to expand rapidly; in the 1959–1962 period the annual rate of increase averaged 17 per cent. In addition, the net external assets of commercial banks continued to fall, and, with the availability of treasury bills, the seasonal fluctuation in the external reserves of commercial banks has decreased considerably. In the first six months of 1960, average external assets of commercial banks were £26 million, while in the first six months of 1963 the average was reduced to only £4 million. The availability of Nigerian treasury bills was not the only cause for this reduction. Another factor was the expansion of loans and advances of commercial banks. In 1959 and 1960 bank credit experienced its normal cyclical swing, although the average credit in 1960 was considerably higher than that in the previous year. In 1961 there was a great seasonal decline in bank credit matched by purchases of treasury bills and a decrease in net external assets. But in 1962 there was no seasonal decline in loans and advances; bank credit expanded almost steadily from £60 million to £80 million.

Of this increase about £2.5 million was loaned to manufacturing concerns, while commercial, agricultural, and miscellaneous loans absorbed the remainder (see Table 8). During the year, banks lowered their liquidity ratio from 39.5 per cent to 29.1 per cent, only 4 points above the statutory minimum, as they mobilized funds to meet heavy credit demands.[13] This growth in credit outpaced deposit growth, and over the three-year period loans and advances, as a percentage of deposits, increased from 56 per cent to 92 per cent. Although bank credit dropped slightly in January and February 1963, it again began to increase through May, exerting pressure on liquidity and external assets.

Balance-of-payments deficits. In the 1959–1962 period, large balance-of-payments deficits and reserve losses created an awareness of the importance of a healthy foreign exchange position. Table 10 gives fragmentary balance-of-payments data for the 1958–1962 period. Prior to 1955, Nigeria maintained a positive trade balance,

[13] Central Bank of Nigeria, *Annual Report and Statement of Accounts,* December 1962, p. 29.

but trade deficits began in 1955 and increased rapidly from £3.6 million in that year to £53.5 million in 1961.

There has also been a growing net deficit on services, which increased from £8.8 million in 1959 to £16.0 million in 1962. The combined deficit on goods and services and private donations was

Table 10

Nigeria's Balance of Payments (£ Million)

	1958	1959	1960	1961	1962
Imports	168.2	180.2	217.5	224.4	205.0
Exports	134.3	162.1	167.0	170.9	166.6
Trade Balance	−33.9	−18.1	−50.5	−53.5	−38.4
Net Service Balance	− 8.8	−15.2	−18.3	−14.6	−16.0
Net Private Donations	− 3.2	− 5.2	− 5.7	− 6.4	− 6.5
Total	−45.9	−38.5	−74.5	−74.5	−60.9
Private Investment	+14.0	+24.0	+19.0	+30.0	+20.0
Gap to Be Covered by Official Aid and Reserve Drawdowns	−31.9	−14.5	−55.5	−44.5	−40.9

SOURCE: Federation of Nigeria, *Quarterly Digest of Statistics.*

£45.9 million in 1958. This deficit was reduced to £38.5 million in 1959, but rose again sharply to £74.5 million in 1960 and 1961. In early 1962, new import duties were introduced which had an immediate effect in dampening demand for consumer items. The result was a 10 per cent reduction of imports which reduced the deficit on goods, services, and private donations to £60.9 million.

Foreign public and private investment (including reinvested profits) during this period has not been sufficient to cover the above deficits, which have averaged about £60 million per annum over the past four years. Estimated private capital investment per annum has averaged £22 million, leaving an average deficit of £38 million per annum to be covered by foreign aid and drawdowns of foreign exchange. Official grants and loans were £19.0 million in 1960, £10.9 million in 1961, and £5.2 million in the first half of 1962. The resulting gap averaged about £23 million per annum.

As indicated in Table 11, the net result of these deficits and the Government's efforts to repatriate overseas investments has been a very rapid drawdown of foreign reserves. In the 1958–1962 period reserves fell from £213.6 million to £124.1 million. This drop in external reserves occurred even though the Central Bank did not repatriate a significant amount of the assets backing the currency. At the end of 1962 the external reserve backing for the currency was still 87.5 per cent, substantially higher than the 40 per cent statutory limit introduced in March 1963.

Table 11
Nigerian External Reserves (December 31, £ Million)

	1958	1959	1960	1961	1962
Federal Government	47.2	29.6	27.0	27.1	28.0
Regional Government	31.5	31.6	23.3	19.5	8.5
Local Government	3.5	3.5	3.9	3.9	3.9
Regional Development Corporations	6.3	5.3	1.9	1.3	0.6
Marketing Boards	31.7	35.2	19.2	—0.4	1.1
Other Semiofficial Agencies	9.4	11.2	8.7	9.4	6.6
Total Official	129.6	116.4	84.0	60.8	48.7
West African Currency Board	70.0	27.4	10.0	6.8	—
Post Office Savings Bank	3.4	3.0	1.7	1.6	—
Net Commercial Bank Balances	10.6	12.2	—2.0	6.1	—1.2
Central Bank	—	57.5	77.6	75.7	76.6
Total	213.6	216.5	172.5	151.0	124.1

SOURCE: Federation of Nigeria, *Quarterly Digest of Statistics.*

The Six-Year Plan

Over-all Plan Targets

It was during this period of tightening bank credit, balance-of-payments deficits, repatriation of overseas assets for investment in Nigerian securities, and rapidly shrinking external reserves that Nigeria's Six-Year Plan was formulated.[14] The Plan's over-all target is a growth rate of 4 per cent per annum to be achieved by investing 15 per cent of the gross domestic product. The economy's total investment over the six-year period is anticipated to be as follows:[15]

[14] Federation of Nigeria, *National Development Plan, 1962–1968* (Lagos, 1961).
[15] *Ibid.,* p. 36.

Federal Statutory Corporations	£ 173.3 Million
Government Capital Programs	471.1
Capital Formation out of Recurrent Revenue	149.4
Private Capital Formation	389.5
	£1,183.3 Million

The Plan states that the figure given for private capital formation is conservative in that the target of £65 million per annum is actually less than the level achieved in 1959 and 1960.[16] However, of the £390 million private capital formation programmed, it is assumed that about £200 million will be capital investment from outside Nigeria. This is an average of about £33 million per annum, a substantially higher level than the £20 million per annum achieved over the 1958–1961 period. In addition to private capital inflow, official foreign aid is assumed to be £327 million,[17] making a total capital inflow of £527 million, or about 45 per cent of the total investment.

Imports are expected to increase 31.8 per cent over the Plan period, while exports are to increase 45 per cent.[18] This represents a marked change from the preceding six-year period when imports increased 65 per cent as against increased exports of 29 per cent. However, these projections are based on the summation of the results of an analysis of specific commodities and thus should be fairly reliable. In 1960 almost one quarter of the total imports into Nigeria consisted of the following items:[19]

Beer, Stout, Ale	£ 3.9 Million
Cement	5.4
Cotton Textiles	22.3
Petroleum Products	10.5
Sugar	3.8
Tires, Tubes	4.1
	£50.0 Million

Since 1960 there has been substantial investment in these industries, and by the end of the Plan period a large measure of internal self-sufficiency will be achieved for each of these products. The

[16] Ibid.
[17] Ibid., p. 39.
[18] Ibid.
[19] Federation of Nigeria, Annual Trade Report, 1960.

outlook for Nigeria's traditional export crops is not particularly favorable, but exports of petroleum and cotton lint should increase rapidly, and both will become important foreign exchange earners.[20]

According to such a pattern of trade, the six-year balance-of-payments deficit is expected to reach £480.5 million and is to be covered by capital imports of £527 million (£200 million private and £327 million official foreign aid). Thus the Plan does not anticipate any severe balance-of-payments problems over the six-year period; in fact, it forecasts an improving external reserve position.

Financing the Plan

Financing the public sector's portion of the Plan will pose very difficult problems for the Federation of Nigeria. Table 12 indi-

Table 12
Financing of Public Development Expenditure
(£ Million)

	Federal	Western	Eastern	Northern	Total
Capital Expenditure	406.9	90.3	27.7	88.9	653.8
Available Funds	200.7	25.2	21.8	15.3	263.0
Percentage of Total	(49%)	(28%)	(32%)	(17%)	(40%)
Assumed Foreign Aid	203.5	45.2	33.9	44.5	327.1
Gap	— 2.8	—19.9	—12.0	—29.1	—63.7

SOURCE: *Nigeria National Development Plan.*

cates the amount of funds that will have to flow from official overseas sources if the public sector plan is to be implemented.

It is obvious from the table that the Regions are particularly dependent on external resources. The Federal Government is (on paper) in a somewhat better position. The sources of funds for Federal Government capital expenditure are as follows:

[20] Exports of crude oil have increased from £1.4 million in 1958 to £16.8 million in 1962 and are estimated to be about £18 million in 1963. By 1965, crude oil production is likely to reach 5 million tons, representing a foreign exchange value of about £26 million. In 1963, crude oil exports will be about 12 per cent of Nigeria's total export earnings. The importance of oil in the Nigerian economy is clear. Without this commodity, Nigeria's trade deficit would be intolerable (Federation of Nigeria, *Quarterly Digest of Statistics*, Vol. 12, July 1963, p. 22; and Barclays Bank D.C.O., *Overseas Review*, August 1963, p. 65).

Recurrent Revenue	£ 27 Million
Statutory Corporation Resources	80
Domestic Debt and Central Bank	63
Mobilized Reserves	10
Other Federal Government Funds	20
	£200 Million

In the budget speech introducing the Plan, the Minister of Finance stated that the Central Bank would be prepared to hold up to £40 million in Government development stock.[21] In March 1962, the Central Bank was holding £7 million; therefore, the Government evidently plans Central Bank purchases of £33 million and sales of £30 million to other financial institutions, organizations, and individuals. In addition to this £30 million, the Government estimates that external balances of various organizations will be further reduced, resulting in sales of an additional £10 million in long-term stock ("Mobilized Reserves").

Since the major pension and provident funds and other institutional investors are purchasing about £6 million of Government stock per annum, the projection of sales to financial institutions seems reasonable. There is some question, however, as to the amount of long-dated stock that the Central Bank will be able to hold during the Plan period.

As mentioned before, the resources of the commercial banking system are being stretched to the limit, and the Central Bank has begun to support them in providing the seasonal credit required to finance crop exports. This is accomplished by the Central Bank rediscounting bills of exchange held by the commercial banks. The Central Bank began this operation in 1962; by the end of the year, it held £14.8 million in discounted bills of exchange. The Minister of Finance has said that he anticipates a rapid expansion of this operation and that at any one time the Central Bank could hold up to £40 million of discounted bills of exchange.[22] If the Central Bank is to hold £40 million of long-dated Government stock and provide £40 million in short-term credit to commercial banks, it will be holding the grand total of £80 million

21 Hon. S. F. Okotie-Eboh, *The Mobilisation Budget* (Lagos, Federal Ministry of Information, 1961), p. 7.
22 *Ibid.*, p. 6.

Table 13

Central Bank of Nigeria: Return of Assets and Liabilities
(£ Million)

Date	Liabilities					Assets					
	Capital and Reserve	Currency	Deposits	Other Liabilities	Total	External Reserve	Federal Government Securities	Other Securities	Rediscounts and Advances	Other Assets	Total
March 31, 1960	1.3	52.4	4.0	0.2	57.9	54.7	2.0	—	—	1.2	57.9
Dec. 31, 1960	1.5	77.1	2.8	1.1	82.5	77.6	1.6	—	1.8	1.5	82.5
Dec. 31, 1961	1.7	80.1	5.1	1.8	88.7	68.5	4.5	7.3	7.0	1.4	88.7
June 30, 1962	1.7	69.0	4.3	1.6	76.6	66.0	8.0	0.8	0.8	1.0	76.6
Dec. 31, 1962	1.9	87.3	3.3	2.0	94.5	76.6	1.5	—	14.8	1.6	94.5
June 30, 1963	1.9	71.9	3.2	1.5	78.5	58.5	8.1	3.5	7.6	0.9	78.5

SOURCE: *Central Bank Annual Reports.*

in local securities. At the end of 1962, £76.6 million out of the Central Bank's total assets of £94.5 million were invested overseas and covered £87.3 million of Nigerian currency (see Table 13). It is difficult to see how the Central Bank will be able to hold £80 million in local securities, in view of its current level of resources. The requisite degree of reserve repatriation is not wholly consistent with current balance-of-payments and foreign reserve problems. Although the combination of increased duties on imports, increased local manufacturing of consumer items, and oil exports helped to reduce the trade deficit to £36 million in 1962 and actually created a surplus of £200,000[23] in the first half of 1963, the shortfall in foreign capital inflow, official and private, from that planned resulted in additional foreign exchange deficits of £27 million in 1962 and £23 million in the first six months of 1963.[24] As of June 1963, foreign reserves amounted to £107 million, or a six months' import cover at current import levels.[25] Thus, the potential for additional drawdowns of foreign reserves to finance development has been greatly reduced. If there are shortfalls in the planned capital inflows and/or excesses in Government consumption over planned levels, there will be difficulty in reaching the level of aggregate investment programmed for the Plan period. Government will have to make a great effort to mobilize domestic capital even to approach the planned level of investment.

Public versus Private Investment

With reference again to the structure of gross investment planned for the Nigerian economy, the private sector's contribution is to be 33 per cent of the total, or £65 million per annum. It was noted that this is less than the actual level of private investment achieved in the years immediately preceding the Plan. Foreign private investment, however, is programmed at £200 million, or £33 million per annum, which is about 67 per cent higher than the equivalent rate in the five-year pre-Plan period. In other words,

23 "Nigeria's Favourable Trade Balance," *West Africa*, No. 2423 (November 9, 1963), p. 1279. However, this surplus, the first in recent years, was largely related to the timing of imports and exports. The more recent data indicate an £8.6 million trade deficit for the first eight months of 1963 compared with £8.7 million in the corresponding period of 1962. "Nigeria Trade Deficit Narrows," *West Africa*, No. 2432 (January 11, 1962), p. 51.

24 Barclays Bank D.C.O., *Overseas Review*, p. 61.

25 Federation of Nigeria, *Quarterly Digest of Statistics*, Vol. 12 (July 1962), p. 19.

the Plan actually calls for a reduction of domestic private invest-ment from a pre-Plan level of about £50 million per annum to about £32 million per annum. This aspect of the Nigerian Plan has not received much attention, but it has important implications for the private credit sector. The Development Plan alludes to this situation in Section 34: "The anticipated inflow of private invest-ment is consistent with the planned growth in domestic savings and especially public savings. The increase of domestic savings, almost all through public agencies, will leave correspondingly less for domestic private consumption and investment."[26] Thus, even if all the projected foreign assistance materializes, there will be strong pressure to channel domestic savings to the public sector for development expenditure. In addition, to the extent that ex-ternal resources for the Plan fall short — and, as mentioned before, this is a distinct possibility — the forces motivating redirection of domestic savings from the private to the public sector are further increased.

As steps are taken to direct domestic savings into public invest-ment, domestic funds available for private investment will be re-duced. This is contrary to another stated objective of Government, which is to encourage Nigerian participation in the private indus-trial sector. There is no evidence that these conflicting goals have been reconciled.

[26] *National Development Plan, op. cit.,* p. 38.

4

ON INFLATION IN GHANA[1]

Robert W. Norris

The path of economic growth in Ghana is currently threatened with an obstruction stemming from the reactions of the Government to inflationary pressures — pressures arising from excessive demand created by an expanding money supply and stagnating gross national product. The ultimate source of the pressures seems to lie in the realm of Government fiscal and monetary policies which are perpetuating an imbalance between consumption and investment demands, on one hand, and, on the other, the supply of funds through savings.

Since Ghana's present problems are latent in many other African states, an examination of them — with particular regard to the motor of inflation and the implications of inflation for Govern-

---

[1] As an aid in analyzing Ghana's inflation, the simple quantity theory of money will be used. See William Fellner, *Trends and Cycles in Economic Activity* (New York: Henry Holt and Company, 1956), p. 174. This theory holds that money supply (i.e., active purchasing power in terms of notes and coins and demand deposits) times the "velocity" of money turnover (i.e., the average number of times money changes hands during a given period against goods and services) equals the total amount of goods and services for which payment is made in the given period times the general price level at which these goods and services are traded. Algebraically this formula is

$$MV = TP$$

where

M = money supply $(£)$
V = velocity of money turnover (dimensionless)
T = total volume of goods and services for which payment is made (units)
P = general price level $(£/\text{unit})$

94

ment development policy — may have considerable admonitory value.

The Motor of Inflation

To restate the initial proposition, the inflationary pressures in Ghana result basically from an interaction between the money supply and the real product of the economy. The velocity of money turnover is significant, but to simplify discussion, this will be assumed as constant.

Money Supply

General trends. Figure 1 shows the development of Ghana's money supply as a function of the money-supply components (the assets of the banking system).

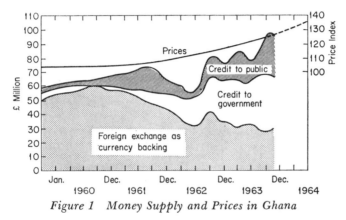

Figure 1   Money Supply and Prices in Ghana

1962 *Economic Survey of Ghana,* June 1963, Bank of Ghana Report, Accra.

The most essential point illustrated by the chart is the change, after December 1960, of the structure of the money supply. Before that time Ghana was on a monetary standard similar to the gold standard, in which the money supply was backed primarily by reserves of foreign exchange. In December 1960, foreign exchange made up 89 per cent of the money supply. A year later, the figure had fallen to 66 per cent, and it continued to decline — though at a reduced rate — to 56 per cent in 1962,[2] and 54 per cent in 1963.[3]

---

[2] *Quarterly Economic Bulletin of the Bank of Ghana,* Vol. 3, No. 1 (March 1963), p. 14, Table 8.

[3] Central Bureau of Statistics, *Quarterly Digest of Statistics,* Vol. 12, No. 4, pp. 62–67, Tables 64–69 (1963 figure is based on stated gold and foreign exchange balances

The decline in foreign exchange has not caused a similar decline in money supply; it has been more than offset by the issuance of Government securities and treasury bills,[4] that is, by increased credit to the Government. Credit issued to the public has also increased, but not at a comparable rate. The trends in these various components of the money supply hold profound implications for Ghana's current inflation problems.

Foreign exchange and the money supply. A distinction must be drawn between foreign exchange that is used as backing for the domestic money supply and foreign exchange balances that represent active purchasing power and reserves against future foreign debt-service charges. The immediate concern in this section is the power of foreign exchange to expand or contract the money supply. In a later section other aspects of Ghana's foreign exchange problem will be discussed.

The decline of foreign exchange as a factor in the money supply is understandable in a new, nationalistic country that is beginning to hold the debts of its own Government, as opposed to those of foreign governments, as its currency backing. As long as the Ghanaian public has reasonable confidence in the ability of its Government to honor the debt, the move is fully within the realm of monetary responsibility. Ghana, like the nations that rejected the international gold standard in the thirties, wants to be master of its economic destiny. By holding a large portion of assets behind the money supply in the form of Government securities and treasury bills, the Government can control the size of the money supply and thus control the level of economic activity in the country. At least, this is the theory. In fact, the ability of the Government to wield this weapon of monetary policy effectively is currently in doubt.

Ghana, like so many less developed countries, has balance-of-payments problems arising primarily out of an unfavorable current account balance. It is the payments balance that determines the level of foreign exchange in the country. Since 1960 Ghana has been running deficits in her balance of payments to such an extent that the foreign exchange reserves of the country have declined

---

of the Bank of Ghana and commercial banks versus the total money supply given in Table 66, p. 65).

[4] *1962 Economic Survey of Ghana,* June 1963, Bank of Ghana Report, Accra, p. 88.

from a balance of £148,635,000 in December 1960 to £43,235,000 in December 1963. After the catastrophic year of 1961, when the balance-of-payments deficit on current account was £52.7 million and reserves fell from £148 million to £73 million, tight import restrictions were imposed.

The arithmetic of the foreign exchange crisis is relatively simple. The money supply is approaching £100 million. Currency is approximately half of the money supply. By law and administrative regulation, the currency in circulation requires 60 per cent backing in the form of foreign exchange (though at the discretion of the Minister of Finance, and after consultation with the Bank of Ghana, the requirement can be reduced to 40 per cent). Thus, £30 million in foreign exchange must be held as currency cover. Current foreign exchange reserves for the country are approximately £40 million. Thus, only £10 million (up to £20 million if the reserve backing requirement is lowered to 40 per cent) remains liquid. Of this amount approximately £6 million must be held by the Government as security for an external loan. Consequently, if Ghana should run a balance-of-payments deficit in excess of £4 million (or £14 million, depending on the cover requirement), there is a danger that there will be insufficient liquidity to meet payments.

As a result of this situation, control of foreign exchange is being consolidated in the Bank of Ghana. In January 1964, the Foreign Exchange Committee was reconstituted with the Deputy Governor of the Bank of Ghana replacing the Minister of Finance as chairman. Virtually all foreign exchange in Ghana, except the £6 million held by the Government as security for the Crown Agents loan, is now held by the Bank of Ghana. Thus, the Government no longer can finance deficits by drawing down past savings of foreign exchange. However, the deficits themselves persist, and the means chosen to finance them constitute the root of Ghana's inflationary problems.

Money supply and credit. The problem of money supply and credit in Ghana is inextricably involved with the cyclical swings of economic activity which result from the economy's dependence on the cocoa crop. Business activity begins to accelerate around the middle of September as the main crop of cocoa is harvested. Commercial banks expand their lending to the public at this time to finance cocoa purchases and the business activity stimulated by the harvest. This increased lending to the public lasts through December, when receipts begin to flow in for the cocoa and the loans are liquidated. Around January, banks experience an increase in idle cash balances. Instead of holding these funds in cash, the banks have invested in Government stocks and securities until

Table 1

External Reserves and Money Supply in Ghana

Period Ending	External Reserves (£ Million)	Money Supply* (£ Million)	Seasonal Contraction†	Peak-to-Peak Expansion‡
Dec. 1960	148.6	68.7		14.5%
Mar. 1961	139.8	63.7		
June 1961	118.1	58.6		
Sept. 1961	98.6	54.5	20.6%	
Dec. 1961	73.7	72.7		
Mar. 1962	70.7	65.8		
June 1962	77.2	64.0		
Sept. 1962	80.3	59.4	18.2%	
Dec. 1962	72.4	81.6		12.2%
Mar. 1963	67.0	75.7		
June 1963	68.7	76.5		
Sept. 1963	64.3	73.8	9.6%	
Dec. 1963	43.5	94.7		16.0%
Mar. 1964	43.0	94.2		
Apr. 1964	na	95.3		
May 1964	na	91.5	3.3%	

* Banking system plus demand deposits in commercial banks. Government deposits in the central bank are excluded. Thus these figures are not directly comparable to Figure 1.
† Peak-to-peak change.
‡ Peak-to-valley change.

the cocoa season starts again. At this time the Government paper is discounted at the Bank of Ghana, and credit to the public begins to increase once again. The money supply traditionally, then, expands during the active season, September to December, and contracts during the off-season from January to September (there is a slight bulge around June for the mid-crops of cocoa, but this is of relatively little importance).[5]

Table 1, which relates external reserves and money supply, illus-

5 See *Quarterly Economic Bulletin of the Bank of Ghana*, Vol. 3, No. 1, p. 17.

trates the seasonal fluctuations of Ghana's money supply and points up two significant trends:

1. The seasonal contractions due to the cocoa crop are decreasing.
2. The money supply is expanding, as measured from increase in the peaks, at an accelerated rate.

In simple terms, the money-supply time series is beginning to resemble a stairway rather than a wave. Behind this phenomenon lie government fiscal and monetary policies which determine the size of the government's deficit and the way in which it is financed, policies which are formulated and implemented against a backdrop of severely constrained foreign exchange reserves.

The Government deficits and how they are financed. Since 1956, the Ghana Government has shown an increasing tendency to spend more than it earns. Figure 2 shows the trends of expenditure and revenue.

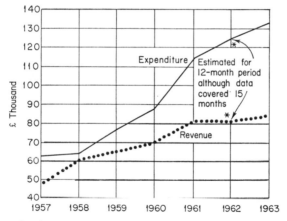

Figure 2   Government Revenue and Expenditure 1957–1963

1962 *Economic Survey, op. cit.,* and *Quarterly Digest of Statistics, op. cit.*

A discussion of the forces underlying this divergence would have to range far beyond the scope of this study, since they lie in the realm of built-in civil servants' wage increases and Government development policy. The limited object here is to analyze how the gap has been financed and what impact the financial policy will have on the future money supply.

Theoretically, deficits can be financed in any of four basic ways:

1. The Government can borrow from the banking system
2. The Government can sell some of its foreign exchange reserves
3. The Government can borrow from foreign or local sources
4. The Government can extract savings from the public

Table 2

Financing Budgetary Deficits in Ghana

Source	June 1960 to June 1961 Amount (£ Million)	%	June 1961 to Sept. 1962 Amount (£ Million)	%	Sept. 1962 to April 1964 Amount (£ Million)	%
Credit from Bank of Ghana	5.4	18.0	5.2	9.7	9.9	15.5
Credit from Commercial Banks	2.8	9.0	12.1	22.5	5.5	8.6
Drawing Down of Government Reserves	18.1	60.0	16.3	30.8	42.4	66.3
(Level of Government Reserves)	(32.0)		(17.0)		(6)	
Other	3.9	13.0	20.1	37.0	6.2	9.6
Total Deficit	30.2	100	53.7	100	64.0	100

* Up to September 1962, figures are derived from *Bank of Ghana Quarterly Reports* of March and June 1963. September 1962 to April 1964 figures represent estimates of Douglas A. Scott, Fellow in Africa, Office of the Ghana Planning Commission.

In June 1960, the Government held £50.1 million in foreign securities. In the ensuing year, it incurred a budgetary deficit of £30.2 million and financed 60 per cent of this deficit (£18.1 million) through the sale of such securities. The banking system was called on for 27 per cent of the deficit (with a direct increase in the money supply of £8.2 million), and other sources external to the banking sector were called on for the remaining 13 per cent.

In 1962, a statistically difficult year because of the change in the fiscal year from June–June to September–September, reserves provided funds for only 30.8 per cent of the deficit, while the banking system provided 32.2 per cent (a direct money-supply increase of £17.3 million). Other sources provided 37 per cent of £20.1 million, made up primarily of public (nonbanking) purchases of treasury bills of £10.7 million.

From September 1962 to April 1964, the primary source of financing the deficit was again foreign exchange reserves — this time to the extent of 66.3 per cent. Since Government reserve coffers were practically empty, the Government had to turn to the Cocoa Marketing Board, which held practically all nonbanking external reserves. This source was tapped through the use of "compensatory stocks," notes of indebtedness which were issued to the Cocoa Marketing Board in exchange for the external reserves, which were then sold to the Bank of Ghana for deposits in favor of the Government.

This transaction marks the virtual end of the supply of foreign exchange to finance deficits. With persistent deficits on internal and external account, the Bank of Ghana is going to have to control strictly the use of foreign exchange to ensure an adequate backing to the currency in circulation. This compounds the inflation problem, because financing deficits through past foreign exchange savings is noninflationary. Borrowing from the banks, however, has direct expansive influence on the money supply. Thus, the trend, shown in Table 1, of increases in money supply will, in the future, be much more closely correlated with Government deficits.

One other important trend illustrated in Table 1 is the decreasing seasonal contraction of the money supply. As explained earlier, the normal Ghanaian business cycle follows the cocoa season, with increased credit to the public in September at the start of harvest. Usually at the end of the cocoa season, credits would fall off, and idle funds would become available for less lucrative outlets such as Government securities. Before the days of large Government deficits and marginal Government foreign exchange reserves, the repayment of loans at the end of the cocoa season caused a decrease in the money supply. Now credit to the Government is more than soaking up these idle balances, with the result that when commercial banks come to the Bank of Ghana in September to discount treasury bills and Goverment paper in order to free funds for more lucrative outlets in credit to the public, the Bank of Ghana Issue Department finds its coffers choked with treasury bills, not cash, and it is becoming increasingly necessary to print money to fill the gap. Thus, Ghana's money supply is taking on the "step" appearance diagrammed earlier.

If the budgetary deficit for 1964 approaches £50 million (not unlikely in view of past trends), the money supply may increase by as much as £15 to £20 million, which could push it to over £110 million, or a 16 per cent increase over December 1963. The rationale for this rough projection is the following:

1. By April 1964, compensatory stocks, as mentioned earlier, had been practically exhausted as a source of finance, and they have only filled £20 million of the 1964 gap.
2. Maximum remaining liquid assets in Government coffers cannot exceed £10 million.
3. Voluntary contributions will probably not exceed £5 million.

With a less than 5 per cent increase in GNP, prices are apt to rise as much as 15 per cent. This follows the trend of prices to date (see price line on Figure 1).

Credit to the public and Government monetary policy. There are essentially two ways of attacking the problem of expanding money supply:

1. The Bank of Ghana can reduce credit to the public, thus lowering the seasonal upswing in September.
2. The government can reduce budgetary deficits and thus the need for expanded bank credit to the Government.

Recent events seem to indicate that the monetary authorities have opted for the former. Evidence in support of this deduction appeared in the *Commercial and Industrial Bulletin* of April 17, 1964, with the announcement of the imposition of stringent reserve requirements on all commercial banks in Ghana. These conditions were as follows:

1. The banks must hold 48 per cent reserves against total deposits from March 1 to August 31 (the off-season in terms of the cocoa cycle) and 54 per cent from September 1 to February 28 (the season of maximum business activity).
2. For these reserves the banks must hold 8 per cent of deposits in liquid assets (cash and balances in other banks), 18 per cent in Government of Ghana stocks, 5 per cent in "special deposits" with the Bank of Ghana and the rest (i.e., 17 per cent to 23 per cent) in Government of Ghana treasury bills, approved agricultural and industrial loans, and other special balances with the Bank of Ghana.[6]

---

6 *Ghana Commercial and Industrial Bulletin*, April 17, 1964, p. 319.

The obvious conclusion to be drawn from these regulations and the foregoing analysis of foreign exchange reserves, Government deficits, and the money supply is that the weapons of monetary control are being used on the "credit to the public" component of the money supply. The regulations require banks to hold large quantities of Government debt paper behind all public deposits, thus guaranteeing a source of finance to the Government and making the banks capable of absorbing virtually unlimited quantities of Government debt. The restrictions are all on loans to the public.

Included in the term "public" are all the State-owned, non-banking enterprises as well as private nonbanking enterprises. Under the new regulations, all loans over £5,000 to the "public" must be approved by the Government. The desire of a basically socialist Government to restrict credit generally makes it seem doubtful that the private sector will receive as much credit as it did before the new regulations.

Another conclusion to be drawn from the data is that monetary policy in Ghana is being called on to fill an essentially fiscal-policy role. When taxation is not adequate to balance Government revenue and expenditure, money is being created to fill the gap. Because of the desire of the Government, particularly at the outset of the ambitious Ghanaian Seven-Year Development Plan, to stimulate economic activity through Government expenditures, it appears unlikely that the gap will shrink. Therefore, a rapidly increasing money supply appears to be assured for Ghana over at least the next few years.

Ghana's National Product

A rising money supply is not inconsistent with stable prices if real product is increasing (see footnote 1). The danger in Ghana is that the money supply is increasing much more rapidly than real product. As was shown in Table 1, the money supply is currently rising at the rate of about 16 per cent per annum. The growth of gross domestic product at constant 1960 prices is given in Table 3.

Gross domestic product and capital/output ratio. From 1958 to 1962 a total of £475 million gross domestic fixed capital formation resulted in £120 million of growth in the gross domestic product. This gives a rough capital/output ratio over the period of 4.1:1.

Table 3

Gross Domestic Product, 1958–1963* at Constant (1960) Prices

	1958	1959	1960	1961	1962	1963†
Gross Domestic Product (£ Million)	382	433	469	477	492	502
Annual Increase	—	13.3%	8.3%	1.3%	3.1%	2%

* Walter, U.N. Report on National Income Accounts in Ghana (1962) (unpublished); *1962 Economic Survey, op. cit.*
† 1963 figures are estimates.

The net capital/output ratio assumed for the new Seven-Year Development Plan is 3:1, but there are many investments currently being undertaken by the Government that tend to reflect less directly productive activity and thus higher ratios.

The scissors effect. Currently Ghana is experiencing the unique phenomenon of unemployment and inflation increasing side by side. The severe import restrictions that have been imposed reduced the available goods and services, as well as investment and replacement goods. Industrial and trading operations have been contracted because of inadequate raw materials, supplies, and replacement parts. This contraction is causing noticeable unemployment. Simultaneously the Government is combating a sluggish economy with deficit-financing policies that continually expand the money supply. In a nutshell, increasing purchasing power is chasing fewer goods and services with the resultant inflationary trends.

This politically volatile and socially painful "scissors" effect is, in a sense, the problem of an economy so tied to external sources for goods, services, and markets that foreign exchange becomes the single most important financial resource of the country. If the world price of cocoa does not rise, Ghana can easily become a financially embarrassed nation that will experience both a severe interruption in her development plans and social unrest.

Implications of the Inflation

As the development history of some countries indicates, inflation can, under certain circumstances, stimulate economic growth. Unfortunately, Ghana does not appear prepared to derive the potential benefits from her price rise. Inflation can increase net per capita national income in four basic ways (the first three can be considered short-run while the fourth is long-run):

1. Profit margins can be increased if wages and other costs lag behind prices.
2. People may be induced to work harder.
3. Buying ahead may be stimulated.
4. Savings and capital accumulation may be encouraged.

To realize these possibilities, investors, public or private, must sense the potential gains and be willing to take the risks. This requires a clear profit orientation to investment decisions. In the author's opinion, governments tend to lack this essential orientation. Expenditure may continue, but the capital/output ratio of the resulting investment is likely to be much higher than corresponding private investment. It is thus more inflationary. Meanwhile, the stringent credit restrictions imposed on the commercial banks will deny the private sector the funds required to realize inflation opportunities, unless capital can be secured abroad.

PART II

PRIVATE INVESTMENT

The Obstacle of Ideology

For a nation in which there is notably little ambivalence toward the right of private persons to have, acquire, and use money for the satisfaction of caprice, as well as necessity, the rather chary attitude of many African governments to private investment presents a curious, confusing, and, to those unfamiliar with its historical antecedents, sometimes irritating spectacle. Michael Roemer, in his article on African socialism, examines the roots of this attitude and discusses its implications for the foreign investor.

John Knapp, who is back in Nairobi continuing his work for the Ministry of Commerce and Industry with the cooperative movement, describes the movement's growth and attributes its promising future both to its organic relationship with regional traditions and to political and ideological enthusiasm for this form of organizing economic effort. Here is one of the most constructive expressions of African socialism.

Incentives and Facilities

Roemer's conclusion that ideological constraints do not yet preclude potentially profitable and useful foreign investment in Africa opens the way to the more mundane discussion of incentives and facilities for private investment. Scott Spangler, who last year was with Ghana's National Investment Bank and is currently working for the Ministry of Finance in Entebbe, Uganda, has written about Ghana's investment incentives program. He states that there now are many government-created economic incentives available to the prospective investor. Whether, from the host country's perspective, incentives such as free land and tax and tariff exemptions are really necessary and desirable in most cases remains an unresolved and, it seems, often an unconsidered question. Probably here, as in most of the world's affairs, it is merely a matter of degree; but Spangler's essay indicates the dilemma inherent in legislative efforts to provide for the discretionary grant of calibrated concessions.

While, if we are to accept Professor John Kenneth Galbraith's suggestion made some years ago, the American stock market continues to display a remarkable indifference to history's chain of burst speculative bubbles, Nigeria's Stock Exchange pursues a quietly conservative course that would do justice to a Zurich banker. In his essay on the formation and operation of this Exchange, Douglas Gustafson concludes that it has an important role to play in facilitating the participation of Nigerian citizens in foreign concerns and in mobilizing indigenous resources for investment in the private sector.

International norms, agreements (between investors and governments and among governments and international institutions, on matters of substance and procedure), and national legislation are the legal bulwarks of foreign investment against injurious governmental intrusion. Some observers are skeptical about the efficacy of international norms and agreements as incentives to the flow of private capital to less developed countries. Yet it is hard to disagree with John Mallamud's point that the interest increasingly manifested by businessmen in the international legal panoply of foreign investment in itself provides substantial evidence that the existence of legal recourse is a factor in many investment decisions. In his essay, Mallamud, who worked on problems of foreign aid and investment while providing legal advice to Uganda's Ministry of External Affairs, outlines existing international legal norms and procedures and examines proposed new international agreements. He argues against excessive reliance on general, multination agreements with strong elements of compulsion, apparently favoring a more *ad hoc* approach. In connection with programs of affirmative incentives such as those described in the Spangler essay, he cautions against the rather unconscious reconstruction of a privileged caste of foreign investors.

Special Problems

Africa seeks, with other developing regions, the elusive solution to the problem of convincing its own residents to invest at home. The problem is particularly acute in East Africa, where there are no effective exchange controls and where there is an industrious and vulnerable racial minority with sizable capital accumulations. The problem is illustrated by Bruce Blomstrom's essay on Asians and capital flight in Uganda. He highlights the Asian's dilemma: The African majority insists that he become a citizen, but, not without some reason in this era of strident racial nationalism, the Asian remains skeptical about the promise of completely equal treatment.

As one palliative, Blomstrom proposes that existing investment-protection legislation be expanded to include all foreign capital, regardless of point of origin, so that Asians will be encouraged to repatriate funds already sent abroad. Mr. Blomstrom spent the years from 1962 to 1964 in Uganda as an Assistant Secretary in the Ministry of Commerce and Industry with responsibility for various international trade matters including Uganda's negotiations with the E.E.C.

East Africa is the continent's principal laboratory for experiments in regional economic cooperation. Though the prospect is uncertain, the region remains Africa's fairest hope for the successful organization of economic activity on a transnational scale. James Stoner, former Project Development Officer with Tanganyika's Ministry of Commerce and Industry, discusses Kenya's, Tanganyika's, and Uganda's mutual embroilment with that peculiarly prickly matter — industrial allocation. As he points out, the failure to work out acceptable arrangements for distributing new private economic activity among the nations of the region impedes development while exacerbating nationalist sentiment. Stoner's essay concludes with a proposal for institutionalized amelioration of the pustulant conflict.

5

AFRICAN SOCIALISM AND THE PRIVATE SECTOR

Michael Roemer

One of the difficulties in understanding African socialism arises from the existence of two schools of thought on the very meaning of the term and considerable variations of emphasis within each school. One group of leaders, the so-called scientific socialists, conceive of it as nothing more than the application in Africa of the teachings of Marx, Engels, and Lenin. The opposed school regards African socialism as a conception different in kind from the socialism known in Europe, a conception emerging from different conditions and employing different means to achieve objectives which are in many cases similar — though not identical to — traditional Marxist goals.

The latter interpretation of African socialism probably owes its genesis to Leopold Senghor, who in any event was the first to use the term.[1] It has been adopted and frequently articulated by Julius Nyerere[2] and Tom Mboya[3] and can probably be taken as the prevailing view among the leaders of East Africa who have been vocal on the subject. It is certainly not the unanimous view; there are outspoken and influential exponents of Marxian socialism in Kenya, Uganda, and Tanzania. Nevertheless, the present weight

[1] Henry Morganthau, "African Socialism: Declaration of Ideological Independence," *Africa Report,* Vol. 8, No. 5 (May 1963), pp. 3–6.
[2] See Julius Nyerere, *Ujama — The Basis of African Socialism,* pamphlet (Dar es Salaam: Tanganyika Standard Ltd., 1962).
[3] Tom Mboya, *Freedom and After* (Boston: Little, Brown, 1963), Chapter 8.

of written opinion and the trend of public policy are on the side of African socialism as a philosophy in its own right.

Elements of African Socialism

Although there are differences of emphasis among proponents of non-Marxian African socialism, the elements of a common philosophy can be pieced together. Its basic premise is that the organization of traditional African society and the human relationships prevailing within that society are generally desirable and should be preserved in modified form within the context of a modern economy. African society was generally communal in its organization, with the individual subordinated to an extended family. Extended families were, in turn, bound together in communities that were usually guided by elders but ruled by consensus. Land belonged to the tribe, and its produce was widely distributed; the needy were customarily provided for through the family and community system. Production was frequently organized on a voluntary, cooperative basis. This communal approach to the organization and distribution of production did not rule out private enterprise, of a sort. Though it belonged to the tribe, land was actually held by individuals or by families, and they did have some control over the distribution of its produce, though they were expected to consider communal requirements in determining appropriate allocation. The only right to hold land, however, was the right established by use. Since land could not be held by title, there could be no transactions involving it. The socially acceptable producer was not acquisitive, but rather gave freely of his goods to those in need.

Particularly as painted in these simple and alluring images, the historical accuracy of this vision is open to some debate. For example, it clearly fails to describe the social arrangements of a host of starkly hierarchic African kingdoms that patched sub-Sahara Africa from Uganda to the Western Sudan. Actually, even for those areas and tribes to which it is generally applicable, it is unquestionably a facile oversimplification. So, one supposes, are most powerful conceptions.

Accurate or not, it is this view of traditional society which guides the Senghor school of African socialists. They seek a modern economy arising within the context of a communal society.

The cooperative movement is seen as one important mechanism for achieving this, as it allows producers to maintain and, in fact, to use their community relationships to meet the demands of a monetary economy. Similarly, self-help schemes are encouraged. Both cooperative and self-help programs permit Africans, who at the dawn of independence have already emerged from the economic and legal relationships of traditional society, to experience a sense of compatibility between traditional values and their new economic and legal position.

Today, many Africans are outright owners of their land, and some have become owners of small industry. These new capitalists have contributed significantly to both the growth and stability of the economy, and there are not many African leaders who would advocate a return of such land or industry to its traditional status (and fewer still who could accomplish it). Nevertheless, African farmers and businessmen are under pressure to satisfy two traditional criteria. First, they must use their assets personally and productively. African socialism glorifies physical work, and absentee ownership is regarded with displeasure, as is the ownership of unutilized assets. Second, they must continue to act in harmony with the expectations of society that the needy will be provided for. The incomes of the modern farmers and businessmen are, in fact, distributed over a wide range of often distant relatives. While the concept of profits (or shall we call it the acquisitive urge?) has become socially acceptable, the retention of too great a portion of them, particularly when other individuals are in need, still is probably considered exploitative. At least, this is the attitude of tribes like the Kikuyu, who do have a deeply rooted communal tradition, though they have been among the quickest to appreciate and respond effectively to the personal economic opportunities presented by the monetary economy. In short, the new private sector is still part of and sensitive to a society that retains considerable respect for tradition.

African socialists view certain features of traditional African society as the basis for establishing modern welfare states. The extended family assumed responsibility for widows, orphans, and the aged. As pointed out before, many aspects of this indigenous welfare society have survived, so that Africans in the monetary economy often distribute their wages or profits among a large number of people. It should be possible to build on these favorable attitudes toward social welfare and give them formal expression through the institutions of a modern welfare state. The 1963 election manifesto of the Kenya African National Union, as a typical example, called for free medical care, provision for the aged (which has resulted in advanced plans for a national provident fund), and universal free primary education.[4]

The typical African socialist's belief that traditional African society can form the basis of a modern nation leads him to reject Marxian socialism. Julius Nyerere is the most eloquent spokesman of this rejection. African society was based on the extended family, he argues in his pamphlet *Ujama,* and all members were, in some sense, brothers. There were no owners of land, the principal means of production; thus there could be no "exploiters" in the society.[5] If in the beginning all men were brothers and none were exploiters, the doctrine of inevitable class conflict, which forms the basis of Marxian socialism, can have no relevance in Africa. Whereas Marx taught that a capitalist society, which would generate its own internal conflict, was the precondition for the transformation to socialism, the African socialists say that socialism already exists in Africa and only needs to be preserved, although in modern dress. The African socialist is fundamentally a conservative in his society and does not contemplate social revolution, although he often seems, to the Western ear at least, to speak in revolutionary language.

The African socialist feels that the intrusion of Western culture has tended to corrupt desirable African customs. For example, Nyerere has cited the renting of land and the abandonment of physical work as antisocial tendencies traceable to Western influence.[6] The achievement of African socialism is often expressed in terms of the elimination of both social injustice and economic exploitation, neither of which, it is said, existed before the colonizing of Africa. Thus, the process of adapting the best of indig-

[4] Kenya African National Union, *What a KANU Government Offers You,* pamphlet (Nairobi, 1963), pp. 3–4.
[5] Nyerere, *op. cit.*
[6] *Ibid.*

enous customs to the modern society must proceed alongside the process of re-establishing those customs which have come under corrupting influences.

A Place for the Private Sector

Because the exponents of African socialism do not adhere to the doctrine of the inevitable conflict between capital and labor, they have exhibited a much more pragmatic approach to social and economic problems than Marxian socialists have normally displayed. In concrete terms this has meant governmental acceptance, indeed encouragement, of a mixed economy rather than suppression of private enterprise. The following excerpt from a speech by Mwai Kibaki, the Parliamentary Secretary to the Treasury, in July 1963, is typical:

Mr. Speaker, Sir, this Government has already made clear the nature of the economy we are working for and it is that of a mixed economy. An economy in which the Government will make its contribution in spheres where the private investor may be hesitant to come in, in spheres where the project takes a long, long time to mature and to show profit. . . . Those areas in which services and goods are being provided by private industry — and being provided very efficiently — we are not going to interfere with. . . . We intend to have an economy where the Government and the private industries cooperate, and an economy where the ordinary individual person, if he has his money, is free to move in the direction he wants to move. . . . This is not to say, Mr. Speaker, that we are not aware that the bulk of the people in this country are poor and that they look to the Government for the provision of social services and incomes which they are not in a position to provide themselves. We are perfectly aware of that position. But we are equally aware, Mr. Speaker, Sir, that the way to help them is not to grab what little exists, or what little has been developed, and to distribute it to these people. . . . That would be the height of irresponsibility. Therefore, Mr. Speaker, our goal for the ordinary man who is poor in this country is for the Government to provide the services we need, on the understanding that he works with us . . . to help increase the national product. Then, Mr. Speaker, we shall have something to distribute to him, and that we promise you. Indeed, we can promise that we shall not allow our economic development to go in a way whereby the bulk of the wealth of this country could continue to be concentrated in the hands of a few people.[7]

The mixed economy of the African socialist is closely controlled. Central economic planning is an essential feature, almost an article of faith, which is intended to ensure that all resources are employed most effectively in the attempt to achieve a fairly equalitarian income-distribution pattern, a welfare state, and rapid increase in per capita gross national product. One of the first tasks of the independent African government is to produce a development plan, showing how all the elements of both private and public enterprise participate in the strategy for growth.

In considering the role of the private sector in an African socialist country, it is important to distinguish between the expatriate and the indigenous private sectors. A significant African private sector has already emerged in East Africa and is growing rapidly. Kenya's development plan emphasizes several programs to encourage greater numbers of Africans to enter the private sector of the monetary economy, as productive landowners, traders, industrialists, and investors.[8] The greater the success of these programs, the more committed Kenya's African socialist government will be to the maintenance of a healthy indigenous private sector. The terms on which it will remain acceptable to the African socialist have already been discussed. The important distinguishing feature of the African private sector, as opposed to its expatriate counterpart, is that at the moment it seems responsive to those traditions the African socialist wishes to adapt to a modern economy.

The more thorny question in considering African socialism and the private sector is the role of the expatriate private enterprises. The key to that role is the pragmatic approach of African leaders to the achievement of African socialism. Recognizing that vigorous economic growth is an indispensable condition for the realization of most of their social objectives, these leaders are encouraging expatriate private investment. The development plans for all three East African countries call for substantial investment of private foreign capital. Under Kenya's Plan, government capital is to be

[7] Mwai Kibaki, *Speech Delivered to the House of Representatives on 24 July, 1963* (Nairobi: Government Printer, 1963), p. 5.

[8] Government of Kenya, *Development Plan 1964–1970* (Nairobi: Government Printer, 1964), pp. 41–44.

concentrated primarily in social services, infrastructure, and security, leaving private capital — a significant proportion of which must come from abroad, since domestic sources are clearly inadequate — virtually alone to develop manufacturing and with the major responsibility for agriculture, fishing, tourism, and housing.

Harmonizing Foreign Investment and African Socialism

Despite the importance of expatriate private investment, it will inevitably experience some difficulty in living harmoniously with African socialism. In the first place, the foreign investor, with the notable exception of the expatriate farmer, is often an absentee owner and, in any case, does not perform the physical work that is revered by African socialists. Moreover, the expatriates who manage private enterprises form an elite that is painfully visible to African leaders, not only because of its obvious wealth but because its existence is contrary to their concepts of a classless society based on the extended family.

There are various avenues open to the foreign investor for the amelioration of latent or potential antagonism. One is to assist in the effort to achieve substantially greater African participation in the monetary economy. When the capital structure of a new venture is being considered, plans should be made to secure African participation. Ideally, shares would be sold to Africans, for that is the most direct way to give Africans the sense of having a stake in new enterprise. Shareholding, however, is probably the last step rather than one of the early steps to be taken in Africanizing the economy. The savings for such investment are not being generated at present in significant quantities, and considerable basic education in the workings of a capital market needs to be undertaken. In some cases, schemes for delayed local participation might be employed. These can be particularly effective in food-processing industries, since the cooperatives of growers who supply the factory can be given a chance to purchase shares out of their earnings. Such schemes for participation by groups or individuals organically related to the enterprise will also help satisfy the preference of African socialists for owners who contribute their own labor to make their assets profitable.

In lieu of immediate direct participation, government participation through a state enterprise, such as a development company,
should be sought. A government committed to African socialism
is likely to feel more comfortable with expatriate enterprises in
which some public agency has an interest. Such an enterprise is
seen as working within the development machinery established
by government and, therefore, as less likely to act contrary to government policies. There is a concomitant benefit to the investor.
Development companies are likely to be staffed with the best business talent available to the government;[9] thus government participation in this form is more likely to be sound and constructive.
Furthermore, the foreign investor may obtain valuable knowledge
of local conditions that he might otherwise lack. He gains this in
addition to what should be enduring governmental favor.

Regardless of whether or not the Government participates
directly in the enterprise, it will probably expect close cooperation
on some matters, particularly those related to social welfare. One
illustration of the type of request that may be made was the Kenya
Government's attempt to alleviate the unemployment problem by
asking employers to increase their labor forces by 10 per cent. The
Government offered to hire an additional 15 per cent itself, while
unions were asked to support a wage freeze for one year. Although
many firms had to hire redundant labor, most large private employers responded to the Government's appeal. Similarly, if a
government's development plans call for expansion or other action
in a certain industry, there is an expectation that existing firms
in that industry will respond, even if the risk may be greater than
normal. While governments in East Africa are unlikely to resort
to immediate compulsion in support of such requests, investors
with long-range interests will undoubtedly discover persuasive
arguments for compliance.

One reason why the motives for cooperation with government
are powerful is the intimate nature of government-company relations in the small African economies, where every new enterprise
of any size represents a significant addition to the economy's productive capacity. A company's favorable public image will promote

[9] [But compare Douglas Gustafson's evaluation of Nigeria's regional development
corporation in his essay "The Development of Nigeria's Stock Exchange" on p. 144.
—*Editor's note*].

cooperation and avoid some of the potentially damaging controls that governments feel philosophically free to impose. Government cooperation may result in valuable concessions to the enterprise in the form of protection, licensing, provision of infrastructure, and other benefits.

One of the important aspects of Kenya's plans to introduce more Africans into the monetary economy is a program to provide loans and extension services to aid African enterprises. The expatriate industrialist can assist in such efforts. He may, for example, donate management time for advisory services to African businessmen, or he may invite fledgling entrepreneurs to his factory on a regular basis for training. In some cases he may find it feasible to assist in the founding of locally owned supply sources as an alternative to producing the supplies himself or importing them.

There remains the question of profits. Africans earning profits are expected to distribute a share to promote community welfare. Analogously, expatriate firms that reinvest locally rather than repatriate the bulk of their profits will find a far more congenial atmosphere for their operations. Most African countries trying to attract investment do have laws guaranteeing the repatriation of profits and capital. Nevertheless, one feature of the working partnership that African socialists are promoting between government and private industry is the expectation that both partners will continue to reinvest in order to develop the country. Rapid repatriation will tend to be equated with exploitation.

In undertaking measures that are intended to reduce the potential conflict with African socialism, it is essential not to adopt a paternalistic approach. The reaction of an American (or European) industrialist or corporation to the social welfare emphasized in Africa may very well be reversion to the paternalism that marked labor-management relations in the United States in the early decades of this country. At that time management began to consider more seriously its responsibility to labor, but did not consider that employees had any right (or ability) to participate in decisions regarding conditions of employment. In Africa the same attitude formed the basis for colonial government. Identification, however inadvertent, with this aspect of preindependence rule would represent the nadir of good public relations. To avoid paternalism, if African participation is invited in a new venture, the shareholders must be given a voice in company policy commensurate with their investment. African managers must really manage and not simply shadow an expatriate decision-maker. Participation in determining appropriate working conditions or welfare plans by worker and — where one exists — by union should be encouraged.

One of the great unresolved questions is whether a modern industrial organization can adapt to the mores and institutions of traditional African society without a serious loss of efficiency. The Japanese have been pre-eminently successful in an analogous effort in their own country. Recruitment methods, the authority structure, and the reward system all closely reflect the traditions of Japan before the turn of the twentieth century.[10] Yet no manufacturer of textiles or electronic devices or a host of other items would today question the efficiency of Japanese industry. Perhaps, with the assistance of indigenous management, a similar integration of the modern and traditional can be effected in Africa.

The Labor Unions

There appears to be little basis in African tradition for labor unions. Landowners were also workers, and cooperative working arrangements meant that everyone served alternately as a worker and a manager. A laboring class, therefore, did not exist. Now, however, labor unions have arisen in response to the emergence of a wage economy, and it seems generally true that African leaders view them with suspicion. They tend to regard labor unions as irrelevant at best and incongruous on the African stage, on the theory that unions are a valid instrument only in a class struggle, which does not exist in Africa. This is, of course, a highly restricted view of the union's role. Moreover, whatever its validity in the context of relations between African entrepreneurs and workers, it does not philosophically preclude the union from being an essential force in defending the interests of labor in industries managed or owned by non-Africans. Actually, the antipathy between African socialists and union leaders appears to be based far more on practical political concerns about the existence of a non-

10 See M. Roemer, "Cultural Influences in African Manufacturing Organizations," Chapter 3, unpublished thesis in industrial management, Massachusetts Institute of Technology, 1962.

governmental power center, which could serve as a base for political opposition, than on philosophical grounds.

Conclusion

If African socialism can be carried to its logical conclusion, ultimately the only private sector will be an indigenous one, part of and sensitive to the traditional African society. By that time, if such a period will ever be reached, possibly new forms of industrial and commercial organization will have evolved, reconciling those African traditions which have been preserved to the needs of a modern economy. But Africa is at least decades away from this outcome, if only because it will take that long to develop the necessary manpower resources and to generate internally the required capital. And whether the normal conflicts between tradition and the monetary economy will ever be resolved remains one of the great riddles of the African experiment. In the meantime there is ample room in Africa for the international investor. Many expatriate enterprises can certainly be planned with confidence that sufficient control will be retained until a healthy return on capital has been earned and repatriated.

While harmonious operations will require some adjustment to the goals of African socialism, it should not be beyond the ingenuity of contemporary Western capitalism. And who knows whether we may discover in the process some answers to a few of our own unresolved dilemmas about the relationship between industry and human community in the machine age.

6

THE COOPERATIVE MOVEMENT IN KENYA

John N. Knapp

Like many other newly independent African countries, Kenya is committed to the development of African socialism. Unfortunately, no one is quite sure exactly what African socialism is or by what means it will be developed. Doubtless, there are many elements which must be reflected in any definition of the term. Among them are (1) dissatisfaction with life under the previous colonial governments, (2) a desire to find a uniquely African personality and to build a distinct African society, and (3) a desire to develop a neutral alternative to communism and capitalism. The cooperative movement aptly reflects these considerations and has begun to acquire importance in the development plans of a number of African countries.

In underdeveloped areas, as well as in advanced societies, the cooperative method has been thoroughly tested as an effective means for organizing people (particularly in agriculture) for the furtherance of economic objectives. Cooperative principles are easily understood by the African peasant, because mutual assistance and cooperation are fundamental to Africa's traditional extended family system. To the African intellectual, the cooperative movement is appealing because it tends to mitigate the centrifugal effects that the process of economic development ordinarily has on traditional communal society, without resorting to the persistent

122

compulsion of Stalinist agricultural organization. It represents a neutral position in the world ideological struggle.

The emerging configuration of cooperative activity in Kenya illustrates how cooperatives may fit into the over-all pattern of development. To place its cooperative movement in context, a few words about Kenya's broad development strategy are necessary. Thus far, Kenya has adopted a moderate, pragmatic approach to economic development. Since the economy has not yet reached the so-called "take-off" stage of development, massive amounts of foreign capital are required. The Government seems to have recognized this fact, and the creation of a favorable investment climate has been one of its major priorities. The Development Plan charts the existence of a large private sector, and its success is frankly premised upon extensive domestic and foreign private investment. Although political pressures, now latent, ultimately may change the Government's attitude, it is apparent that the present leadership recognizes the negative effects on the flow of private capital which such impeccably socialistic policies as nationalization of industries would have, and hence are avoiding their use. It is sometimes difficult, however, for the leadership to rationalize its development strategy with the commitment to African socialism, particularly since the strategy tends to increase foreign domination of the economy. Critics of Government policies demand specific examples of African socialist development.

If a vast edifice of welfare services could be established, it could be cited as a "socialist" achievement. But only modest programs can actually be supported with available funds and staff. By a process of elimination, therefore, the cooperative movement emerges as the principal hope for the immediate and effective expression of African socialist principles. Its idealism, the similarity of its work patterns to those of the extended family, its democratic structure, and its involvement of large numbers of people as active participants make the cooperative movement particularly well suited to this task.

The tendency to identify cooperatives with African socialism is already quite clearly demonstrated in Tanzania and Uganda; both countries are developing their cooperatives at an extremely rapid pace, and large investments are being made in cooperative training programs and extension work. Planning is now being undertaken in Kenya that will provide for similarly intensive development.

The Extent of Present Cooperative Development

Kenya's first cooperative society was registered in 1932, but serious efforts to introduce cooperatives in the African sector did not begin until after World War II. A milestone in their development occurred in 1957 when the annual turnover of African produce-marketing societies first surpassed £1 million. By the end of 1962, the turnover of these societies had reached £4.5 million, of which £3.6 million was accounted for by 146 coffee-marketing societies. The membership of African societies in 1962 was over 220,000. By way of comparison, the turnover in 1962 of essentially European societies and unions was £23 million (8,300 members), and of Asian societies £5.5 million (3,000 members). It can be seen from these figures that by the time Kenya became independent in December 1963, the cooperative movement was firmly established. Although African producers played the smallest economic role in the agricultural cash economy, it was, nevertheless, a significant one. With independence and the rapid departure of many European farmers, the African role is expanding rapidly, and it is likely that African cooperatives will become one of the dominating social and economic forces in the country.

Most of the approximately 650 African cooperatives are produce-marketing societies. The typical pattern is for a group of small holders to join together in a cooperative that collects the members' produce and arranges for marketing. Sometimes, as in the case of coffee cooperatives, the society or union will itself own factories to process or partially process the crop. In the past, most cooperatives have been organized on the basis of a single commodity. However, the schemes organized to resettle Africans in formerly European farming areas have led to the introduction of cooperatives dealing with a variety of products. Over fifty settlement cooperatives have been formed on farms that typically are engaged in mixed farming carried out on small, individually owned plots. The cooperatives purchase and operate any machinery required for cultivation and market the entire range of products. A start has been made toward actual farming on a cooperative basis, and, as the Government now is attaching more importance to the problem of keeping large-scale European farms intact, it is likely that the incipient pattern of communal ownership and operation will be considerably extended.

Problems of Cooperative Development

The fundamental problems of the cooperative movement in Kenya are as follows:

1. The large number of uneconomically small societies
2. The lack of skilled management, or the unwillingness on the part of members to pay for good management
3. The failure by societies to keep adequate records and accounts
4. Tribal or sectional jealousies, which lead to the fragmentation of previously viable societies
5. Inadequate government staff resulting from the fairly low priority attributed to the cooperative movement by the colonial administration and the continuing low salary scales
6. The lack of full understanding of the cooperative movement among most members
7. The almost complete lack of training facilities either for Government staff or for members and officials of the movement.

The majority of present cooperatives are too small to be economically viable. Many of them are either unwilling or unable to hire a bookkeeper, and accounts are kept either by Government inspectors or not at all. In the past, the movement has suffered because of inadequate or inferior supervision by Government. Most cooperative inspectors have only a primary school certificate. While being paid a salary equivalent to that of a Grade II clerk, they have been required to carry out audits and to give managerial advice. Not surprisingly, many of the more competent officers have been hired away by private firms.

As the Government staff has been totally occupied with the problem of keeping abreast of the accounting and auditing functions, it has not been able to carry out the training programs that are properly its duty. Consequently, member education and training of committee members and elected officials has been sadly neglected. Hardly any facilities have been available for training the Government's own Cooperative Department staff, and the Government is now faced with an enormous problem if it is to build up a competent department quickly enough to avoid a breakdown here at one of the most critical points of the development effort. At a time when the Government is turning to the cooperative movement as the answer for a wide variety of problems, the movement and its governmental counterpart are both sadly lacking in organization and resources and are ill prepared to cope with the challenge of new development. Fortunately, the groundwork is now being laid for a new start with revised legislation and a comprehensive reorganization and revitalization of both the Cooperative Development Department and the movement itself. Whether the planned reforms will be in time, or be sufficiently comprehensive, to reverse present trends cannot yet be determined.

The cooperative movement in its present condition is extremely wasteful of managerial manpower. Normally there are about ten members on each management committee; hence approximately six thousand people are required at the present time to staff over six hundred management committees. If, as even the most modest conceptions of efficiency require, each society is to employ its own bookkeeper and society secretary, there is an immediate need for an additional 1,200 trained individuals. If the experiences of Tanzania and Uganda offer any guide, the number of societies may double or triple in five years. There is at present little hope of training a sufficient number of bookkeepers, society secretaries, or committee members to cope with a proliferation of this magnitude.

The seemingly obvious solution to this dilemma is to change the present pattern of small societies and thus to concentrate management resources. But there are serious problems inherent in any effort to change the present pattern. Cooperatives are like community development groups; that is to say, they are usually formed by a group of people who are neighbors or who at least live in fairly close proximity to one another. Ideally, this propinquity produces a "cooperative spirit" which permits the society's affairs to be run democratically with active participation by all members. Attempts to change this pattern will inevitably lead to a different type of cooperation, and much of the cooperative spirit may be lost in a bureaucratic embrace. The attempt to consolidate cooperatives may also run afoul of the powerful tribal antagonisms which still persist.

A Strategy for Consolidation

The strategy that has been adopted in Kenya is to consolidate development in an administrative district through the formation of District Cooperative Unions. The plan was recently described in a speech by the Parliamentary Secretary for Commerce and Industry (the responsibility for cooperatives is under the Ministry of Commerce and Industry) as follows:

> The Department of Cooperative Development is going to encourage the formation of new cooperative unions which will be organised on the basis of one district, one union. The purpose of these District Unions will be to coordinate cooperative development within a District, to provide, where necessary, centralised accounting services to primary societies, to organise crop marketing, and to provide administrative advice and support. . . . The creation of the District Union involves a revision in the relationship between primary societies and unions. The District Unions will be given powers which will enable them to supervise certain aspects of the administration of primary societies. In particular, the District Unions will be given powers over financial matters and the recruitment and grading of staff. In the future the Department will concentrate its supervisory activities on the District Unions, which will, in turn, supervise the operations of primary societies. The effects of this reorganisation will be to conserve staff and eventually to generate self-discipline and better management in the cooperative movement.

The District Unions will be the hub around which the cooperative movement will be built. They will coordinate all cooperative development within the district and will assume some of the supervisory and accounting functions which previously have been the burden of Government Inspectors. New legislation will give the Commissioner for Cooperative Development additional supervisory powers that will enable the Government to exercise fairly strict controls over future development. The new legislation will also facilitate mergers of societies, and efforts will be made to consolidate the uneconomically small societies into larger units.

At the level beneath the District Union there are two organizational alternatives. It is possible to divide a district into a number of small, geographically or ethnically congruent areas and create multipurpose societies. The alternative is to develop specialized societies that will concentrate on the production or marketing of a specific crop. Studies are now in progress to determine the structure that best conforms to conditions in Kenya. It may develop that in different areas different structures will prove optimum. There are, of course, many difficulties to overcome in any attempt to disturb the *status quo,* especially at the grass-roots level of the primary societies. However, with active support from District Unions and careful guidance of future growth, the changes previously discussed have a fairly good chance for successful implementation. The success of the program will very much depend on the quality of the Government's leadership and its astuteness in securing the vigorous support of the leaders of the cooperative movement.

At the national level, the Kenya National Federation of Cooperatives has recently been formed as the apex organization. The Federation is composed of representatives of cooperative unions and will be responsible eventually for mass education, publicity, policy coordination, and some of the development functions currently being performed by the Government. The objective is to create a structure that will, insofar as possible, allow the cooperative movement to become self-sustaining. Some of the Federation's initial tasks will be to assist in the formation of a cooperative bank and to study the movement's educational needs. It will also attempt to establish an audit union. If the Federation is able to provide an effective vehicle for the unification of the cooperative movement, it could become a considerable political force.

Nonagricultural Cooperatives

The programs that have been described primarily concern the development of agricultural marketing cooperatives. Other types of cooperatives have not thus far been developed on a significant scale in Kenya, but certain kinds are now becoming objects of considerable governmental interest. These are credit unions, consumer and wholesale societies, housing cooperatives, and rural industry cooperatives. The extent to which these types of societies can or will be developed will be dependent on the Government's ability to support a large group of experts to organize and supervise their growth. Since the Government must effect a very sizable enlargement of cooperative staff merely to catch up with present needs and to cope with the growth expected in purely agricultural societies, it is doubtful that considerable growth can be achieved in other fields in the near future. While it should be possible to obtain overseas experts for the organization of cooperatives in these new fields, the problem of subsequent supervision of societies is a formidable barrier to growth, unless one accepts a very high rate of failure. Widespread introduction of nonagricultural cooperatives will probably have to be delayed until a solution to the manpower problem is in sight. At the present stage of development, it is far more important to assure the success of cooperatives in the agricultural sector; the development of nonagricultural cooperatives should not be allowed to dilute this effort. But as the electorate begins to identify cooperatives with African socialism, there will be increasing political pressure to extend them into other sectors. There already are indications that such pressure is developing in Kenya.

7

PROMOTING PRIVATE INVESTMENT IN LESS DEVELOPED COUNTRIES

Scott M. Spangler

Many governments striving for economic development have spent considerable time and energy in designing investment incentive laws. However, once the legislative instruments have been enacted — often with extremely generous benefits and encouragement for "pioneer" industries — their intent has in many cases been thwarted in the course of implementation. Frequently, this is a significant reason why the private investors who enter the economy under the benefits of the act are neither as numerous nor as economically desirable as the legislators had hoped.

My object here is to examine some of the problems occurring in the implementation of investment incentive acts and in the creation within a country of an institution for the promotion of private investment. Although based on the experience of a specific country, most of the problems noted and the solutions proposed should be applicable to any less developed country.

Private Investment as a Growth Ingredient:
The Ghanaian Experience

Newly developing countries require large capital investment in infrastructure projects as the first step to industrialization. The poorer governments are quickly forced into heavy debt to provide these vital investments in social overhead projects which often bring little or no financial return on the investment. Additional extensive investment in agricultural or industrial projects may, therefore, be beyond their means. Some more fortunate countries, by reason of cash crops or mineral resources, accumulate government revenues sizable enough to permit substantial investment in both categories. But even they lack sufficient domestic financial resources or the human resources of managerial and technical skill needed to provide the rates of growth desired by ambitious populations wanting to "catch up" with the advanced nations. Hence, regardless of ideological orientation, virtually all of the less developed countries have recognized the need for some private investment.

Ghana is one example of a new state that is relatively wealthy and has committed itself to the ultimate achievement of a socialist society, yet seeks private investment. Income from cocoa and substantial mineral resources has made it one of the richest (per capita) African nations. The goals of the Government, as stated in the new Seven-Year Plan[1] and other publications, are to create a true socialist state and to attain a rapid rate of economic growth. The Government intends to finance each year a major proportion of the productive investments made in the economy so that the country will become progressively socialized. It is intended that by the end of the Plan period the State will control the dominant share of the economy. The Ghanaian Government has acknowledged, however, that, during the transition to pure socialism, the economy of the country will have to remain a mixed one, in which the contribution of private enterprise will be essential to the attainment of substantial industrial growth.

At present, Ghanaian industry makes a relatively small contribution to the gross national product, averaging only 30 per cent from 1960 to 1962. The two sectors of mining and construction alone contribute about 70 per cent of the value added by all industries. This reflects the early stage of economic development in which Ghana finds itself, with extractive industries aimed toward export markets and a construction industry booming at the initial

---

1 *Seven-Year Plan for National Reconstruction and Development,* presented by the President to Parliament, January 1964 (Accra, Ghana: Government Printing Department, 1964).

stages of infrastructure development. Within the manufacturing sector, the greatest activity has occurred within the small-scale establishments employing mostly family labor and little capital. Until recently, large-scale establishments were really important only in beverages, tobacco, and wood products; but these industries accounted for 75 per cent of the value added in all manufacturing industries.

In its Plan, the Ghanaian Government envisages successive stages of industrial development in the country. At first, emphasis will be on manufacturing local substitutes for imported staples of consumer demand and on processing local raw materials to increase export earnings. Subsequently, local production of building materials and other basic metals and chemicals will be established. Finally — probably in the next Plan period — Ghana intends to produce machines, capital goods, and other products of heavier and technologically more advanced industries.

The successful completion of the first two stages should reduce considerably existing foreign exchange constraints. Domestic supply of the present demand (now satisfied by imports) for staple consumer goods and basic building materials is also advantageous, because industries producing such goods as clothing, shoes, processed foods, cement, and furniture do not require a sophisticated technology and will give Ghana's new industrial labor force an opportunity to serve its apprenticeship. These first steps will prepare the economy for the advanced stages of industrialization.

Ghana's planners recognize that, more than capital or skilled labor, the availability of adequate management is potentially the most serious impediment to each stage of successful industrialization. The procurement of the entrepreneurial skills to initiate projects and the managerial skills to operate them is a prerequisite to the achievement of the country's goals. It is not physically possible for Ghana's educational system to turn out sufficient business administrators and engineers to run both the state enterprises projected for the next seven years and the dozens of other industries, large and small, that must be developed. Further, it is doubtful if any educational system can teach that rare combination of business and technical skills and risk-taking ability which makes the successful entrepreneur. Two of the basic purposes of Ghana's investment-promotion institutions, therefore, must be the encouragement of business risk-taking and the provision of a managerial cadre. The third basic purpose of these institutions is to encourage from private sources an additional flow of investment funds.

The average contribution of private domestic savers to total investment funds in Ghana in recent years has been about £40 million per year. The Plan baldly states that "even though a large proportion of [private] domestic savings has to be transferred to the Government sector in order to meet the deficit in the Government account, the remainder should be enough to provide an average of £55 million per year over the Plan period." This represents a target increase of 38 per cent in the annual rate of domestic private investment. The Plan also calls for expansion of the flow of foreign private capital into Ghana from a level of £5 million per year, which has been observed in the past, to £8 million per year. This represents a target increase of 60 per cent in the annual rate of foreign private investment.

Recent trends cast doubt upon the probable achievement of these rates of private foreign and domestic investment. In 1960 the recorded increase in total (private and Government) investment in Ghana was 28 per cent over the previous year, but in 1961 the increase was only 8.3 per cent, and in 1962 total investment *dropped* 7.7 per cent![2] Since during this period the Government's development expenditure remained constant or increased each year, it is apparent that the rate of increase of private investment has declined considerably over the period, and in fact was negative in the last year.

In the light of this evidence, the planned increase in annual rates of domestic and foreign private investment of 38 per cent and 60 per cent, respectively, indicates a vital need for an effective investment-promotion institution in Ghana, if the total private investment projection over the next seven years is to be fulfilled.

Development of Ghana's Program of Investment Incentives

The development of Ghana's program of investment incentives started with a section of the Income Tax Ordinance of 1943, in which a procedure for the declaration of pioneer industries and the certification of pioneer companies was laid down. Once a com-

2 *Bank of Ghana Annual Report of June 30, 1963* (Accra: Government Printer, 1963).

pany had been certified as a pioneer company, which meant that
it was a new company in an industry considered vital to the economy, it was eligible for an income tax holiday of up to five years.
All applications were handled by the Income Tax Department.
By 1959, when a new Pioneer Industries and Companies Act was
passed, forty industries had been declared pioneer and thirty-two
certificates issued. In this time, several major problems had become apparent.

One of the first was the lack of criteria for the definition of a
pioneer industry. A second problem was measurement of the need
of a company for pioneer benefits — that is, what degree of profitability or rate of payback of investment should eliminate the company from benefits or cause the benefits to be reduced. The third
problem was the question of balance between benefits gained from
a new enterprise and the loss of revenue to the Government. The
final problem was the lack of significant success in attracting new
investors.

An attempt at solving the second of these problems was made
in the Pioneer Industries and Companies Act passed in 1959. The
new legislation eliminated the maximum of five years' tax holiday
and provided instead that the pioneer companies would be granted
tax relief until they had recovered their initial investment in full.
The implementation of the Act of 1959 was somewhat haphazard.
It was not significantly more successful than its predecessor in
promoting foreign investment in Ghana.

At about the time of the enactment of the Pioneer Industries
and Companies Act, the Import Duties Act was passed; the latter
allowed companies to be granted remission of import duties on
their raw materials. The importance of this benefit to local manufacturers is indicated by the results of a study of twenty-four firms
that were eligible under the law. In 1960 the average rate of duty
applicable to the principal raw materials of these firms was 35
per cent ad valorem; at the same time, the average rate of duty
applicable to imports of competitive finished goods was only 33
per cent. After the austerity budget of 1961, which was designed
to reduce imports by raising import duties, the same manufacturers
reported (1) an average increase in the rate of duty on principal
raw material of 33 per cent, (2) an average increase in sales price
as a result of duty of 23 per cent, (3) an average increase in working

capital requirements of about £50,000, and (4) an average reduction in utilization of 1963 capacity of 45 per cent (some companies faced closure).

The Import Duties Act and the Pioneer Act were nominally in effect until the Capital Investment Act of 1963 was passed. During this period there were a number of changes in the agencies responsible for implementing the legislation. Contacts with the companies applying for pioneer status were handled by several different governmental bodies. Once accepted as a pioneer company, a firm might be either completely ignored or badgered with requests for information. Many of the problems of implementation experienced under the previous investment incentive act still existed, especially (1) difficulty in selecting criteria for pioneer status, (2) inefficient processing of applications, and (3) lack of real success in stimulating new industries.

In 1962, the Government suspended all of the benefits to all companies in order to review the cost of the pioneer incentives. At this time, twenty-four companies were enjoying the import-duties remission at a total accumulated cost to the Government of less than £50,000. On an annual basis, this represented only about 0.5 per cent of the Government's import-duty revenue. A total of forty-two companies had received Pioneer Status certificates since the initiation of the program in 1943, or about two per year. (There may have been more than this, but the somewhat sketchy records dating back to 1953 indicate forty-two as a total.) The revenue loss to Government from income tax holidays was incalculable because of the lack of financial reporting by most of the firms. The firms provided employment for about 5,000 Ghanaians and manufactured products ranging from building materials to food and tobacco products to textiles and simple consumer products.

In the light of this experience, a new Capital Investments Act was drawn up and put into effect in early 1963. The Act establishes a central authority called the Capital Investments Board whose primary functions are to initiate and organize activities for the encouragement of investment of foreign and domestic capital, to provide a liaison service between prospective investors and the sundry Government departments they must contact, and to grant certain or all of the incentive benefits provided for in the Act.

The incentives provided for in the Act are quite extensive and attractive. They include a guarantee of compensation for nationalization and of no restriction on transfer abroad of principal, interest, or profits on foreign investments; an income tax holiday of up to ten years; exemption from purchase and excise taxes, and import and export duties; deferment of payment of fees to Government agencies normally due upon establishment of a company; exemption from property and similar taxes; and special capital allowances.

The Act stipulates that the prospective investor must provide a significant amount of information about the proposed project. Although not stated explicitly, it is the apparent intention of the Act that the Capital Investments Board grant benefits only where they appear to be a necessary precondition for a project's prospects of success. Thus, the old problems of selecting applicants and deciding upon the minimum amount of benefits that are needed were passed on to the Board. As the Board is made up of prominent and able Government officials, each of whose services are in demand in several other agencies, the technical investigation of each application had to be subcontracted to the research department of the National Investment Bank.

In the first thirteen months after the Act was passed, a total of thirty-two applications was received by the Board. Of this total almost 75 per cent were from companies which were "old friends," in the sense that they were either companies that had enjoyed the benefits of the Pioneer Act and that wanted reinstatement or were locally esablished firms wishing to add to or expand their interests. They could not be considered as new investors attracted by the Act. On the positive side, however, about 75 per cent of the applications involved an inflow of foreign capital. Further, 13 per cent of the applications were from businesses wholly owned by Ghanaians, and 55 per cent had a Ghanaian interest. An unfortunate trend is that most (55 per cent) of the applications were received in the first three months after the Board opened its doors. After this period there was a noticeable decline in the application rate. In fact, only three applications were received in the last three months of the period studied. At least in part, this appears to have been due to the increasingly poor investment "climate."

Although to date the Capital Investments Board has only proc-

essed nine applications (only one of which was granted the benefits), both the strengths and weaknesses of the institution are
already becoming apparent. Some problems are new, created by
the new powers of the Board and the changing conditions in
Ghana, but many are persistent old ones stubbornly remaining
unresolved. Many of the problems are actually outside the Board's
powers as defined in the Act, yet they directly affect the Board's
chances of success. As the following discussion should indicate, the
strengths and weaknesses that have characterized Ghana's investment promotion programs over the years are likely to occur in
those of many other African states.

Some Problems of Investment Promotion

Institutionalization

One of the primary problems that Ghana's experience has high-
lighted is the need for an official body or institution to implement
the provisions of any investment incentives act. The principal
missing element in Ghana's initial investment-promotion efforts
was an agency with responsibility for assuring that the intent as
well as the letter of the law was carried out, and with the authority
necessary for imaginative implementation and prompt decision-
making. Effective solutions to most of the problems outlined in
this study require the existence of a permanent institution with a
full-time staff.

"Pioneer" Criteria Definition

As suggested before, a very important initial problem confronting legislators attempting to promote private investment is the
definition of criteria for "pioneer" statutes. To a large extent,
industries and companies can be defined as pioneer on the basis
of economic factors that are easily ascertained, factors such as
employment and training of local labor, earnings or savings of
foreign exchange, utilization of unexploited local resources, provision of opportunity for peripheral industries, and so on. Since
such criteria can be measured and documented fairly easily, caprice
and arbitrariness on the part of officials can be substantially circumscribed and an aura of rationality and impartiality developed.

Moreover, the applications can be processed at a relatively low level in the Government. If the criteria are not well defined, or if a separate decision must be made in each industry as to whether private enterprise is to be encouraged, the decision often is pushed higher and higher in the Government hierarchy until it sometimes is decided at the Cabinet level.

Benefit Allocation

When the number or the magnitude of benefits to be awarded to companies qualifying for pioneer status is not standard, the attempt to reduce the process of benefit allocation to a virtually mechanical level is rendered more arduous. The argument in favor of variable benefits is that they protect the Government against unnecessary loss in revenue and enhance the opportunity for selective promotion of industry. However, they greatly increase the cost of administering an investment incentives program. For instance, if a tax holiday of one to ten years can be awarded, how long a holiday should be granted to a company whose projected capital payback period is four years, as opposed to one whose payback period is six years? This type of decision-making is more likely to be referred higher in the Government hierarchy than when the tax-holiday and other benefits are standard for all pioneer companies. Variation of benefits also is an encouragement to applicants to "color" their application to appear more necessitous, and requires extensive financial investigation into each application to ensure fairness in awarding the benefits. Therefore, if the act provides for variation in the number or the life of the incentives, effective implementation requires a trained staff of analysts.

The Capital Investments Board of Ghana has found that the average number of professional man-hours required to analyze each application is about forty. The report of the Board's analysts is derived from data provided by the applicant. It briefly summarizes the information about the applicant and his project. An analysis of the internal and external market for the product is made to estimate the market share for the enterprise, the state of competition, and the probability of success for the venture. A financial analysis presents a pro forma profit-and-loss projection and estimates the rate of return on the investment. The report also sets out the benefits, if any, to the economy deriving from foreign exchange savings or earnings or local-resource utilization and points out detrimental factors such as consumption of scarce resources (e.g., water) or elimination of cottage industries. The report presents only a technical evaluation and makes no judgments regarding the award of benefits. After the report is prepared by the professional staff, the Board itself must meet to exercise its judgment on each case. The total number of official and professional hours per application may exceed fifty. This is an expensive proposition, but necessary to ensure that the intent of the Government is carried out.

Incentive Design

An additional problem in setting up institutions to attract private investment is the identification of effective incentives. This requires careful consideration of the economic conditions within the country and must involve some understanding of the motivation of potential investors. Here a differentiation is necessary between the domestic and the foreign investor. In view of the exchange controls operative in most less developed countries, the domestic investor is not able to choose between one country and another.[3] Therefore, different economic conditions in another country do not have to be offset. He cannot be entirely disregarded, however, since he can opt between alternative investments in his own country. An investment-promotion institution can channel his funds into desirable (as opposed to illegal or speculative) investments, or into high-risk or long-payout productive enterprises, by providing the proper incentives.

Attracting the foreign investor, on the other hand, requires not only that the benefits be designed to channel funds as desired, but also that the benefits provide economic conditions attractive in comparison with other parts of the world. There are, of course, many economic conditions that cannot be changed by legislation, such as the presence or absence of a sizable market for a product and the availability of the necessary resources for production. In their absence, incentives are irrelevant. Other factors such as political stability, cost of living, and legal or government red tape are

[3] [As Bruce Blomstrom points out in his essay on capital flight in Uganda, this is not yet true of East Africa, where exchange controls are very mild. — *Editor's note*]

also more or less resistant to legislative amelioration, though they can sometimes be offset by attractive incentives.

The importance of incentive design cannot be underestimated. In Ghana, for example, where provisions against nationalization of private property are already included in the Constitution, it was still important — in terms of investor confidence — to restate this provision and define in the Capital Investments Act itself a procedure for fair compensation in the case of take-over in the national interest. This provision and a guarantee of unrestricted repatriation of profits are an extremely necessary first step in putting any country on an even footing in competing for capital. The importance of tax benefits was demonstrated by Ghana's experience with the Import Duties [remission] Act.

A problem that inevitably occurs in designing the tax benefits to be granted in an investment incentive act is: How much? This question can be excruciatingly difficult for a government that is hard pressed to balance its own budget. Every additional tax holiday granted seems to many politicians to represent, not an additional industry for the economy, but another decrease in the government revenues. The question always is: How much profit should a pioneer enterprise realize as a result of the benefits granted? The answer, of course, is as much as it takes to attract the promoters of the enterprise. When companies in Europe and the United States are realizing an average of 15 per cent after taxes on their new domestic investments, it is obvious that it will take at least this much to attract them to an underdeveloped country. In fact, at a recent Caribbean conference on development[4] when a number of delegates had been maintaining that 8 per cent or 9 per cent was an adequate return for foreign investors (and complaining that they could not attract outside capital), a representative of Puerto Rico shocked the participants by bluntly stating that his government believed from experience that it required at least a 30 per cent return on investment (20 per cent on sales) to bring United States investors to Puerto Rico, where political stability is linked directly with their own country.

A rate of return as high as 20 per cent or 30 per cent, whether earned by a domestic or a foreign investor, presents significant

4 See William H. Stead, *Fomento — The Economic Development of Puerto Rico*, National Planning Association Pamphlet No. 103 (Washington, D.C., 1958).

public relations problems in many countries like Ghana where strong feelings against "exploitation" and "capitalism" are held by a very vocal and influential section of the population. (That it is not a uniformly experienced emotion in the country is suggested by rough calculations of rates of return on investment in inventory realized by an equally influential section of the population — the market women. Conservative estimates are seldom as low as 200 per cent.) This public relations problem provides an area in which an effective investment-promotion institution, which is more than just a clerical body, can greatly contribute to economic development.

Creating an Investment Climate

In spite of the voluminous literature written about him, the entrepreneur is a rare bird. In many small, less developed countries, the number of local individuals or organizations who have accumulated and can manage sizable investments in productive assets is very limited. As mentioned before, even an educational system as advanced as Ghana's cannot mass-produce the skills and attitudes needed by an entrepreneurial class, particularly when the educational process is often regarded only as a steppingstone to the civil service. Unless a country succeeds in establishing policies and institutions that create an environment in which risk-taking, productivity, and — as the reward for success in these activities — the accumulation of wealth are regarded as social virtues, the society will lose its basic sources of initiative. If this happens, and the only remaining center of initiative is the Government, business innovation seems unvaryingly to diminish, and consequently the rate of economic growth is retarded.

The institution responsible for promoting private investment can be a central force in the effort to provide a favorable public environment. It can do this first by acting as the advocate within the Government for present and potential investors. Simultaneously, it can be a clearing house and publicity organ for Government departments whose actions affect private business. By keeping informed on the business conditions within and outside the country and by becoming familiar with particular problems of local businesses, it can initiate Government programs designed to assist the private sector. It can expand the opportunities for public participation in business by encouraging large investors to sell shares in their enterprises to small domestic savers and can bring foreign know-how into the country by facilitating investment by foreigners in incipient or established local enterprises. In short, such an institution can act as a "go-between" for business interests, the public, and the Government.

Another problem experienced by Ghana that has direct relevance to this public relations aspect of the investment-promotion institution is the classic and literal "run-around" often inadvertently provided for potential investors. One recent foreign visitor (the problem also exists for domestic investors, but is not so acute) listed the Government departments he and his staff visited during their inquiries into a potential investment. In addition to the Capital Investments Board, there were seven departments, several of which they had to visit more than once. He seemed resigned to the process, apparently because it is the same in almost all developing countries. But what a difference it would make if a foreign or domestic investor could visit one office and find there the answers to all his questions, and perhaps even obtain definite action on most of the steps involved in establishing a business. If this were done, even visitors with a casual investment interest would be encouraged to investigate potential investments thoroughly.

The problem of promoting business investment extends beyond the creation of a favorable climate within a country. The investment-promotion institution must also aggressively sell the country to external investors. Here again Ghana's experience has direct relevance to many other new countries. The Capital Investments Act of 1963 represents a sophisticated attempt to provide an effective investment-promotion agency for the country. Unfortunately and paradoxically, many of the same political forces that passed the Investment Act had previously, and have since, provided an unfavorable atmosphere for private (and especially foreign private) investment. At present, it takes an experienced investor in new countries and one very knowledgeable about Ghana's political environment to regard with reasonable equanimity the abuses of the Government-controlled press. The seeming antagonism to private enterprise has probably been the major factor in the recent significant downturn in the rate of private investment in

Ghana and in the drying up of applications coming in to the Capital Investments Board. It is not surprising that the number of new foreign investors investigating Ghana as a potential site diminishes during a period of shrill recriminations against local businessmen by the Government and press. Nor should it surprise anyone that a great deal of local investment capital has been diverted from low-return, productive enterprises to quick-return speculation in inventory and real estate.

The responsibility for maintaining an economic atmosphere conducive to private saving and investment must necessarily be shared among a number of institutions in a country. The responsibility for mobilizing the internal and external information services and other influences on public opinion, however, can and should be centered in one agency that will seek to publicize the goals of the country, to show the importance of private investment to the economy, to provide favorable local publicity for investors committed to domestic projects, and to advertise on an international basis the favorable aspects of investment in the country. Particularly in countries where a very vocal segment of the political spectrum is antagonistic to private investment, an effective investment-promotion institution must undertake energetically this difficult and delicate task of reassuring investors and educating the electorate.

8

THE DEVELOPMENT OF NIGERIA'S STOCK EXCHANGE

Douglas Gustafson

In an environment where capital investment can effectively take place, the provision of capital itself is an essential component of the growth process. Less developed countries face the task of improving the processes whereby domestic savings are first created, then channeled into productive investment, whether it be by encouraging the development of private institutional channels, government saving and investment programs, or a combination of these methods. In tropical Africa, Nigeria has made relatively large strides in the development of an active capital market. An examination of its experience in institutionalizing a market for both governmental and private securities should provide useful insights into the methods and utility of encouraging such a development in the African environment.

The Pre-Exchange Investment Environment

The Private Sector: Governmental Attitude

The private sector in Nigeria is composed of two distinct parts: the indigenous private sector and the foreign private sector. The former is associated with the traditional occupations of farming, trading, small-scale craft manufacturing, and service operations. The foreign private sector was traditionally involved in large-scale trading, both import and export, and the development of natural resources. This pattern is now undergoing change as the private foreign sector is gradually being restricted to investment in manufacturing. The Development Plan states:

Nigeria's economy is a mixed one. The Governments have taken an active part not only in providing the social but also the basic economic services, such as a steel plant and an oil refinery. The attitude of the Governments of the Federation, however, is entirely pragmatic and accepts the desirability of a mixed economy. At the same time, the Governments are convinced that no amount of Government activity can effectively replace the effort of a broadly based and progressive private sector.[1]

The use of the word "pragmatic" is noteworthy. It indicates governmental realization that a key element in the development of the economy is a degree of investment in industry that is possible only with the injection of foreign capital, management, and technology. With severe limitations on the funds available for even the public investment required to provide a framework for economic growth, the Government has found it to be a practical necessity to invite foreign private investment. Neither the capital nor the skills required to generate industry are available within the economy. This places Nigeria in a rather uncomfortable position because a large inflow of foreign capital and manpower representing foreign private interests is, by its very nature, distasteful to a country only recently in possession of its political independence. The Plan hints at this in stating:

. . . Governments will insist upon the fullest Nigerian participation in ownership, direction, and management at the earliest possible time.[2]

Nigeria has gone a step further toward acceptance of private investment in industry in that the Governments' avowed aim is an economy where private Nigerian individuals control a substantial block of the modern manufacturing sector and the organizations required to support this activity. This philosophy has yet to be put to the test, as there are relatively few economically successful Nigerians in the private sector who have attracted attention.

1 *National Development Plan, 1962–68* (Lagos: Government Printer, 1961), p. 21.
2 *Ibid.*, p. 360.

Moreover, it is not difficult to detect distinct qualms not only about the existence of an economically prominent foreign community but also, though less overtly, about the existence of a really powerful group of Nigerian "industrialists."

Nonetheless, a decision has been made by the current generation of politicians that a strong private sector should be encouraged, particularly if it involves Nigerians. Foreign investors are beginning to realize that their presence constitutes a political problem and that it is in their interest to encourage Nigerian participation in the capital structure of their firms to enhance their acceptability.

"Nigerianizing" Foreign Investment

In general. Just as the development of a capital market for government securities was assisted by the rapid expansion of financial institutions, the development of a private securities market was assisted by the existence of these institutions. It was also facilitated by the rapid increase in the number of industrial concerns operating in Nigeria and the growing awareness of the desirability of "Nigerianizing" investments. In 1957, there were very few manufacturing facilities in Nigeria, and manufacturing accounted for only 1.3 per cent of Nigeria's gross national product.[3] Since 1957, a large number of important manufacturing facilities have been established, and the output of the manufacturing sector has increased approximately four times. Data from the most recent *Industrial Directory* give some indication of the size of the manufacturing sector. The *Directory* lists about thirty plants employing 100 to 200, twenty-five plants employing 200 to 500, four plants employing 500 to 1,000, three plants employing 1,000 to 2,000, and two plants employing over 2,000 persons.[4] Many of these plants have commenced operations in the 1957–1962 period, and most are at least partially financed and managed by foreign investors.

The economic reason for Nigerianizing the capital structure of private firms is, of course, to broaden the incidence of risk. While initially the major motive to Nigerianize has generally been political in nature, there are indications that firms are also becoming interested in Nigerianization as a means of reducing their own investment of risk capital.

---

[3] Okigbo, *Nigerian National Accounts* (Lagos: Federal Ministry of Economic Development, 1961).

[4] Federal Ministry of Commerce and Industry, *Industrial Directory,* 1963.

The foreign investor has four basic ways to Nigerianize the capital structure of his company. The first is to invite direct governmental participation. The second is to invite the participation of quasi-governmental or private development corporations. The third is to make an effort to line up a few, usually one to five, Nigerian individuals who have some resources to contribute to a given project. (This may mean a cash contribution, a contribution of land, or some other services.) And the fourth method is a public security issue designed to attract both a relatively large number of individuals, each holding small amounts of the security, and institutional funds.

Direct government investment. Each of the four Regional Governments has included funds in its development programs for investment in industry.[5] Looking at the past pattern of direct Government participation, one can see that normally these funds are reserved for large projects of strategic importance in the economy. The proposed steel mill and oil refinery are examples of projects where the Government wants a substantial equity participation. There are also a few smaller investments, however, where the Government participates directly as a shareholder. These include investments in cement, flour milling, textiles, sugar and rubber plantations, and tire factories.

The foreign investor often seeks governmental participation because this provides him with some assurance that the Government supports the project and will be interested in its success. However, the foreign investor normally wants to control the management of the enterprise. This has not proved a problem in many cases, since the Government has had neither the desire nor the funds to secure a majority shareholding.

Local development corporations. The second alternative is to seek the participation of regional development corporations. This alternative has not been exercised as frequently by foreign in-

[5] The Federal Government has allocated £5 million for direct investment in industry plus £4 million for the new National Industrial Development Bank. In addition, £38 million is allocated to the proposed steel mill and oil refinery *(National Development Plan, op. cit.,* p. 53). The North Plan calls for a direct industrial investment of £7.55 million *(ibid.,* p. 299); the East Plan allots £10 million *(ibid.,* p. 239); and the West Plan allots £10 million *(ibid.,* p. 299). If the Regions' resources are not adequate to finance planned public expenditures, either their investment in foreign-controlled industries will have to be restricted or public programs will have to be cut back.

vestors as it potentially could have been. There are several reasons for this, probably the most important being the poor reputation of these agencies. Another reason has been the desire to avoid potential political pressures and the delays commonly resulting from partnership with these corporations. The Coker Commission of Inquiry[6] examined the operation of the Western Region's finance and development corporations; the ensuing exposure of poor management practices confirmed their prevailing reputation. In business circles it was felt that the other regional agencies were in no better condition than the West's. All of the Regions have announced plans to reorganize their development corporations on commercial principles, but at the present time is is not clear what role they will have in providing industrial finance.

In 1950 the Investment Company of Nigeria was established as a private development finance company to provide both loan and equity capital to medium- and large-scale projects. This company has recently been reorganized and expanded and is now called the Nigerian Industrial Development Bank. The firm operates on the principle that its equity holdings, when marketable, will be sold to the public. Ownership of the N.I.D.B. is international, but it is essentially a privately controlled Nigerian institution which can be a valuable local business partner for both Nigerian and foreign investors alike.

Nigerian partners. Occasionally foreign investors wish to locate a few Nigerian individuals to participate in their projects. These projects are normally of a smaller scale than those referred to previously. In many cases this type of arrangement is motivated by the services the Nigerians can provide rather than the capital contribution involved. These services may include the acquisition of land or assistance on other aspects of a project's organization. Since, at the present time, the number of individuals capable of making significant financial, managerial, or other contributions is limited, it is unlikely that this method of securing Nigerian participation will be used frequently by foreign firms undertaking medium- and large-scale manufacturing investment.

Public share offers. The fourth method, to offer shares or debentures for sale to the public, is the most recent method that firms

[6] Federation of Nigeria, *Report of Coker Commission of Inquiry*, 1962, Vol. II, Chap. 1; Vol. III.

have used to Nigerianize their capital structure, and it is around this activity that the development of a genuine market in Nigeria for private, local securities has centered. The public offer of securities has advantages over the other three methods of Nigerianizing the capital structure of firms and in many cases can be used in addition to those other methods to optimize results.

The most obvious noneconomic benefit of a public issue is that it signifies the willingness of the foreign investor to allow anyone to participate in the benefits that may accrue as a result of the investment, if he is willing to assume the risks of an investor. One frequently heard complaint is that foreign investors constitute "selfish interests" and that Nigerians do not participate in the benefits of foreign investment. This, of course, is an unfair, if not untrue, statement; but it is a natural attitude in a less developed country. By taking the trouble to enlarge the equity ownership of the firm, the stigma normally associated with a foreign investment can be reduced. Partnership with Government, one of its organizations, or individual Nigerians does not necessarily accomplish this to the same degree as a public issue, since sections of the public may be just as wary of Government or the elite's association with large industry as they are of the foreign companies themselves. If a company is able to build up a sizable group of Nigerian shareholders, it reduces the chances that Government would find it politically advantageous to take arbitrary action inimical to the shareholders' interests.

The economic benefit of public issues is that they open up entirely new sources of capital for investment in private industry. These sources are individual and institutional and are discussed later in connection with the development of the private securities market.

The Record of Private Securities Issues

Nigerian Cement Company Limited. The first public offering was made by the Nigerian Cement Company, Limited (Nigercem) in February 1959. The sponsors of this project were the Federal Government, the Eastern Region Government and some of its agencies, the Colonial Development Corporation, and the project manager, Tunnel Portland Cement Company, Limited. Located in Eastern Nigeria near excellent deposits of raw materials and on the Nigerian Railway Line, the plant had an initial capacity of 100,000 tons, or about 20 per cent of the Nigerian market for cement at that time. The import tariff on cement was about 15 per cent, and this protection, as well as the factors previously mentioned and efficient management, combined to make the venture financially attractive. With Government agencies absorbing the major portion of the financial cost, the public could anticipate strong Government support for the profitability of the project.

Certain basic mechanisms had to be created in order to make the public issue of Nigercem practicable. Three requisites for a public issue of stock are an orderly registration of the ownership of that stock, a method to transfer ownership, and a method of selling the stock to the public. The only institutions with wide coverage in Nigeria that could efficiently handle subscription moneys were the commercial banks. Barclays Bank D.C.O., one of the largest banks in Nigeria, decided to establish a registrars department in its Lagos head office. The decision to do this was based not on prospects of immediate profitability but on the belief that the development of modern financial mechanisms would be in the over-all interest of the banking community and that the department would eventually become self-sustaining as the number of accounts it handled increased.

The pattern of marketing, which has been more-or-less duplicated in subsequent issues, was to advertise the issue by printing the prospectus in the major newspapers for several days with advertisements inviting the public to make application through commercial banks, by direct contact, or by mail. This marketing pattern allows maximum diffusion of information about a stock issue and minimizes the application effort.

The response to the Nigercem issue was very encouraging. Approximately 2,150 Nigerians applied for £125,000 of stock. (About 1,100 of these were for £10, and 348 were for £20 of stock.) One hundred expatriates purchased about £20,000 of stock. Most of the applicants were from Lagos (700) and the Eastern Region (950); together these applicants purchased about £100,000 of stock. Over one third of the proceeds came from the fifty applicants subscribing for £500 or more of the stock.

The success of the Nigercem issue, both from the company's and shareholders' points of view (in the first year shareholders received a 10 per cent dividend free of tax), paved the way for other firms in Nigeria to consider public share offers. It also provided impetus to the formation of a market to deal in private securities. Several private businessmen became interested in developing a mechanism to allow orderly security exchange transactions; and the Government, through the offices of the Central Bank, endorsed this effort and began to assist in the formation of a securities trading market.

Nigerian Tobacco Company Limited. During this period three other firms made public share issues. The first of these was the Nigerian Tobacco Company (N.T.C.), a wholly owned subsidiary of British American Tobacco Company, Limited. This firm had been operating in Nigeria since 1951 and had declared gross dividends of 16.7 per cent, 13.33 per cent, and 13.33 per cent in the three years prior to the public offer.[7] The company had a good record; it was the sole producer of cigarettes in a highly protected market, and it had excellent management resources. The project appeared to be a "sure thing."

The purpose of this offer was not to raise capital. (The company held about £1.3 million in reserves in 1959 and had adequate plant capacity for the foreseeable future.) Rather, as stated in the prospectus: "Nigerian Tobacco Company Limited is the leading manufacturer and supplier of cigarettes in the Federation of Nigeria and its products cater for all sections of the public. The Nigerian public is now being offered a share in the equity of the company in order to strengthen this bond of common interest."[8]

The amount of the original public offering was 100,000 £1 par value shares at par. The offer was oversubscribed; and in order to satisfy all applications up to £1,000, the offer was doubled, and £200,000 of the stock was taken up. At the present time, 1,647 Nigerian individuals hold £120,000 of the N.T.C. stock, and 157 expatriates hold £40,000 of this security. The remaining £40,000 of publicly owned stock is held by pension funds, insurance companies, and other corporations.

John Holt Investment Company Limited. In August 1960, John Holt became the third company to offer shares to the public. This particular operation is of interest because it deviated in type and

---

[7] *Nigerian Tobacco Company Limited Offer for Sale* (Lagos), prospectus dated April 25, 1960.
[8] *Ibid.*

style from the previous two issues. John Holt was a name familiar to almost every Nigerian. The company's history goes back to the 1880's, when John Holt, a Liverpool merchant, began trading along the Nigerian coast. From this modest beginning Holt's grew to be one of the most important trading firms in Nigeria. Toward the end of the 1950's it became obvious that the control of trade by expatriate firms such as Holt's was objectionable, and these firms began to switch their operations from trade to production. One of the main reasons for a public issue was to dispel some negative feeling toward the company name arising from its association with the colonial period.

By 1959, John Holt and Company (Liverpool) Limited had a wide range of interests in Nigeria, including agricultural exports, wholesale and retail trade, property development, travel, and direct minority investments in manufacturing enterprises. In 1953 the company transferred some of its residential and commercial property holdings to a subsidiary company, Guinea Coast Holdings. The tenants of these properties were in most cases associated with some activity of the John Holt group. In 1960 Guinea Coast Holdings was reorganized into the John Holt Investment Company Limited. Some of its properties were sold, and the new firm purchased about £400,000 worth of Nigerian industrial securities from the parent company. At the time of reorganization these securities were revalued, and the gains (about £200,000) were capitalized. The amount of the capitalization was then offered for sale to the public.[9]

The John Holt Investment Company was unique to the public because it was not associated with any single product or activity. At the time of the share issue, the major portion of the company's assets were invested in the firms indicated in Table 1.[10]

Another factor that made this issue distinctive was that £100,000 of the issue was in the form of ordinary shares of par value 5/–, whereas the N.T.C. and Nigercem stock was issued at a par value of £1. Furthermore, the remaining £100,000 was issued as 7½ per cent preference stock in 10/– par value units. The reason for introducing new stock unit values was not made explicit. With a lower

9 *John Holt Investment Company Limited Offer for Sale* (Lagos), prospectus dated April 25, 1960.
10 *Ibid.*

Table 1

*John Holt Investment Company Limited — Major Assets,
September 1960*

Land and Buildings at Cost Less Depreciation		£245,000
Investments		
Nigerian Breweries Ordinary Stock	£216,000	
Costain (W. A.) Ltd. Ordy. (Construction Co.)	45,500	
Holts Nigerian Tanneries Ordy.	64,943	
Crittal-Hope Ordy. (Metal Windows, etc.)	15,000	
Thomas Wyatt & Son Ordy. (Stationers)	23,475	
P. S. Mandrides & Co. Ordy.	20,000	
Asbestos Cement Products Ltd. Ordy.	13,600	
Investment Company of Nigeria Ltd. Ordy.	5,000	£403,518
Total		£648,518

unit value more shares could be purchased for a given amount of funds, and the shareholder held more "paper." The company may have felt that a lower unit price would encourage the small saver to participate in share ownership.

On the other hand, a smaller share price than that of the other available stocks (N.T.C. and Nigercem) might imply to an unsophisticated public that instead of being a "better buy" the stock was "not as valuable" as the higher-priced stocks. The issue, while not as successful as the previous ones, still succeeded in a diversification of the ownership. Approximately 1,100 Nigerians, 75 expatriates, and several companies and pension funds applied for £37,890 preference stock and £70,267 ordinary stock.

Nigerian Breweries Limited. This firm is the major producer of beer in Nigeria and also an important producer of soft drinks. The company was formed as a joint venture between a European brewer and the large expatriate trading firms in Nigeria. The company realized profits almost immediately and since 1958 has enjoyed gross earnings of at least 40 per cent on capital and reserves. It decided to invite its distributors to take an equity position in the company, and the existing shareholders privately sold some of their holdings to these distributors. The sales price was established at 50/- per £1 unit, and the existing shareholders also loaned money to the distributors to assist them in purchasing shares. The stock is not quoted, and transfers are effected by private arrangement. In order to retain the existing balance of Nigerian stockholders, the company's Articles of Association restrict share transfers.

The issue was very successful; one thousand individuals purchased £200,000 of stock. The company's auditors fix a valuation periodically, and potential sellers are informed of this quotation. The turnover in this security has been very small, with about half a dozen transfers completed in the past two years. This is partly because many of the existing certificates are still pledged on loans and partly because of the restriction on transfer. This type of issue is useful in building a good relationship between a firm and its distributors, but the benefits of identification with the populace as a whole are missing.

The Need for an Exchange Mechanism

By the end of 1961 a substantial amount of money was invested in Federal Development Loan Stock and three ordinary shares and one preference share of private sector businesses. It became clear that the practicality of many individuals holding small amounts of stock (individual holdings in Nigeria are typically in the £10–£200 range) is directly related to their ability to dispose of that stock. The creation of a mechanism for selling and buying became crucial to the widening of ownship of securities in Nigeria.

Providing a market mechanism for Government stock, which is supported at par by the Central Bank's agreement to purchase any such stock on offer, was not as difficult a problem as providing an exchange mechanism for private securities. Institutional funds are expanding rapidly and require investment outlets; hence, the Government hardly risked a deluge of sales of stock by agreeing to buy any offer for sale at par. The Central Bank was easily able to absorb or sell the small amounts of stock offered by individuals who wanted cash. Another factor that simplified the transfer of ownership of Government stock was that with the price of such stock fixed, and transactions taking place at par plus or minus accrued interest to the day of the transaction, there was no need for a real market to determine price. The Central Bank, being a highly regarded public institution and also the registrar for the stock, was a natural clearing house for buyers and sellers.

Yet there were some problems with having the Central Bank deal directly with stockholders. The whole environment of the Bank was not amenable to direct communication with private firms and individuals. Established to counsel the Government on monetary affairs, to control and manage the currency, and to supervise the operations of commercial banks, the Central Bank had neither the staff nor the desire to act as a conventional stockbroker dealing with the public, particularly with respect to the normal advisory function of independent brokers.

It was the administrative problems of acting as a broker for Government stock that proved particularly burdensome. Stockholders are scattered all over the country, and communication is difficult. People's signatures (and even their names) have a remarkable tendency to change between the date of purchase of a given amount of stock and the time they wish to sell. Occasionally people bring in stock to sell, sign a transfer, and then vanish. Payment for purchases can become an involved process. Hence, although the Central Bank was a logical place to begin the marketing of Government stock, and indeed did do this for some time, there were reasons for removing this activity from the Central Bank if the marketing could otherwise be handled in an orderly and controlled fashion.

In any event, the Central Bank really could not serve as an effective broker for private securities. Trading of private stocks differs significantly from the buying and selling of Government stock. The first difference is that, although the volume of private securities transactions in Nigeria is much smaller than the volume of Government stock transactions, the dealings in private securities involve more "trading." That is, most of the volume of transactions in Government stock is accounted for by sales from Central Bank holdings to an institution's portfolio, whereas transactions in private securities are characterized by sales from one individual to another. In the case of Government stock the Central Bank represented a pool where buyers and sellers could satisfy their requirements. On the other hand, an individual who wanted to buy or sell £50 of N.T.C. Ordinary Stock had to find another individual to complete a deal. There was no place where he could in effect "meet" buyers or sellers as the case may have been. Barclays Bank Registrar, who was responsible for registering the changes in ownership for these private securities, was occasionally able to match buyer and seller and perhaps give informal advice on prices, but many of the same reasons given for the Central Bank's reluctance to deal in securities also applied to Barclays. Barclays was a commercial bank and a registrar, but not a stockbroker. (This is not to say that the banks could not act as brokers if they set up a separate organization as such, but only that there was no bank organization particularly geared to stockbroking activities.)

The other major difference between transactions in Government and private securities is that the price of the former is daily established down to the last pence, whereas private securities have freely fluctuating prices. With no efficient market place providing a price determination function, each individual had to act as his own agent, and the market in private securities had a large built-in chaotic factor. Even after an effective market was established, individuals have been observed making "private deals" that were patently unfair. With the potentially large gaps in sophistication, knowledge, salesmanship, and ethics that can exist between two given individuals, one can imagine some of the financial feats that could be, and have been, accomplished.

In Nigeria, such considerations led the business community, the Central Bank, and the Government to consider various ways of establishing a securities market. The effort was spearheaded by a firm interested in the marketing of its own shares and in the development of the financial sector in general. As the plan developed, the Investment Company of Nigeria (I.C.O.N.) took an increasingly active interest, since it looked forward to the day it would be turning over its equity holdings to the public.

Two factors that greatly influenced the organization of the securities market were the thinness of the market and the necessity of building investor confidence. The exchange mechanism required checks and balances — no Government experience existed that could serve as a regulatory influence — to build public confidence in security ownership and trading. Theoretically, one prudently managed firm, subject to some form of regulation, could handle all the business of a simple exchange and by careful manipulation of its own portfolio offset some of the instability inherent in a small market. The disadvantage of this is that some market freedom is sacrificed and the system becomes less practical as trading volume increases. A sole broker would have monopoly control, and even with the most public-spirited management could lay itself open to charges of mismanagement to a greater extent than if other firms existed to provide alternative points of view, advice, and opportunity for brokerage business. In some cases it may be necessary to depend on a single organization to handle the market for securities. Where this is the case, the problems inherent in such a situation should be recognized, and adequate controls should be devised and installed. In the Nigerian case, the founders of the exchange mechanism felt that the development of the private securities market would be maximized by using a group of brokers.

Formation of the Lagos Stock Exchange

Quite simply, the process of formation was initiated by the organization of a limited-liability company under Section 21 of the Companies Ordinance.[11] The name of the company is the Lagos Stock Exchange. The provision under which it was organized is that pertaining to the formation of nonprofit associations, limited by guarantee, formed to promote commerce. Under Section 21, any income must be applied to the promotion of its objectives as established in the association's Memorandum of Association. No income can be transferred by any means to present or past members of the association.

As laid down in the Memorandum of Association, the objects of the Lagos Stock Exchange are to provide facilities for share sales and purchases, to control the requirements for listing on the Exchange, to establish and supervise the rules of brokerage firms in Nigeria, and in general to oversee and promote activities associated with security dealings in Nigeria. The founding members of the Exchange each purchased five £10 shares in the Exchange. It was a group that was diverse, yet fairly representative of the business community.[12]

Under the Articles of Association methods are prescribed for becoming a member and for electing a Council out of the members. This Council, meeting a minimum of once a month, controls the affairs of the Exchange. The Council is given the final power of adjudication of complaints between members, and between members and nonmembers, provided the latter consent in advance

[11] Laws of Nigeria, *Companies*, Chap. 38.

[12] The founding members were: C. T. Bowring (Nigeria) Ltd., insurance brokers; Senator Chief T. A. Doherty, Nigerian businessman and Federal Government Senator; John Holt (Nigeria) Ltd., merchants and finance house; Investment Company of Nigeria Ltd., development finance company; Sir Odumegwu Ojukwu, K. T., O.B.E., Nigerian businessman; Akintola Williams, Nigerian chartered accountant; and Alhaji Shehu Bukar, company director.

to the Council's rulings. The Council has the sole power to issue licenses to members for the purpose of dealing in stocks, shares, and all securities. Finally, the Council has power to make, alter, or revoke regulations for carrying on the business of the Exchange and to regulate the conduct of members.

There is no official tie between the Exchange and any Government agency other than that specified in the Lagos Stock Exchange Act.[13] This Act makes it illegal for nonmembers of the Exchange to act as stockbrokers for securities listed on the Exchange. Contravention by individuals is subject to a maximum £1,000 fine and/or two years' imprisonment; corporate bodies are subject to a £5,000 fine. The Act also requires a quarterly report of activities to be made to the Governor of the Central Bank. Finally, the Act requires the Council to inform the Central Bank and the Federal Minister of Finance when an application for membership is rejected and to cite the reasons for rejection. While apparently giving this power to review membership rulings of the Council, the Act does not set forth any provision by which the Government could alter Council decisions. Evidently the purpose is to provide some public perusal of Council activity in order to ensure basic fair practices. It is obvious from this minimal relationship between Government and the Exchange that the regulatory function falls on the Council of the Exchange. In view of conditions in Nigeria, this has been a practical and effective method to regulate securities activity and should prove adequate for some time to come.

Operation of the Lagos Stock Exchange

In discharging its regulatory function, the Council of the Exchange has published two documents setting forth conditions to be observed. One pertains to members' activities,[14] and the other deals with the requirements for listing on the Exchange.[15]

The following is a partial list of areas where the Regulations prescribe conditions to be met by members:

1. Dealing members are required to follow specified record-keeping practices.

13 Laws of Nigeria, *Lagos Stock Exchange Act, 1961*.
14 Lagos Stock Exchange, *Regulations of the Lagos Stock Exchange*, Appendix II.
15 *Ibid.*

2. Strict limits and controls are placed on the degree and form of advertising members may use in soliciting business.
3. Members' associations with nonmembers are subject to Council approval.
4. Dealing members are required to post a security of £1,500 with the Exchange and must pay a fee of £150 per annum;
5. Procedures are outlined for the investigation and settlement of defaults.
6. The schedule and procedure of call-overs is specified.
7. Minimum commission rates are established.
8. Members are allowed to share their commissions with agents provided the Council has formally approved the agent. (Only 25 per cent of a commission may be shared.)
9. Provision is made for the publication of a daily list indicating share prices.
10. The method for becoming a member of the Exchange is specified.

Appendix II of the Regulations prescribes in detail the procedure that firms, statutory bodies, and governments must follow in seeking a listing on the Exchange. One's impression on reading the Regulations and observing the listing of new firms on the Exchange is that it is an involved and difficult process. There are occasional complaints that this discriminates against the smaller, less experienced, indigenous firms. Many small enterprises have naively considered the Exchange as a source of funds in itself, rather than a mechanism for linking investor to business, and are disappointed when they discover that a listing for them is out of the question. However, the success of the development of business on the Exchange is dependent on investor confidence. It was necessary, therefore, to set high standards of disclosure and reporting from the outset of Exchange activity.

The Regulations are so designed that companies obtaining permission to list their securities on the Exchange will necessarily have reported their operations, completely and accurately, to the public. The Exchange has been concerned with the occasional "handbill" approach used by small companies offering stock to the public. The effort to build confidence in security ownership can be damaged if the public is misled. Occasionally firms print fliers asking for share subscriptions with incomplete, even false, information. The only control over offerings is Section 242 of the Companies Act, Chapter 38. The requirements of this section relate to the prospectus, and they are minimal. There is no provision for preoffer inspection of the prospectus by the Registrar of Companies unless the company is incorporated outside Nigeria. Even in the cases where the Companies Act has been violated, prosecution is unlikely and is not necessarily what is needed. The object is not to close the door entirely to public offers by small companies but to sift the reasonable from the unreasonable. A simple way to control the cases that appear to border on fraud would be to tighten the prospectus requirements and to provide for Company Registrar approval for public issues not handled over the Lagos Stock Exchange. In addition, if the Company permits or requires applications to be made through banks (which some have done), the commercial banks should exercise reasonable judgment in lending their names to such issues, and if their names are used without consent, they should of course take steps to protect themselves.

Before the existence of the Lagos Stock Exchange, the potential danger of unsound public issues was perhaps not as great as it now is. Once the Exchange has established confidence in public issues, it is possible for firms to mimic this success, and undiscriminating investors can be exploited in the process. This has not been a significant problem yet, although there have been a few very flimsy attempts at public stock issues. However, it is something that must be watched, particularly in the early period of educating people about security ownership.

The financial arrangements for the Exchange are of importance, since finances have been a continuing problem. Brokers' commissions are set as follows:[16]

		Nominal Value	Commission
1.	Government Stock (Including Local Government and Statutory Corporation Securities)	0–£4,000	3/8%
		£4,000–10,000	1/4%
		over £10,000	1/8%
2.	Private Securities	1% on Consideration	
3.	Minimum Commission	10/—	
4.	On matching deals between the National Provident Fund and the Central Bank, the rate can be 1/32 per cent.		

16 *Ibid.*, Section 57.

The Exchange's income is derived from the annual charge of £150 for each dealing member, an initial listing fee per security of £2 per £10,000 authorized capital of the company, subject to a maximum of £50, and a £25 annual charge to companies listed on the Exchange. No charge is made on Government listings.[17]

The Lagos Stock Exchange opened for business in June 1961. There were three founding members (or associates) who applied for licenses to deal: C. T. Bowring, I.C.O.N., and Nigerian Stockbrokers (John Holt). A fourth dealer, Inlaks, was subsequently licensed. Space was provided in the Central Bank Office Building, where I.C.O.N. was located, and a Nigerian was hired full time to take care of the day-to-day administration. The first Secretary of the Council, Mr. T. F. Griffin was supplied by I.C.O.N. Prior to taking up this position, he spent a period in London gaining additional familiarization with the operation of securities markets.

With the Exchange housed more or less in I.C.O.N. offices and with the Secretary's dual obligation to the Exchange and I.C.O.N., it made sense to have I.C.O.N. manage the affairs of the Exchange and to support the Exchange with its secretarial and clerical staff. This made it possible for the Exchange to exist without an independent staff. In return for its services, I.C.O.N. received an annual management fee from the Exchange.

The mechanics of operation are simple. The Exchange convenes at 2:30 daily (except Saturday and Sunday), the stocks are called over, and bidding takes place among the four brokers. A daily summary of transactions is circulated showing the prices at which bargains were made and the closing prices.

The following stocks were the Nigerian securities originally available:[18]

1. Federation of Nigeria

5% Development Stock	1964
5½% Development Stock	1969
6% Development Stock	1979

---

[17] *Ibid.*, Schedule IX.

[18] Lagos Stock Exchange, "Official List," No. 20, June 30, 1961. In addition to these securities, arrangements were made to deal in the shares of certain firms operating in Nigeria which already had quotations on the London Stock Exchange. By establishing a method of utilizing security deposit receipts, it was possible to purchase these stocks in Lagos at London prices without being subject to United Kingdom Transfer Stamp Duty. The securities included under this arrangement are Bisichi Tin, Ex-Lands Nigeria, Gold and Base Metal Mines, Bank of West Africa, Jantar Nigeria, and Amalgamated Tin Mines of Nigeria.

5% Second Development Stock	1967
5½% Second Development Stock	1977
6% Second Development Stock	1985

2. Nigerian Industrials

John Holt Investment Company Ordinary Stock (5/– units)
John Holt Investment Company 7½% Preference (10/– units)
Nigerian Cement Company Ordinary (£1)
Nigerian Tobacco Company Ordinary (£1)

One point causing some concern about stock ownership in Nigeria is the investing done by expatriates temporarily resident in the country. Apparently on the assumption that the foreign community has a degree of knowledge permitting unfair speculation and exploitation, there has been some fear that the Stock Exchange would serve only expatriate interests and would lead to some form of exploitation. But because of the market, the nature of the Exchange, and the type of companies listed, these fears are patently unjustified.

Companies seeking a listing on the Exchange are normally large manufacturing concerns that from the start have at least a substantial amount of foreign corporate participation. If, in principle, foreign corporate investment is necessary to the economy, foreign individual investment should not be treated differently. In fact, from a political standpoint, one could argue that it is better for the individual foreign investor with limited capital to invest in listed securities rather than investing directly in small firms where his visibility is greater. (Economically, portfolio investment is not as useful as direct investment because the securities investor does not make a technical or managerial contribution.) Moreover, records are kept of his investment, and income arising from his activities is measurable. Thus, rumors of huge, secret profits can more readily be scotched. Since only small portions of the listed companies are held by the public, there is no danger that individuals will be able to build empires. In addition, with the low trading volume and the stabilizing activity of four dealing brokers, there is very little, if any, room for speculation. In particular, I.C.O.N. has endeavored to stabilize any severe movements in the market by dealing into or out of its own holdings.

Practically speaking, foreign influence is simply not an important consideration. First, very few expatriates have any real knowledge of the operations of security markets in their own country, let alone a knowledge of Nigerian markets. Second, the days of the long-term expatriate resident are over. Most people are in the country for an 18- to 24-month tour, with perhaps another term of duty following, but are then off to some other assignment. Individual savings are directed home, where the foreigner has more intimate knowledge and confidence. In most cases he will not bother to invest locally because he will not want to run the risks of final sale and exchange control when he leaves Nigeria. The expatriate has no long-run commitment in Nigeria, and he does not want to risk his savings there.

Consequently, the regulations prescribe that in order to obtain a listing, a company's ". . . fully-paid shares shall be free from any restriction on the right of transfer other than [such restrictions as] may be approved by the Council and shall be free from all lien."[19] In practice, the Council has required that transfer be free of restriction, and this has been a rational policy. Restricting share ownership to Nigerians would not have had any "real" (i.e., non-political) benefits, but in the initial stages of operation, it could have adverse effects. In a small market, the more buyers and sellers there are, the better. The exceptional cases are companies where there is a specified Nigerian/foreign ratio. If, for example, a Nigerian/foreign equity ratio of 51/49 were desired, and some of the shares were publicly held, transfers would have to be controlled to avoid a potential shift of foreign ownership above the 49 per cent level. The most efficacious method for handling this problem is the creation of two classes of shares, with foreigners restricted to one class. (Nigerians could theoretically be allowed to hold either class.) This would allow a partial equalizing effect if the supply-demand relationships were different for the two classes of investors. If the price of the foreign-held shares was lower than the local class of shares, Nigerians could buy the foreign class, which would tend to balance the price. However, if the demand for the foreign-held shares was such that the price of this class was higher than the local class, arbitrage would not be possible, and the price would remain differentiated until other conditions changed.

Now that the market for securities is established and foreign involvement is becoming less significant, there is less need to main-

19 Lagos Stock Exchange, *op. cit.* Schedule VI, Part A, A-2.

tain free transferability. Firms and/or the public may press the Exchange to allow entire public issues to be restricted to Nigerians. In some cases this would have favorable political implications, but there would be no significant change in security trading because of the minor involvement of foreign personnel. (See the ownership patterns of recent public issues described later.) What is important is the citizenship attributed to institutional investors. If, for example, the life insurance companies were not allowed to purchase stock classed as Nigerian, the market would be very much affected. This would be detrimental to both the insurance companies and the securities market.

Government Policy and Legislation Affecting the Private Capital Market

The Government has passed two important pieces of legislation indirectly affecting the securities market. In April 1961, the Income Tax Management Act[20] was passed. Among other things, this Act stipulates that for pension and provident funds to retain their tax-free status, and for contributions and withdrawals from these funds to be tax-deductible and tax-free, respectively, funds approved by the tax authorities after April 1, 1961, must maintain 50 per cent of their investments in securities issued by or under the authority of any Government in Nigeria, while funds approved prior to April 1 are required to maintain 33.33 per cent of their investments in these securities. (The deadline for meeting these requirements was March 31, 1962.) This Act was passed to implement the Government's decision to encourage repatriation of the overseas investments of private and corporate pension funds. However, it should be noted that the provision is not satisfied merely by investment in Nigeria; qualifying investment is limited to stocks issued by or under governmental authority. To date, this has been restricted to Federation of Nigerian development stocks and treasury bills, plus a small debenture issue by the Broadcasting Company of Northern Nigeria Ltd.

The second item of legislation is the Trustee Investments Act.[21] This Act gives trustees the power to invest in the debentures and

20 Laws of Nigeria, *Income Tax Management Act, 1961.*
21 Laws of Nigeria, *Trustee Investments Act, 1962.*

fully paid-up shares of any public company, subject to the following limitations:

1. Nominal value of the company's paid-up shares exceeds £500,000.
2. The debentures or shares are quoted on the Lagos Stock Exchange.
3. Dividends of at least 5 per cent have been paid for three consecutive years preceding the current year.
4. No more than 33⅓ per cent of the fund can be so invested.
5. No more than 10 per cent of the fund can be invested in a single company.
6. No more than 5 per cent of the fund can be invested in the shares of a single company.

Thus, pension funds have been restricted in their purchase of private Nigerian securities by tax requirements and the Trustee Investment Act. An additional development with significant implications for the private securities market has been the decision of the National Provident Fund (N.P.F.), the largest institutional source of individual savings, to invest its entire proceeds in Federation of Nigeria Development Stock.[22] The N.P.F. is being used as a quasi-taxation device to raise funds for the Federal Government and to channel funds from private to public sectors.

Post-Exchange Development in the Securities Market

New Issues

Since the Exchange was opened in June 1961, three firms new to Nigeria, one statutory corporation, and a company with considerable experience in Nigeria have undertaken public issues and listed their issues on the Lagos Stock Exchange.

[22] In the 1963 Budget speech the Federal Minister of Finance stated: "In effect, these monies constitute a trust fund to secure the benefits assured to each individual contributor. We have, therefore, taken great care in deciding upon the manner in which they should be invested. Clearly the monies must be invested within Nigeria but only in such a manner as will ensure their safety whilst yielding a satisfactory return. We have, therefore, decided that investment will be limited to those securities enjoying trustee status and for the present this will be further limited to investment in Federal Government securities." (Text by Federal Ministry of Information, p. 13).

Broadcasting Corporation of Northern Nigeria Limited (B.C.N.N.). The first new issue to be made after the formation to the Lagos Stock Exchange was the debenture stock of the B.C.N.N., a statutory corporation that operates the Government radio station in Northern Nigeria. It issued its debenture at a time when pension funds and insurance companies were under pressure to find profitable investment outlets in Nigeria (as a result of the legislative requirements discussed earlier). In order to meet the requirements of the Trustee Investments Act of 1962, the Corporation decided to have a public issue and sought quotation on the Lagos Stock Exchange. The Investment Company of Nigeria was engaged to handle the issue.

The debenture was medium-term, maturing in 1972–1976, and carried a 6¾ per cent rate of interest. Having been issued under the authority of a Government of Nigeria, it met the requirements of a Government security as specified in the Income Tax Management Act of 1961. (It remains as the only such security other than the Development Loan Stocks of the Federal Government.) There was, in these circumstances, no difficulty in placing the £210,000 issue. Since most of the stock is held by institutions, there has been very little activity in this security on the Exchange. Eleven applicants, nine of which were pension funds, absorbed the issue. About 97½ per cent of this debenture is now held by pension funds.

The success of this issue, due to the fact that it was in effect a Government security which yielded ¾ per cent more than the longest-dated Government stock, would indicate that similar issues by other statutory corporations in need of capital would find a ready market. The amount of funds that could be raised on the local market by statutory corporations will be related to (*a*) the competition for funds for private industry and (*b*) the Government's need for funds, since the Government can control the debt financing of the statutory corporations.

Alcan Aluminum of Nigeria Limited. The next public issue made in Nigeria was the Alcan offer of £425,000, 7½ per cent First Mortgage Convertible Debenture Stock, 1970–1972 (payable at £99). The conversion rights are for full or partial conversion at the rate of £88 of ordinary per £100 debenture on January 1, 1967, or £72 of ordinary per £100 debenture on January 1, 1970.[23] This

---

[23] *Alcan Aluminum of Nigeria Limited, Offer for Sale* (Lagos), prospectus dated May 8, 1962.

company, established by the Aluminum Group, has recently begun a rolling-mill operation producing semifabricated aluminum coil, sheets, and tubes. The company has been granted tax relief for a five-year period, and its prospects appear favorable. The issue was made in June 1962, and subscriptions were received by Barclays Bank D.C.O. and the Investment Company of Nigeria, which acted as broker to the issue. The Council of the Lagos Stock Exchange granted permission for listing the debenture on the Exchange. Subscriptions were required in multiples of £25; therefore, the offer was not directed to the very small saver.

There has been some discussion in the Lagos press to the effect that minimum subscription levels should be low enough to allow all categories of savers to invest in the industrial concerns operating in Nigeria. The reluctance to set the minimum subscription at very low levels is, however, supported by several factors. Although it may sound desirable to have the very small saver participating in the financing of industry, this person's savings objectives are probably maximized by other forms of savings such as the 5 per cent tax-free savings certificates, the Post Office Savings Bank, or a commercial bank savings account. His savings should be liquid, and the charges for servicing his savings should be minimal. When the holder of £5 of stock wishes to sell, he will have to pay the minimum brokerage fee of 10/– equivalent to 10 per cent of his investment. If he needs cash in a hurry, he runs some risk of not finding a buyer at a reasonable price, particularly for small amounts of stock. From the issuing company's point of view, the amount of capital to be raised from the very small purchaser is marginal, and the administrative costs of handling the accounts is disproportionately increased. In all the issues other than the Alcan issue, the minimum subscription rate has been £10 or £20, and in view of the above considerations, this would seem to be a reasonable range.

The Alcan issue differed from previous private issues in two essential ways:

1. The company had neither an operating record in Nigeria nor Government participation in the equity of the firm. Thus, the general public was not familiar with the company, and the element of "guaranteed profitability" resulting from Government participation was missing.

2. The convertible debenture was a new type of security to the

public, somewhat more difficult to understand than either a straight debenture or ordinary stock.

The issue was publicized by advertisements in the press and the distribution of the prospectus by I.C.O.N. and Barclays Bank. The subscription lists were open for three weeks. The issue was over-subscribed by institutional investors, but their allotments were cut in order to satisfy all individual subscriptions. Individuals purchased £30,000 of the issue, while £395,000 was allotted to institutional investors. Tables 2 and 3 indicate the pattern of subscriptions.

Table 2
Alcan Subscriptions — Institutions

	Type	Number	Amount
1.	Insurance Companies	5	£ 45,400
2.	Pension and Provident Funds	4	66,275
3.	Investment Company of Nigeria	1	50,475
4.	Indag (Eastern Region C.D.C. Operation)	1	141,750
5.	Other Miscellaneous Funds	4	91,475
		15	£395,375

Table 3
Alcan Subscriptions — Nigerian* Individuals

Size of Purchase	Number	Percentage of Total	Cumulative Percentage	Total Value	Percentage of Total	Cumulative Percentage
25	41	29	29	1,025	4	4
50	31	22	51	1,550	5	9
75	2	1	52	150	$\frac{1}{2}$	$9\frac{1}{2}$
100	41	29	81	4,100	15	$24\frac{1}{2}$
125	1	1	82	125	$\frac{1}{2}$	25
150	1	1	83	150	$\frac{1}{2}$	$25\frac{1}{2}$
200	8	5	88	1,600	$5\frac{1}{2}$	31
250	2	1	89	500	2	33
300	3	2	91	900	3	36
400	1	1	92	400	2	38
500	6	4	96	3,000	11	49
550	1	1	97	550	2	51
1,000	3	2	99	3,000	11	62
10,500	1	1	100	10,500	38	100
Total	142			27,550		

Lagos		East		West		North	
No.	Amt.	No.	Amt.	No.	Amt.	No.	Amt.
55	£17,125	51	£6,125	18	£2,575	18	£1,100

* Thirteen expatriates applied for £2,175 of stock.

Several points are of interest:

1. Only thirteen expatriates applied for the stock. Three of these subscribers purchased an average of £400 each, while the other ten applied for an average of £100. Some of these people were connected with the Alcan project and thus had a special interest in the stock. The important point is that the foreign community did not participate significantly in the issue even though they may have possessed a more thorough understanding of the issue and its merits.
2. Of the 142 Nigerians who applied for the stock, eleven of them (8 per cent of the total) accounted for £17,050, or 62 per cent of the proceeds. This weighting was, to a large extent, due to a single £10,500 purchase.
3. Most of the Nigerian subscribers were either from Lagos or the Eastern Region, where the plant was located.
4. The institutional investors were key to the successful sale of the issue.

Even though this issue offered a good fixed return and a chance of capital appreciation resulting from the conversion feature, many Nigerians were not motivated to invest.

Dunlop Nigerian Industries Limited. The first ordinary stock offered to the public after the formation of the Lagos Stock Exchange was that of Dunlop Nigerian Industries Limited. The offer for sale was made in October 1962, shortly before production of tires by the company commenced. The initial share capital of the firm was £1.5 million, and of this total the Western, Northern, and Federal Governments held £225,000. The company's prospectus stated that it would take several years for a plant of this size to reach a level of production where dividends could be paid, but foresaw a dividend for the operating year 1966.

Since a return on the stock was some years off, the issue was not made in the hope of securing a large number of subscribers. However, the company did want a public listing and also wished to give its Nigerian distributors an opportunity to participate in the company. With these factors in mind, the company arranged to make available 200,000 shares to the public, to be purchased through I.C.O.N., which would be available from October through December 1962. During this period about thirty purchasers took up about £20,000 of the stock. Seven purchased less than £100,

while one insurance company purchased £5,000. The average purchase of the twenty-two other applicants was about £750. Many of
the purchasers were Dunlop dealers personally contacted by the
broker. The issue was, in effect, more of a private placing than a
public issue. There is not likely to be any trading in this security
until the income prospects of the company are more definite.

Nigerian Sugar Company Limited. The most successful public
issue in Nigeria to date was the issue of U.K. £2,100,000, 7½ per
cent Sterling Convertible Debenture Stock of the Nigerian Sugar
Company Limited in September 1962. This company is the result
of a great deal of research and effort to organize a sugar-growing
and refining industry in Nigeria. Governmental support of a
project of this nature is of prime importance. The final agreements
reached between the company and Government included the following:[24]

1. All four Governments would participate in the £1.5 million
   equity of the company, and together they would hold 50 per
   cent of the equity capital.
2. A five-year tax holiday was granted to the company.
3. Protection against imports was guaranteed within limits of
   "reasonable remuneration to an efficient producer."
4. A large block of land (15,000 acres) would be provided at
   an annual rent of 1/– per acre.
5. The Federal Government would underwrite the issue to the
   extent that subscriptions were not forthcoming up to a maximum of £1.5 million.
6. The Federal Government exempted the debenture interest
   from Nigerian tax for stockholders, companies, or individuals resident outside Nigeria.

Of the £2.1 million offered, I.C.O.N. and Phillip Hill, Higgin-
son, Erlangers Limited agreed to place £1.1 million, in effect leaving £1.0 million on offer to the public. Applications were received
for £460,000, and the Federal Government purchased the remaining £540,000. Of I.C.O.N.'s placing, about £300,000 was with several institutions in or related to the Nigerian financial community;
therefore, the private capital raised internally for this company

24 *Nigerian Sugar Company Limited* (Lagos), prospectus dated September 7, 1962.

by means of the issue was approximately £760,000.[25] This is the largest amount of private capital raised in this manner to date in Nigeria. Some of the reasons for the success of the offer have already been given. In addition to the strong Government support for the project, the stock satisfied the requirements of the Trustee Investments Act of 1962, and the yield was higher than that available on long-dated Government stock. Furthermore, the management of the company is experienced, and the participation of respected overseas interests in the equity of the company created confidence in the project.

The minimum subscription was set at £20 as compared with the N.T.C. and Nigercem minimums of £10. This higher minimum probably eliminated a large number of potential subscribers. Nevertheless, subscriptions were received from about 960 individuals; of these 929 were Nigerians. Table 4 indicates the pattern of the applications.

Table 4
Nigerian Sugar Company Debenture Applications

	Number	Amount	Percentage Total
Nigerian Individuals	929	£125,780	28%
Expatriate Individuals	33	12,240	2%
Business Firms	5	9,000	2%
Pension Funds, Insurance Companies, etc.	12	312,980	68%
	979	£460,000	100%

Thirty-three expatriates applied for the stock. Eight were associated with the Sugar Company, while the rest were miscellaneous business people, professionals, teachers, etc. Their average subscription of £370 was quite high, but the impact of their total contribution was marginal. Even provision for tax-free payment in sterling of interest and principal to residents outside Nigeria did not result in a heavy demand from expatriates.

Pension and provident funds were the largest single source of funds for this issue, as in others, and they will undoubtedly continue to be the most important factor in the capital market of Nigeria. Of the £312,980 subscribed by institutional investors,

---

25 In addition, some of the Phillip Hill placing was to financial institutions with business interests in Nigeria.

three of the statutory corporation pension funds bought £230,000, while a private pension fund purchased £25,000. Two insurance companies purchased a total of £40,000, and six miscellaneous organizations subscribed for the remainder.

Over nine hundred Nigerian individuals made application for the debenture. Table 5 shows the geographical distribution of the subscriptions. The largest bloc of applications, both in value and

Table 5

Geographical Dispersion of Sugar Debenture Applications

	Number of Nigerian Individuals	Amount	Percentage Total
Lagos	243	£ 38,260	30%
Western Region	106	18,000	14%
Northern Region	160	16,380	13%
Eastern Region	411	53,140	43%
	920	£125,780	100%

numbers, came from residents of the Eastern Region, who subscribed for about 43 per cent of the stock purchased by Nigerian individuals. There do not appear to be any factors in the project itself that would make it of more interest to Easterners than to residents in the West, North, or Lagos. The company is located about seventy miles north of the Western Region in Ilorin Province and is geographically distant from the East. No special publication effort was made in the East. The marketing plan was typical, with advertisements in the major newspapers, and applications were made through all the major banks in Nigeria or by mail. The banks were probably not making any special effort to sell the issue in any of the regions. Indeed, the banks would normally find it advantageous to encourage customers to maintain savings account balances rather than suggesting a transfer into long-term securities. Of course, the first major Government project that was extremely successful (Nigercem) was in the East, and the demonstration effect of this project might be stronger there. Nevertheless, the subscriptions from the East seem to indicate that the Easterner is more amenable than others to participate in security ownership. The Western Region had the lowest number of applicants (106 subscribing for £18,000). However, the political crisis in the Western Region at this time had created a mood of uncertainty, and this could have affected investment decisions. Since there is a filtering of Western Region activity into the Federal Territory, another possibility is that many Westerners subscribed through banks in Lagos. Subscriptions from the Lagos area accounted for 30 per cent of the total.

Table 6 breaks down the applications on the basis of amount of debenture requested. The minimum subscription allowed was £20;

Table 6
Value of Individual Applications — Sugar Debenture

Amount of Application	Number	Percentage Total	Cumulative Percentage	Amount	Percentage Total	Cumulative Percentage
£ 20	217	23.6	23.6	£ 4,340	3.4	3.4
40	102	11.0	34.6	4,080	3.2	6.6
60	42	4.6	39.2	2,520	2.0	8.6
80	20	2.3	41.5	1,600	1.3	9.9
100	340	37.0	78.5	34,040	27.2	37.1
120–180	10	1.1	79.6	1,680	1.2	38.3
200	102	11.0	90.6	20,440	16.2	54.5
240–260	3	0.3	90.9	820	0.6	55.1
300	14	1.5	92.4	4,220	3.2	58.3
400	16	1.7	94.1	6,400	5.1	63.4
500	32	3.5	97.6	16,000	12.8	76.2
600	2	0.2	97.8	1,220	1.0	77.2
800	3	0.3	98.1	2,400	2.0	79.2
1,000	13	1.5	99.6	13,020	10.4	89.6
2,000	1	0.1	99.7	2,000	1.6	91.2
3,000	2	0.2	99.9	6,000	4.8	96.0
5,000	1	0.1	100.0	5,000	4.0	100.0
	920			£125,780		

and 217, about 24 per cent, of the applicants, subscribed for this minimum. The proceeds from this group were relatively unimportant, as they contributed only 3.4 per cent of the total capital invested by Nigerian individuals. In fact, the total value of subscriptions for less than £100 was only 9.9 per cent of the total proceeds from individuals, while these subscriptions were 41.5 per cent of the total number subscribing.

The largest grouping of applications was in the £100–£200 range. Almost 50 per cent of the applications fell in this range, and they accounted for about 45 per cent of the proceeds from Nigerian individuals. Fifty-four Nigerians subscribed for £500 or more of the debenture, and the proceeds from this group were almost 37 per cent of the total. There were relatively few applications from Nigerian individuals for very large amounts of stock. Thirteen applied for £1,000, one applied for £2,000, two applied for £3,000, and one applied for £5,000. The extremely wealthy were evidently not motivated to subscribe for large amounts of this security, and to the extent that they contributed to the issue, their applications were not for large amounts.

Tables 7 and 8 give data on the occupations, location, and application amounts of Nigerians applying for stock. The largest occupational groups applying for stock were traders. A total of 336 traders purchased £38,660 of stock, and 232 of these traders were from the East. The next important occupational grouping was the civil servants; they, however, numbered only about half of the applications from traders. Teachers and doctors each purchased about £10,500, although the number of applications from teachers (78) far exceeded those from doctors (24). Employees of commercial firms and professionals other than doctors and lawyers purchased about £15,000 of the stock.

Daily Times of Nigeria Limited. The most recent public issues were the *Daily Times* of Nigeria offers of £50,000 Ordinary Stock and £300,000, 7 per cent Convertible Debenture Stock, 1969–1973, at a subscription price of £99 per £100 debenture, made in July 1963.[26] This company publishes an independent news daily that enjoys the highest circulation of any of the Nigerian newspapers. Founded originally by a prominent Nigerian, Sir Adeyemo Alakija, the company became a member of the Overseas Newspapers Group in 1947. In addition to the *Daily Times,* the company prints some weekly, monthly, and annual magazines, does a substantial amount of commercial printing, and is entering into the light packaging field. The proceeds of the issue are being used to finance expansion and modernization. Although the company is associated with a foreign press, the paper maintains an independent outlook, and the management, editorial staff, and writers are almost all Nigerian.

Data on the issue are given in Tables 9, 10, and 11. Almost five hundred Nigerians applied for £31,070 of ordinary stock. Twenty-one expatriates applied for £4,910 of the ordinary stock. Five of these applicants purchased £500 or more, and these five purchases

[26] *Daily Times* of Nigeria Limited (Lagos), prospectus dated July 16, 1963.

Table 7

Size of Application by Occupation—Sugar Debenture

Size of Application £	Civil Servants	Traders	Teachers	Doctors	Nurses	Lawyers	Employees	Commercial Private	Contractors	Labor	Miscellaneous	Politicians
20	33	76	11	1	6	—	5	5	4	14	55	—
40	17	41	6	1	1	—	4	4	1	3	17	—
60	8	16	3	1	4	1	1	—	3	3	10	—
80	3	4	3	—	—	7	2	—	1	—	3	—
100	58	138	33	9	7	7	11	32	9	9	30	1
120–180	4	4	2	—	2	—	4	2	—	—	—	—
200	21	35	15	1	2	—	—	16	3	—	7	—
240–260	1	1	—	—	—	—	—	—	—	—	1	—
300	4	3	2	2	—	1	—	—	1	—	1	—
400	5	4	1	1	—	3	—	1	—	—	3	—
500	4	9	3	3	1	1	—	7	1	—	—	—
600	1	—	—	—	—	1	—	—	—	—	—	—
800	—	5	1	4	—	—	—	1	1	—	—	—
1,000	2	—	—	—	—	—	—	1	1	—	—	—
2,000	1	—	—	1	—	—	—	—	—	—	—	—
3,000	—	—	—	—	—	—	—	1	—	—	—	—
5,000	—	—	—	—	—	—	—	—	—	—	—	—

Table 8

Applications by Location and Occupation—Sugar Debenture

	Lagos		West		East		North		Total	
	Number	Amount	Number	Amount	Number	Amount	Number	Amount	Number	Amount
Civil Servants*	57	£ 6,520	28	£ 5,520	43	£ 6,500	34	£ 3,520	162	£ 22,060
Traders	43	6,460	10	1,120	232	26,860	51	4,220	336	38,660
Teachers	17	2,980	20	2,100	30	3,400	11	2,240	78	10,720
Doctors	7	3,420	8	1,740	7	5,260	2	200	24	10,620
Nurses	10	1,100	8	800	3	220	1	60	22	2,180
Lawyers (Private)	5	1,580	3	800	7	2,000	—	—	15	4,380
Bank Employees	11	1,280	4	80	8	600	5	560	28	2,520
Employees of Commercial Firms,† Professionals, etc.	28	5,460	5	3,900	19	3,380	18	2,180	70	14,920
Contractors	4	1,160	1	200	11	860	8	1,360	24	3,580
Labor — Skilled	10	540	1	20	13	600	5	320	29	1,480
Misc. (Clerks, Students,‡ Housewives, Others)	50	2,760	18	1,720	35	1,860	25	1,720	128	8,060
Politicians	1	5,000	—	—	12	1,600	—	—	13	6,660
Total	243	£38,260	106	£18,000	420	£53,140	160	£16,380	929	£125,780

* Excludes doctors, nurses, and teachers, if possible.
† Includes salesmen, professional people, senior staff, etc., who are nongovernment.
‡ Housewives, clerks, students, and others not specifically classified.

Table 9
Daily Times Ordinary Stock Issue

	Number of Allottees	Value
Nigerians	495	£31,070
Institutional Investors	4	13,945
Expatriate Individuals	21	4,910

totaled £3,450. A few of the expatriate applicants were "close" to the issue. That is, they were associated with the *Daily Times* in some way or worked in banks taking part in the distribution of the prospectus.

The company made a special effort to encourage its employees and vendors to purchase stock. Special application forms were sent to the 600 direct employees and 100 newspaper agents associated with the company. The list of applicants does not enable the writer to determine the employment of all applicants, but the data indicate that at least forty of the applicants were associated with the company. Even though the effort to encourage employee participation was moderate, the educational effect is important because it confronts many individuals with the possibility of a new form of investment that probably they had never before seriously considered.

Table 10 shows the distribution of Nigerian individual allottees of the ordinary stock. The minimum subscription was set at £10, and 39 per cent of the total number of applicants subscribed for this amount. About 60 per cent of the applications were for £30 or less, and this group contributed 14 per cent of the proceeds. Half of the proceeds came from the forty-two applicants allotted over £100 of stock. Lagos was by far the most important source of funds, as about 57 per cent of the applications and 53 per cent of the proceeds originated in Lagos.

The number of applicants and the proceeds were less than in the preceding ordinary stock issues. Yet, in light of the relative image and visibility of the company, the type of business involved, and the potential political risks, the ordinary stock issue was successful.

The £300,000 convertible debenture was completely subscribed. About 120 Nigerian individuals purchased £11,270, while sixteen institutional investors, mostly insurance firms, purchased about

Table 10
Daily Times Ordinary Stock Applications

Size of Application	Lagos		West		East		North		Total		Percentage of Total		Cumulative Percentage of Total	
	No.	Amt.	No.	Amt.	No.	Amt.	No.	Amt.	No.	Amt.	No.	Amt.	No.	Amt.
£ 10	118	£ 1,180	25	£ 250	28	£ 280	21	£ 210	192	£ 1,920	39	6	39	6
20	44	880	11	220	13	260	9	180	77	1,540	16	5	55	11
30	14	420	9	270	5	150	2	60	30	900	6	3	61	14
40	4	160	2	80	3	120	—	—	9	360	2	1	63	15
50	46	2,300	6	300	12	600	8	400	72	3,600	15	12	78	27
51–99	3	190	1	70	1	70	1	80	6	410	1	1	79	28
100	36	3,600	17	1,700	6	600	8	800	67	6,700	13	22	92	50
101–199	2	240	—	—	—	—	2	300	4	540	1	2	93	52
200	8	1,600	1	200	3	600	1	200	13	2,600	2	8	95	60
250	2	500	—	—	3	750	1	250	6	1,500	1	5	96	65
300	2	600	2	600	1	300	—	—	5	1,500	1	5	97	70
500	4	2,000	4	2,000	1	500	—	—	9	4,500	2	14	99	84
800	1	800	—	—	—	—	—	—	1	800	¼	2	99¼	86
1,000	2	2,000	—	—	—	—	1	1,000	3	3,000	½	10	99¾	96
1,200	—	—	—	—	1	1,200	—	—	1	1,200	¼	4	100	100
Total	286	£16,470	78	£5,690	77	£5,430	54	£3,480	495	£31,070	100	100		

£288,000 of the debenture. The issue coincided with the Government's drive to repatriate overseas investments of insurance companies operating in Nigeria; this explains their interest in the debenture stock.

Table 11
Daily Times Debenture Allottees

	Number	Value
Nigerian Individuals	121	£ 11,270
Expatriate Individuals	3	260
Insurance Companies	9	192,300
Pension Funds	2	45,200
Other Institutions	5	50,970
		£300,000

Volume of Transactions on the Lagos Stock Exchange

The volume of trading on the Lagos Stock Exchange has shown appreciable growth in the two years the Exchange has been operating, although the absolute volume is still small (see Figures 1 and 2). The volume of trading is dominated by the purchases of

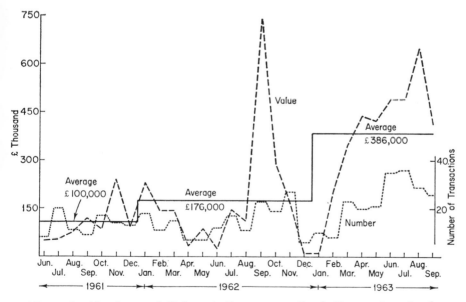

Figure 1   Number and Value of Government Stock Transactions in the Lagos Stock Exchange

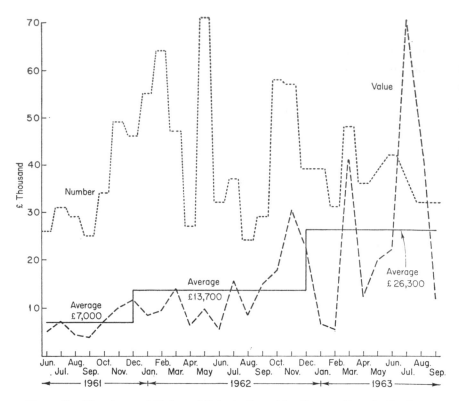

Figure 2   Number and Value of Private Securities Transactions in the Lagos Stock Exchange

Government stock from the Central Bank by institutional investors. The monthly average for Government stock trading was £100,000 in the last half of 1961, £176,000 in 1962, and averaged £386,000 in the first nine months of 1963. (The low volume of Government stock transactions in December 1962 and January 1963 was due to the nonavailability of stock from the Central Bank. This problem was alleviated by the £15 million Federation of Nigeria Fourth Development Loan issued in February 1963.) The rapid growth of the trading volume was largely due to the purchases of the National Provident Fund, whose contributions have increased rapidly since they commenced in April 1962.

Over the same three periods just mentioned, the average monthly volume of private securities transactions has been £7,000, £12,000, and £26,000. Although the number of Nigerians holding private securities has increased with every new issue, the number of private securities transactions has not grown proportionately. The average monthly number of transactions corresponding with the three periods noted were 34, 43, and 35.

The total volume of trade in private securities over the Lagos Stock Exchange for 1963 was probably close to £300,000. This volume is not impressive in absolute terms, but there is no doubt that in the context of the Nigerian economy the Exchange has had a very successful beginning. The future growth in activity on the Exchange is dependent on the number and quality of new public offers, the performance and yields of the listed securities, and the amount of local savings available for investment in private securities.

As previously mentioned, the Exchange has been extremely cautious about promotional activity. The only publicity the Exchange has received is the indirect publicity in the newspapers accompanying new issues, plus occasional newspaper and television announcements giving the day's closing prices. Unfortunately, there have been some newspaper articles critical of activities related to the Lagos Stock Exchange that were written without reference to the facts and thus were erroneous and misleading. Their objective was not analysis but exciting copy. (One such article appeared in the *Daily Times* shortly before the firm came out with its public offer. Typically, no one got very excited about it, but the management of the newspaper did agree that its reporter could benefit from some education on security dealings and sent him to the Exchange for correct information.) The Exchange could probably do more than it has done to promote and educate. One simple way of doing this would be to make an effort to assist the commercial news reporters in writing educative articles about securities markets and their role in Nigeria. Similar assistance could be given to people working in other news media.

Performance of Private Securities

The performance of securities listed on the Exchange has been very favorable, and, in general, investment in the listed securities has been profitable, particularly for individuals who have insufficient savings to enter into direct participation in trade, transport, or housing. The convertible debentures pay either 7 per cent or

7½ per cent, which is considerably higher than the currently available maximum Government yield of 5¾ per cent. In addition, the conversion features add to the attractiveness of these issues. With these fixed yields available, it does not pay an individual to maintain long-term savings accounts at banks that pay only about 3 per cent interest.

The gross dividend yield on John Holt preference stock has been between 8.3 and 9.3 per cent since the stock was listed. (Gross dividend is the dividend before income tax.) John Holt ordinary stock has shown no capital growth, but the dividend yield over the past eighteen months has been about 11 per cent, and the security is backed by substantial earnings as indicated in a price/(before-tax) earnings ratio of 4.5 in 1961 and 4.1 in 1962. Nigerian Cement Company ordinary stock has been a very good investment; from June 1961 the price rose from a par value of 20/– per share to about 45/– preceding a one-for-two stock split and one-for-three 20/– rights issues in October 1963. After these issues, the price fell to 32/– but has since increased to between 35/– and 36/– per share. This firm enjoys Pioneer Status; thus, its dividends are free of tax and will remain so for several years to come. It has paid a regular 10 per cent tax-free dividend while at the same time carrying out a large expansion program that has quadrupled its original capacity. In the financial year 1960/61, the price/earnings ratio calculated on a 39/6 share price was 5.9, and even this will be improved as a new plant is put into production. There has been a high demand for this security, and the government agencies holding this stock would have no difficulty disposing of portions of their holdings to the public. Such a course of action is doubtful despite the capital appreciation that could be realized, since the governments, in spite of their budgetary problems, are reluctant to dispose of a profitable investment.

The Nigerian Tobacco Company ordinary stock has had an average gross dividend yield of 11.3 per cent in 1961 and 15 per cent in 1962 and has had price/(before tax) earnings ratios of 6.5 and 5.5 in these two periods. Subscribers to the recent *Daily Times* ordinary stock are almost assured of a 10 per cent gross dividend yield within a year of their purchase, and prospects of increasing dividends are good. The Dunlop ordinary stock is the only exception to the high yields available on the listed securities.

With these yields it is not surprising that the demand for securities, particularly the well-known ordinary stocks, has at times exceeded the supply. On the contrary, it is unusual that more individuals have not taken advantage of investing in the private securities available, as many individuals maintain substantial long-term savings in low-yield assets such as savings account balances. There does not seem to be an awareness of the yields available relative to yields on other forms of savings. However, once an investment is made by individuals who have moderate sums to invest, they often become very enthusiastic about the advantages of stock ownership and continue to utilize this form of investment.[27]

Maintenance of the Exchange

One of the continuing problems of the security business in Nigeria is finances, particularly the cost-benefits of brokerage activity. Dealing members must pay an annual fee of £150 to the Exchange; they must send someone to the Exchange daily to take part in the call-over; they must maintain clerical and secretarial staff to handle correspondence and accounts associated with transactions, and they must share 25 per cent of the commission with other agents (such as commercial banks), if these agents obtain the business. In order to minimize the cost to individuals trading stock, the commission rates have been kept low. The commission on private stocks is 1 per cent regardless of value. Since the bulk of the transactions are for relatively small amounts of stock, the small volume of trading can hardly support four brokers.[28]

Table 12 shows an approximation of the commissions paid on securities traded over the Exchange since it was opened. For a variety of reasons, the business has not been evenly split among the four dealing members. The Central Bank has simplified its transactions by specifying one broker, I.C.O.N. Securities, to

27 Some Nigerians find it advantageous to reduce their cash balances to purchase securities for other reasons than the yields available. Facing pressure from relatives for cash, they find it easier to maintain savings if the savings are not easily accessible; stock ownership is more "tied up" than bank balances.

28 Although no direct comparison of broker commission rates is legitimate between developed countries and Nigeria because the activities of brokers are not comparable, it is interesting to note that a purchaser of a small amount of stock over the New York Stock Exchange must pay commissions of 6 per cent on a $100 purchase, 2.75 per cent on a $400 purchase, and 1.7 per cent on a $1,000 purchase.

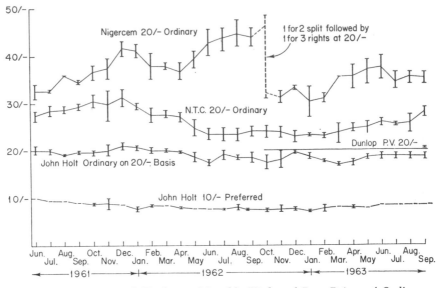

Figure 3   Lagos Stock Exchange Monthly High and Low Prices of Ordinary Stock

handle all sales of Government stock from the Central Bank's portfolio. I.C.O.N. Securities is the only one of the four dealing members that has been able to devote a substantial amount of funds to its brokerage activity. This fact, plus I.C.O.N.'s special situation in regard to establishing and managing the Exchange and its proximity to the Central Bank offices, has made it the logical firm to handle the Central Bank's business. Of course, other brokers are free to solicit orders for Government stock from institutional investors, and a small amount is handled by them. But I.C.O.N. Securities has been the broker for the National Provident Fund and some of the other important buyers of Government stock and retains most of the Government stock commissions.

In addition, I.C.O.N. Securities is in a unique position as far as the trading of private securities is concerned, since it has been able to devote manpower to soliciting and advising. Furthermore, I.C.O.N. Securities has acted as an issuing house for all the private issues made since the Exchange was formed and therefore is in a special position to build its reputation. Many individuals naturally gravitate to I.C.O.N. Securities when they wish to purchase or sell securities because they have heard more about I.C.O.N. Securities

Table 12

Estimated Commissions on Lagos Stock Exchange Turnover

	Date	Private Stock Commission	Government Stock Commission
1961	June	£ 75	£ 190
	July	105	235
	August	65	270
	September	60	355
	October	105	360
	November	150	720
	December	175	405
		735	2,535
1962	January	125	690
	February	145	420
	March	210	525
	April	95	130
	May	150	210
	June	80	120
	July	230	250
	August	125	175
	September	225	1,260
	October	270	440
	November	450	320
	December	345	38
		2,450	4,578
1963	January	100	38
	February	80	215
	March	615	350
	April	185	600
	May	300	735
	June	330	650
	July	1,035	650
	August	805	1,110
	September	180	465
		£3,630	£4,813

SOURCE: Estimated from Lagos Stock Exchange turnover data.

than the other members. The role of commercial banks in servicing their customers' requests to buy or sell securities is important because none of the brokers maintain offices outside Lagos. The banks have endeavored to distribute the business evenly among the brokers. However, this has not significantly balanced the brokerage volume. It is unlikely that any of the brokers other than

I.C.O.N. Securities has received commissions totaling more than £250 in 1961, £750 in 1962, and £900 in 1963. These are very rough estimates, but they do underscore the problem. It is no wonder that these brokers look on their activities as a public service rather than a profitable business. Even I.C.O.N. Securities is not profiting a great deal on its business because it subsidizes the activities of the Exchange by providing space and services at less than their actual cost. If the income of the brokers continues to be marginal, certain economies should be introduced, if the number of brokers is to be maintained.

It would also be in the interests of Government to support the brokers indirectly. One way to do this would be to direct the applications for the new issues of Government stock by governmental or quasi-governmental organizations through the brokers, allowing them the application commission. In the past, the Central Bank has directed these orders through its own offices to avoid paying this commission. Support in this manner has much to commend it because it is flexible. Other potential economies include a reduction in the frequency of call-overs and less dependence on revenues from brokers to finance the Exchange's operating costs, perhaps making up any of the losses by increasing the listing that fee companies are required to pay. At this particular stage of the Exchange's development, the listed companies are obviously its principal beneficiaries. The ideal solution is an increased trading volume distributed among the brokers in a way related to the quality of services they are able to render their clients; perhaps this pattern will gradually emerge. In the meantime, however, other steps may have to be taken to increase the profitability of brokerage activities.

Conclusion

The early operations of a capital market in Nigeria have been encouraging, and the prospects for continued progress are favorable. This development has resulted from the following factors: first, the financial condition of Government and its need for funds; second, the existence of reserves in the form of sterling assets which the Government could, directly or indirectly, mobilize for internal investment; third, new savings created in the economy (particularly those associated with financial institutions) which are available for investment; and fourth, the pace of foreign private investment in industry and the desire of foreign firms to secure both institutional and individual investment funds in Nigeria.

From 1959 through the end of 1963, the Government had issued £24 million of ninety-day Treasury Bills and £39 million of long-dated stock. In the private sector about £2.165 million had been raised from public share offers by private companies. The private issues have been greatly assisted by the presence of the Lagos Stock Exchange. Without this trading mechanism, the sales of private securities to the public would have been severely retarded.

The continued development of the market for private securities will be related to the dissemination of information about stock ownership, the returns available, and Government policy regarding the level of domestic investment in the private sector. The substantial financial requirements of the Six-Year Development Plan are likely to put pressure on the Government to absorb domestic savings for public programs, leaving correspondingly less for investment in the private sector. This pattern has already been established by the investment of the National Provident Fund's resources in long-term Government stock. Moreover, other trust funds are restricted by tax and trustee investment legislation to holding the major portion of their portfolio in Government securities.

On balance, the groundwork that has been laid for the marketing of Government and private securities is solid. As more experience is acquired and the public becomes better informed about security ownership, the public issue of securities should be an important positive force in the industrialization process in Nigeria. An active capital market for public securities is the key to financing development. The existence of a private securities market has proved useful at this stage of Nigeria's development both because it provides an incentive for foreign investment by reducing the foreign investor's capital commitment and because it provides an effective way to Nigerianize the capital structure of new and existing firms.

It is hoped that both the Government and private interests will continue to recognize the benefits accruing from the short but successful operation of the Lagos Stock Exchange and will continue to support the development of this institution.

9

LEGAL SAFEGUARDS FOR FOREIGN INVESTMENT

Jonathan Mallamud

In large measure because the flow of critically needed foreign capital to the developing countries does not seem commensurate with the available opportunities for profitable investment, scholars, administrators, and others concerned with economic development have been examining the existing legal institutions and norms affecting foreign private investment. Few would argue that legal safeguards constitute any sort of panacea for investor trepidation. At best, litigation is a long and costly process. This is true of commercial litigation between private citizens in any country. When a sovereign state is involved, cost, length, and, particularly, unpredictability of outcome all are increased by a very considerable factor. On the other hand, foreign investors — perhaps unduly influenced by their legal advisors who might, not unnaturally, place a slightly disproportionate emphasis on the efficacy of legal remedies — have manifested a genuine concern over the existence of legal avenues of redress for the various forms of state interference with investment. Hence, the assumption that improvement of the presently available avenues, or the development of new ones, will stimulate additional private investment in the less developed world does not seem unwarranted.

In certain cases the internal legal order may be sufficient to enforce a government's adherence to its commitments, or fair play, as the case may be. The minimum requirements would be an independent judiciary and legislative or preferably Constitutional provisions permitting the sovereign to be sued in specific cases. Both requirements vary vastly in degree from country to country, as do the length and cost of litigation.

In certain cases international law may provide redress. But the precedents in this field are hardly calculated to instill intense confidence in the hearts of potential investors. Aside from the inordinate length, complication, and expense often associated with international tribunals,[1] the state of international law is such that only the most egregiously arbitrary acts of governments are clearly unlawful. In case of expropriation, for example, there is no international consensus — and, in the absence of treaty, covenant, or other instrument, international law is nothing more than such a consensus — as to the proper definition of fair compensation. Nor is there a consensus as to what degree of interference with a man's investment constitutes expropriation. The sudden imposition of exchange controls may preclude repatriation of one cent of profit or capital, but, in itself it violates no rule of customary international law. Even where a violation is clear, the injured party has no personal standing before an international tribunal; rather he must convince his government to adopt and press his claim.[2]

Legal measures designed to enhance the security of foreign investments have fallen into three categories:

1. National legislation, which may be either general internal law (tax laws, company laws, etc.) or laws designed exclusively to stimulate foreign investment;

---

[1] International arbitration, however, has not infrequently been a fairly efficient means for the resolution of disputes.

[2] The rights of persons, individual and corporate, are doubtful in present international law, which developed mainly as a law regulating relations between states and does not generally afford remedies to individuals except insofar as their states may adopt their claims. This situation may be changing. Note the following statement at pp. 737–738 of William W. Bishop, *International Law: Cases and Materials* (second edition; Boston: Little, Brown and Company, 1962):

> We may not be far from recognising frankly that the individual does have such rights, and that interposition of the claimant's state is now necessary only because there is no procedure whereby the claimant may bring his case before any tribunal in his own right. Once the existence of such a right is recognised, it might in turn not be too long a step to provide machinery by which he could pursue his own remedy against the respondent state, without need for interposition by the claimant state. This, in turn, might support the notion that individuals may have certain rights under international law, regardless of their nationality and even against the state of which they are nationals. . . .

2. Specific legal arrangements (agreements) between the host government and foreign investors;

3. Bilateral or multilateral treaties to which the host state, as well as the state of the investor, are parties.

For the developing countries, changes in the legal order to protect foreign investment often are thought of as a limitation on their power over the national economy. Yet, as measures required to attract essential capital, they properly should be conceived as exercises of sovereignty designed to achieve an appropriate objective. From the standpoint of the developing country, the value of new legal arrangements should be measured in terms of the kind and quantity of investment such arrangements may be expected to attract. One approach would be to examine the obstacles to investment and then consider what steps (in the context of this discussion, what legal measures) would tend to eliminate or counterbalance the obstacles.

Of course, how to attract the investor is not the only decision developing countries must make, and it would be unwise to attract now without considering the possible requirements of future policies and contingencies. It must also be borne in mind that the creation of a class of foreign investors with privileges and immunities considerably more extensive than those of the indigenous population can lead to an ultimate deterioration in the "investment climate," not to mention political disaster.

In this context of attracting foreign investment, the legal framework of investment and possible changes in it — including measures proposed and actually taken — will be discussed.

The Internal Legal Order of the Host Country[3]

One aspect of the internal legal order is general legislation of the host country that affects both foreign and domestic investors. Illustrative of such general legislation are laws relating to com-

---

[3] The internal legal order of the investor's country, while not discussed here, can also be important. For example, the tax laws of an investor's country may play a large role in determining whether he invests abroad and can certainly be designed to encourage such investment, as the U.S. tax system to some extent demonstrates. One could imagine many other areas of law affecting the economy being designed to encourage nationals of a country to invest abroad (and of course the laws can be designed to have the opposite effect). The omission of a full discussion of such laws here does not by any means reflect a judgment that they are not an important aspect of the subject.

panies, taxation, corporate reporting procedures, labor, social security, and exchange control. Fairly comprehensive general legislation was operative in the developing countries at the time of independence, and since independence considerable legislative revision has been undertaken in an effort at clarification and modernization.

Another aspect of the internal legal order is special legislation to encourage foreign private investment. Such special legislation is broadly described as protection and incentive legislation and is illustrated by the recent proliferation of laws providing for, among other things, compensation in the event of expropriation, convertibility guarantees, exemption from taxation, exemption from customs duties, tariff protection, and cheap land. The special legislation has taken a variety of forms. Some countries have enacted comprehensive laws that embody a complex of provisions such as those already enumerated; other countries have enacted separate laws governing each type of benefit. A common characteristic of all this legislation is a discretionary power given to a minister to withhold or grant the privileges or immunities created by the legislation; this discretionary power provides a basis for specific negotiation with each investor.

One example of special investment legislation is the Tanganyika (now Tanzania) Foreign Investments (Protection) Act of 1963 (Act No. 40 of 1963). The main thrust of the Act is to provide "full and fair" compensation in the event of expropriation for "approved" foreign investments. The Act contains no guarantee against expropriation, nor even a statement that the expropriation will be only for a public purpose. Provision is made for arbitration in the event of a dispute arising over the value of the property taken (Section 6). Approval of an enterprise may be given by the responsible minister in his discretion "in any case in which he is satisfied that the enterprise would further the economic development of, or benefit, Tanganyika" (Section 3). In this way the Government is able to sort out investments and to encourage only those which will enhance the economy and not offend political sensitivities or obstruct social policies. Another important element of the Tanganyika Act is its guarantee of substantial rights of convertibility even in case of the imposition of rigorous exchange controls.

Insofar as the Tanganyika Act provides for compensation in the case of expropriation, it may be compared with Section 22 of the Uganda Constitution, which circumscribes governmental power to deprive an individual of his property. Unlike many Constitutional guarantees, the exceptions do not materially detract from the main protection. In its essentials, this section provides that no property or right over or interest in property shall be compulsorily acquired except for a public purpose or in the public benefit, and except where the necessity justifies the hardship to the owner, and where provision is made for the prompt payment of adequate compensation. It also guarantees the owner the right of access to the High Court to determine the legality of the taking and the amount of compensation, and for the purpose of obtaining prompt payment.

Some doubts have been expressed about the investment-attracting qualities of Section 22. The Constitution was, after all, an integral part of the independence parcel and hence was not entirely the creation of the Uganda Government. In examining the investment climate, legislation sponsored by a postindependence government may be more significant as an expression of national policy toward investment.

Although the Tanganyika Act is specifically aimed at attracting foreign investment, it falls very short of being a comprehensive investment code, such as the one adopted by Ghana. Ghana's new Capital Investments Act provides not only a guarantee of compensation for nationalization and the right to repatriate principal, interest, or profits from foreign investment, but also an income tax holiday of up to ten years, exemption from purchase tax, excise tax, and import and export duties, deferment of payment of fees to government agencies upon establishment of a company, exemption from property and similar taxes, and special capital allowances. The Ghana Act also establishes a central authority called the Capital Investments Board, whose primary functions are the initiation and organization of activities for the encouragement of investment of foreign and domestic capital, the provision of liaison services between prospective investors and the sundry Government departments that they must contact, and the selective granting of the incentive benefits that the Act establishes.

As far as the actual benefits that an investor may be able to obtain are concerned, the difference between the existence of comprehensive legislation and the conferring of benefits under scattered acts may be more of form than substance. In fact, even without specific investment-incentive acts, governments can usually find the means to confer benefits on desired industries. Sometimes, however, the form can be important. Particularly for the medium-sized investor, new to a country, it may be difficult to discover the benefits available in scattered legislation. A comprehensive act provides a clear summary of the benefits available. It may consequently serve an important public relations function. Of course, a widely publicized policy statement may perform the same function almost equally well.

The fact that the Ghana Act applies to domestic, as well as foreign, investment may avoid the serious possibility that special investment legislation will produce a class of foreign investors with privileges and immunities considerably more extensive than those of the indigenous population. But the creation of a privileged class is not the only problem beginning to emerge from the rash of incentive legislation. Another is the potential effect on tax revenues, a problem that does not appear to have received sufficiently serious consideration by the policy-makers of the less developed countries. Still another problem in this field is generated by legislation enacted specifically for the benefit of one investor, sometimes named, but in any case identifiable. This type of legislation is generally to be deprecated, for it casts suspicion on the legislative process and can place the beneficiary in a vulnerable position as a focus for nationalist antagonism. The objectives of such legislation can easily be effected by the host government and the investor entering into an agreement.

For the enforcement of the rights and privileges accorded by both the general and the special legislation, the investor should be able to look to the municipal courts. As suggested earlier, the availability of a forum, the civil procedure, and, very importantly, the independence and reliability of the local judiciary should become significant factors in determining the investor's attitude toward the value and usefulness of the offered privileges. The investment-attracting force of internal legislation is easily and quickly suppressed by a judiciary that is unreliable or subservient to the executive.

Even if the existence of legislative safeguards and an independent and reliable judiciary capable of enforcing them is assumed, the private foreign investor in a one-party state is subject to the risk that legislation, and even constitutions can quickly be amended. Particularly in such states, policy statements emanating from party or high government authorities encouraging foreign investment may be far more indicative of the long-range investment climate than particular laws. And in all less developed countries, an obsession with legal benefits and remedies unaccompanied by acute regard for the nation's political propensities would be naive and could be disastrous.

Host Country–Investor Agreements

For a variety of reasons, any major investment in a developing country (such as the construction of a harbor, an oil refinery, a cement plant, a fertilizer factory, or a truck assembly plant) usually is the subject of a detailed agreement between the host country and the investor. This is true regardless of whether the government participates in ownership or management. Often the agreements represent attempts to relate the investment directly to the national development plan.

The main purpose and value of these agreements is the articulation of mutual rights and obligations, which are far more elaborate than those contained in traditional agreements, which often involved nothing more than the payment of a fee for the right (and not the duty) to exploit certain natural resources. Today, all agreements must be justified in terms of national economic objectives. The investor often undertakes — as an obligation toward the host government — the exploitation of a mineral or the construction of a dam, plus a host of ancillary obligations, such as the construction of roads, the widening of a harbor, the training of indigenous technicians, the employment of local labor, and the building of houses, schools, and hospitals. In return, the host government commits itself to specified actions with regard to imports of key materials and the allocation of the necessary foreign exchange, the entry and rights of foreign personnel, the repatriation of capital and earnings, tax concessions, guarantees against expropriation for a stated period of time, and so on. Sometimes, these mutual rights and obligations are underpinned by an arbitration clause, providing for arbitration by a tribunal headed by an impartial chairman. Where the subject of the agreement is the exploitation of a natural resource, there is an arrangement for the sharing of profits, since the host state now universally claims ownership over all natural resources. Quite often, as in the case of the Tanganyika Kilombero Sugar scheme or the Liberian Iron Ore Consortium (Lamco), the agreement is made by the host government with a plurality of foreign investors of different nationalities and with various national or international lending institutions. And with increasing frequency, these arrangements are linked with partnership associations (joint international business ventures) in which the host government, the foreign investors, and sometimes a lending institution (such as the I.F.C. or the C.D.C.) take various equity participations. The distribution of equities does not always correspond to that of management responsibilities. Some of the partners do not take any equity but associate themselves through management contracts, credits, or long-term sales contracts.

These international economic development agreements are becoming increasingly important, and must be examined as a new type of institution that is evolving in response to the cooperative relationship between large private investors and governments of developing countries. Traditionally, international law regulates relations between nations and comprehends wrongs to individuals only insofar as the wrongs have been considered wrongs to the state of the individual and have been presented by that state.[4] In recent years, a considerable body of opinion has developed to the effect that an individual should be able to press his claim directly against the offending state.[5] The use of arbitration clauses in such agreements may tend to reinforce this view, for it can be argued that the acceptance by states of such clauses constitutes recognition that what was once considered only a wrong to another state is now a wrong to the injured alien.

These contemporary agreements mark a break with tradition in another respect. In the past, a simple breach of contract by a state was not considered an international wrong; a wrong arose only when a state used its sovereign position in order to do what

---

[4] See Bishop, *op. cit.*, p. 737.

[5] *Ibid.*, pp. 737–738, and Article 22 of Louis Sohn and Richard Baxter's *Convention on the International Responsibility of State for Injuries to Aliens* (Draft No. 12, Cambridge, Mass.: Harvard University Law School, 1961), pp. 25 *et seq.*

a private individual could not, such as annulling the contract by statute or failing to obey a court's judgment.[6] Even if these agreements do not stand under the protection of international law, arbitral tribunals can still give effect to them by applying either the law that would be applicable under normal principles of conflicts of law or some generally accepted principles of contract law.[7]

International Legal Protection

Customary International Law

Primary responsibility and capability for the protection of rights continue to rest with national governments. From a purely legal perspective, the best source of security for an investment is a strong legal order in the host country. International law has for a long time provided in certain circumstances some additional protection.

Just exactly what those circumstances are and what the measure of redress should be remain questions that provoke unremitting controversy among legal theorists. In evaluating the respective positions in this controversy, it is useful to recall that the history of foreign investment is not free from abuse by investors, as well as host governments; nor should one forget the compelling moral and political obligations of governments to improve the social order where certain segments of the population are severely underprivileged. As Judge Philip C. Jessup of the International Court of Justice has written:

---

[6] See materials quoted by Milton Katz and Kingman Brewster, *The Law of International Transactions and Relations* (Brooklyn, N.Y.: Foundation Press, 1960), pp. 138–141. For example, Charles C. Hyde is quoted there as follows (from Hyde, *International Law Chiefly as Interpreted and Applied by the U.S.*, Vol. 2, para. 303 (Boston: Little, Brown, 2nd rev. ed., 1947):

> It may be doubted, however, whether the mere breach of a promise by a contracting State with respect to an alien is generally looked upon as amounting to internationally illegal conduct, or as constituting a violation of a legal obligation towards the State of which he is a national. . . . In the estimation of statesmen and jurists, international law is probably not regarded as denouncing the failure of a State to keep such a promise, until at least there has been a refusal either to adjudicate locally the claim arising from the breach, or, following an adjudication, to heed the adverse decision of a domestic court. Upon the happening of either of these events the internationally illegal conduct is regarded as first apparent. There is then seen a failure to respect a duty of jurisdiction which is distinct from the breach of contract and subsequent to it in time.

[7] To what extent the latter course would in fact be the creation of "modern public international law" or "transnational law" is, as they say, a "nice question."

The history of this branch of international law during the nineteenth and twentieth centuries exemplifies the way in which a body of customary law develops in response to the need for adjustment of clashing interests. It was inevitable that the states which had achieved a large measure of local industrial and financial development should seek outlets for the investment of surplus funds and for the energies of their ranchers, bankers, mining engineers, railroad builders, constructors of ports, and other trained personnel. In many instances those energies found an outlet in colonies. In other instances colonial outlets were few and attention was turned to those independent countries which were on the threshold of their economic development. In the background as a driving force was the desire of governments for political influence in certain countries, the scramble for markets and for sources of raw materials which induced organized state support for the export of capital and industrial skill. The history of the development of the international law in the responsibility of states for injuries to aliens is thus an aspect of the history of "imperialism" or "dollar diplomacy." It is remarkable that in this struggle which so generally involved the relations between the strong and the weak, international law, for all its primitiveness, developed as a balance for conflicting interests. The fact that several strong states found themselves simultaneously interested in the welfare of their nationals in states which were "exploited" may have assisted the legal development.[8]

At this point in the law's development, the position of the individual, as pointed out earlier, generally remains subject to the possible concern of his state for his plight, and the substantive law governing his rights remains more a source of controversy than confidence. For example, while expropriation of an alien's property without compensation is clearly unlawful, there is vociferous disagreement as to the nature of the compensation required to render the expropriation valid. Capital-exporting countries generally insist on "prompt and full" (whatever that may mean) compensation. But many jurists, and not only those from the poorer countries, have been quick to point out that the rigorous application of such a criterion would in effect deny the right of a poor state to expropriate even to effect vital economic and social reforms. This, among other factors, has precluded the evolution

[8] Philip C. Jessup, *A Modern Law of Nations* (New York: The Macmillan Company, 1959), pp. 95–96.

of a consensus on valid expropriation. Some states have gone to the length of contending that the time and manner of the payment of compensation must be determined exclusively by the law of the expropriating state.[9] This view is only another mode of expression for the hoary proposition that what's good enough for our own nationals is certainly good enough for foreigners who had the alternative of not coming here in the first place. It has, fortunately, found little support.

Although the potential political and economic effects (for example, reduction or termination of economic assistance by the investor's state or, more often, a sharp fall-off in foreign investment) of expropriatory and related actions should seem to be more potent guardians of foreign investment than the threat of legal action, investors have often demanded additional protection in the form of specific legal obligations — regarding substance and procedure — assumed by host countries pursuant to bilateral or multilateral international agreements, that is, agreements between sovereign states.

International Agreements

Bilateral. Bilateral agreements covering the treatment of foreign property have been negotiated on a considerable scale by the United States, West Germany, and Switzerland. The Friendship, Commerce, and Navigation treaties negotiated by the United States provide at least for nondiscriminatory treatment of its nationals and for the settlement of disputes by arbitration. The more recent investment guarantee agreements, on which the investment insurance program is based, permit the United States to acquire the investor's claims against the host country (subrogation), and often include clauses on the means for settling disputes. In defining appropriate standards of treatment for American investors, these bilateral agreements contain at best some general provisions on nondiscrimination and "adequate" or "just" and prompt compensation in cases of expropriation. Some recent Swiss agreements with African states go well beyond this and guarantee, among other things, the convertibility of earnings and principal —

9 See Mexican-American Correspondence quoted by Herbert W. Briggs, *The Law of Nations* (London: B. F. Stevens & Brown, Ltd., 1953), pp. 558 *et seq.*

within defined limits — for investments approved by the host country.

Multilateral. There have been a number of recent efforts to establish a multilateral convention for the protection of foreign property. One is represented now by a draft prepared by experts from some fifteen European countries under the auspices of the O.E.C.D. and its predecessor, the O.E.E.C. The O.E.C.D. has not yet taken any official position with regard to the draft, but soundings taken among governments of developing countries have revealed rather negative reactions.

The O.E.C.D. draft convention is allegedly an attempt to codify customary international law and practice. Yet its substantive norms remain very general and thus ambiguous on many points: private property may not be expropriated, directly or indirectly, except for a public purpose; host countries must abide by the terms of undertakings given to investors; if property is taken or if the terms of an undertaking are not followed, full and prompt compensation must be paid; violations of the convention entail an obligation to make "full reparation." The draft further provides that "each Party shall have regard to the principle that any measures taken by any State, whether or not a party to the Convention, which are in conflict [with the basic provisions regarding expropriation] should not be recognized within the territory of that Party as valid." This goes beyond existing international law. Finally, the draft convention provides for compulsory jurisdiction of an arbitral or "any other international tribunal" either for litigation between the investor's country and the host country, or, in certain cases, between the individual investor and the host country.

What would be the value of a convention of the O.E.C.D. type? Parties would, in the first place, recognize that the treatment of foreign property in accordance with certain standards — including those derived from the terms of investment agreements — is part of international law. More important, the convention would establish an international mechanism for the compulsory settlement of investment disputes, thus enhancing the legal enforceability of the accepted norms of international law. On the other hand, it must be recognized that a multilateral convention of this "code of good conduct" type would do little to spell out what these international norms really mean, and might thus engender misunderstandings, conflicts, and international litigation. Bilateral agreements are more flexible and would seem more appropriate means for spelling out the concrete obligations to be undertaken by host countries with regard to, for example, indirect expropriation, convertibility, procedural due process, and other matters that normally can be dealt with more effectively and fairly on an *ad hoc* basis. The formulation of general norms, as found in the O.E.C.D. draft, coupled with compulsory jurisdiction, would empower the international tribunal to determine the permissibility of a wide range of governmental acts, and to do this without precise guidelines or possibilities of appeal. It seems highly doubtful that such a limitation of governmental power will prove acceptable at this time to many sovereign states. This is particularly true with regard to the many acts or omissions (e.g., the denial of residence permits to foreign management) that might amount to indirect expropriation or might be contrary to undertakings contained in agreements with investors, though not in conflict with international norms.

A more limited multilateral convention is being considered by the International Bank for Reconstruction and Development. It would establish a permanent center for the settlement of investment disputes by conciliation or arbitration between the individual investor (or exceptionally, in cases of subrogation, the state of the investor) and the host country. This convention has only procedural significance; it does not purport to lay down substantive legal norms with regard to foreign investment. At least in principle, the jurisdiction of the proposed I.B.R.D. Center would be voluntary; in practice, however, host countries might find it difficult to refuse advance commitment to I.B.R.D. arbitration in their major investment agreements. The provision in the convention that arbitration awards would be directly enforceable in signatory countries should significantly heighten the prospect for voluntary compliance with decisions.

In conclusion, it appears that international law does provide some general standards for the treatment of foreign investment, but they are both vague and rudimentary. Further definition of mutual rights and obligations, better mechanisms for the settlement of disputes, and improved prospects of enforceability are gradually being sought through bilateral and multilateral agreements. Whether comprehensive and highly elaborated norms and compulsory recourse to international tribunals for their application are feasible or wholly desirable at this stage is another matter. It seems fair to say, in any event, that excessive reliance on laws and procedures that protect only aliens tends to create a privileged class of foreign property owners and investors and to distract attention from the task of raising the social and legal order in the host country to a level that can offer adequate security to foreign and domestic investors alike.

Investment Insurance

Investment insurance has been offered for a number of years by the United States, Japan, and West Germany to protect investors against noncommercial risks[10] in developing countries.[11] It has covered outright expropriation, indirect expropriation, nonconvertibility of income and principal, and losses due to war and insurrection, and is granted to investments approved by the capital-exporting and the host country. In certain exceptional cases the United States Government will guarantee an investment against ordinary business losses as well. A small nonactuarial premium is charged. The United States and German schemes require investment guarantee agreements with the particular host country for which coverage is granted. Coverage does not necessarily have to correspond, however, to the obligations assumed by the host country, which, as previously indicated, are not very extensive either under these agreements or international law. Therefore, it can be and generally is quite comprehensive and definite.

The United States program now covers investments aggregating two billion dollars in some fifty countries, and investor demand for coverage has tended to grow. Investors in countries without national guarantee schemes, especially in Northern Europe and

[10] Comprehensive coverage including commercial risks may now be granted under the U.S. scheme.

[11] The U.S. and Japanese schemes are not specifically restricted to developing countries, although the general authorization for the U.S. program states that the program is undertaken "in order to facilitate and increase the participation of private enterprise in furthering the development of the economic resources and productive capacities of less developed friendly countries and areas . . ." 22 U.S.C. § 2181(a) (1961). Moreover, A.I.D. policy appears to restrict guarantees to investments in countries it classifies as "developing."

Canada, are putting pressure on their governments to establish similar guarantee programs. There also is support for some sort of international program. At the United Nations Conference on Trade and Development, a Turkish-Pakistani initiative supported by most developing countries resulted in a request addressed to the I.B.R.D. to study the possibility of establishing a multilateral guarantee scheme.

The study was actually initiated by the O.E.C.D. in close co-operation with the I.B.R.D. The O.E.C.D. recently concluded that the project is technically feasible. The next probable step will be the establishment of a service institution, possibly and preferably within I.B.R.D., which could initially write investment insurance on behalf and at the request of some ten capital-exporting O.E.C.D. countries willing to join such a scheme. Terms could be similar to those of national guarantee policies. The United States has indicated that it wishes to participate in such a scheme without abandoning its national guarantee program. It is envisaged that any predetermined capital fund risk-sharing among the partici-pants will be proportionate to the origin of guaranteed invest-ments, that is, to the actual use made of the scheme by the partici-pants. Host countries would not be required to share losses, but their participation in administrative expenditure and management and their advance commitments with regard to subrogation and arbitration of disputes are considered essential. Indeed, the prin-cipal value of such a multinational venture is the establishment of a nonpolitical forum for discussion and negotiation on subjects and conflicts regarding the treatment of foreign investment. In addition, such a multilateral scheme would permit coverage of joint ventures and multinational investments that, at present, can-not qualify under any single national insurance scheme.

It may well be that for some years to come investment insurance will be the most effective means for the protection of private in-vestors against political and unusual economic risks, without inter-ference with the exigencies of social change in the host country. As internal and international legal security become more firmly established, the need for investment insurance should decrease. The existence of a multilateral guarantee scheme, grouping devel-oping and developed countries, may facilitate and, indeed, accel-erate the gradual growth of a more secure legal order for invest-ment.

10

CAPITAL FLIGHT IN EAST AFRICA: THE CASE OF UGANDA

Bruce A. Blomstrom

The Asians

Although there have been Asian traders on the coast of East Africa for several hundred years, the first large influx of Asians occurred during the period 1896–1901, when 32,000 were employed on the construction of the Kenya-Uganda railway. At its conclusion, about 6,000 decided to remain. Today there are some 350,000 Asians in East Africa, accounting for 1.3 per cent of the total population.

In Uganda there were 82,000 Asians in 1963, equivalent to just over 1 per cent of the population. Forty-five per cent of the Asian community in Uganda live in the five major towns and account for about one third of their population. The average Asian wage in 1963 for a male was £597, while for an African it was £97.[1] Asians are now being forced to sell their cotton ginneries to co-operatives, but in 1948 they owned 90 per cent of the industry.[2] Asians held 97.5 per cent of the trade in the main city, Kampala, in 1953.[3] Almost the entire sugar production of the country is still in Asian hands.

---

[1] *Background to the Budget 1964–65,* Uganda Government pamphlet, May 1964, p. 25.

[2] George Delf, *Asians in East Africa,* London Institute of Race Relations (London: Oxford University Press, 1963), p. 57.

[3] Guy Hunter, *The New Societies of Tropical Africa: A Selective Study,* London Institute of Race Relations (London: Oxford University Press, 1962), p. 147.

Capital Flight

The Raw Figures

Capital has been flowing out of Uganda in large amounts for at least the past ten years. The World Bank estimated that from 1954 to 1959 the outflow averaged £5 million per year.[4] This rate increased significantly between 1960 and 1962, and the increase was sustained in 1963. Estimates for 1964 suggest that, at best, there will be no decrease in the rate of outflow. From 1960 to 1963, capital outflow was roughly £20–£35 million. This estimate could be in error by 100 per cent or more, because balance-of-payment statistics are calculated only on an East African basis. At best, these figures just give an indication of the magnitude of the funds that have left Uganda.

Consequences

This heavy capital flight has contributed to the stagnation, since 1957, of Uganda's economy. From 1957 to 1962, the gross domestic product grew by only 6.8 per cent, or £10 million (see Appendix I). Although the 1963 and 1964 estimates, in comparison, indicate an extraordinary increase of £37.7 million, or 24 per cent, in two years, the major reason for this is unusually high coffee prices, with a resulting increase in production and processing. This sudden spring upward not only illustrates the tremendous fluctuations that can occur in a two-crop economy, but has tended to obscure the fact that the rate of capital outflow remains undiminished.

The problem created by this outflow becomes more apparent when gross capital formation is examined (see Appendix II). From 1955 through 1963, the annual rate of capital formation decreased from 21.3 per cent to 13.6 per cent, or by about one third. Except for 1960 and 1963 (estimated), the actual value of gross capital formation in the private sector has been falling since 1956. It leveled off in the 1960–1962 period at £10 million. For 1963/64 the high coffee prices are likely to boost it to the 1956 level of £13 million.

The World Bank has interpreted the decrease in capital formation as indicative of a lack of investment opportunities, but it is more likely that investors have not been searching for them. Certainly this is true of the Asian community.

[4] *The Economic Development of Uganda,* a study prepared by the International Bank for Reconstruction and Development, October 1961, p. 24.

Although bank deposits have been increasing since 1960 (see Appendix III), advances have been increasing even faster, to the extent that banks are now drawing on their overseas offices for loan funds. Most of the new loans have been used to finance the two major crops—coffee and cotton. Except for short-run crop financing, credit is now tight for all but the largest businessmen. The capital flight has certainly contributed to this situation, for it has drained off such a substantial quantity of potential investment funds that practically the entire residue of available private funds has been able to find short-term, low-risk outlets.

The Asian Component

The private banking community has displayed a keen reluctance to loan on a long-term basis. An important part of this reluctance is derived from the fact that loans granted to Asians are normally used to export cash rather than for investment. Among Asians there has been a sharp trend in the past few years to mortgage themselves to the hilt and to secure overdrafts which are then sent overseas as protection against devaluation, exchange control, or political persecution. There are instances of men on small salaries sending up to four fifths of their pay out of the country. The current situation was summed up by one man who said that "everyone who has any money has sent it out of the country; it is the only prudent thing to do."

No statistics are available that would clearly define the amount of capital outflow attributable to the Asian community, but talks with a few leading Asian businessmen confirm that it is significant. They estimate that a minimum of £3–£10 million would be returned to Uganda in the next two or three years, if the Government were to pursue a deliberate policy of trying to attract these funds. One estimate by a well-informed source ran as high as £50 million. If this is correct, then the amount of money that could be attracted back to Uganda from the Asian community over the next few years could be more than double the amount of external financial assistance that Uganda is likely to receive for the entire period from 1961/62 to 1964/65. During these four years, external financial aid will total £18.3 million.[5] This figure is equivalent on

[5] *Background to the Budget 1964–65, op. cit.,* p. 38.

an annual basis to one third of current gross capital formation in the private sector.

This estimate of the amounts available for repatriation to Uganda, should there be a restoration of confidence among the Asians, does not, of course, include the amount of capital that will continue to be generated and exported each year. These sums in themselves are substantial, even though they will decrease as Asian cotton ginneries are sold to African cooperatives.

Asian Insecurity

In the past the Asian community has done dangerously little to lay a secure foundation for its position in Uganda. One of the most frequently voiced criticisms of the Asian is that he has not identified himself with Uganda, but has lived a clanlike existence related more to his country of origin and to his caste than to his present homeland. Sons are still sent to India to find their wives. More importantly, some Asians have manifestly regarded the African as an inferior being and have treated him accordingly.

Among ordinary Africans there is a pervasive belief that they have been exploited by the Asians. Asian awareness of this feeling is reflected by continual reference to the treatment received by the Asian minority in Zanzibar during the 1964 revolution.

The African position is that an Asian must become a citizen if he wants nondiscriminatory rights to participate in the economy. It has been stated that, once an Asian becomes a citizen, he will be accorded the same rights and opportunities that other citizens possess. This has yet to be demonstrated conclusively. It may be true that Asians who become citizens will be permitted to retain their present positions, but it remains to be seen whether an Asian citizen more qualified than an African citizen will receive a job for which both apply. More importantly, the Asian suspects that, if he becomes a citizen, his right to travel or live abroad may suddenly be circumscribed.

The most immediate Asian fear is that of restrictive exchange controls. Almost the first comment from an Asian on the subject of investment is that exchange control is bad. Warned that complete exchange control will be introduced in the future, the first thought of an Asian with money is to send it out of the country, where it will be available in the event that he must leave Uganda. The uncertainty associated with future exchange-control policy forces the Asian (and others) to assume that controls will be imposed. The result is that rather than capital being attracted by Uganda's liberal policy, it is driven away. The only solutions to this aspect of the capital flight problem are either a Government guarantee that there will be no exchange control for a specified period or the introduction with the greatest possible rapidity and suddenness of complete exchange control.

To attract funds back to Uganda, the Asian investor must be given an assurance that he can re-export them at will. If the Asian is not a Uganda citizen, he may bring himself under the Foreign Investment Protection Act of July 29, 1964, which provides the necessary assurance; but since he is under increasing compulsion to become a citizen if he wishes to remain in Uganda, he soon will be left only with the option of administrative assurances. The obvious problem with the administrative alternative is that the guarantee is not as firm and can be changed at will. Such administrative assurances are now given to approved investments by the Uganda Exchange Controller. If the Investment Protection Act were altered so that its benefits were applicable to foreign capital regardless of ownership, the incentive for capital repatriation by Asians would be substantial.

Finding Investment Outlets

If stringent exchange control were to be introduced, Government assistance in identifying investment projects for the trapped funds would be required. Asian businessmen, when interviewed, indicated an absence of investment ideas outside the commercial processing fields in which they have congregated. Ideally, the Ministry of Commerce and Industry should be able to describe in detail the size and kind of available investment opportunities. Initial feasibility studies of a summary nature would be necessary. These could be undertaken in conjunction with similar efforts to lay out projects for foreign investors.

Should the Government embark on a positive policy of encouraging Asian investment, there will be an opportunity to use the Asian group as innovators. As a vulnerable minority group, the

Asian community will be inclined to do those things which are approved by the Government. Furthermore, its insecurity could be harnessed and used to broaden Uganda's economic base by Government encouragement of Asian investment and entrepreneurship in areas where significant African activity is highly unlikely in the foreseeable future.

Industrial opportunities identified by Government must pay more than the 3–4½ per cent which is available in gilt edges on the London Stock Market. Since Uganda Government bonds are, in fact, paying almost 10 per cent at today's valuation and can be purchased on the London Exchange payable in pounds sterling, and since some of the stocks listed on the Nairobi exchange are paying between 11 and 15 per cent, the Uganda Government should aim at identifying opportunities that offer a return on investment of at least 10 per cent.

If the Government of Uganda wishes to use the Asian community as an asset for its economic development program, it must take positive steps to do so. To overcome the fears inherent in the racial situation, continued statements are necessary from the highest to the lowest levels of political authority giving assurances against discrimination and outlining both the kinds of guarantees available to Asian investors and the way in which the Government would like to see this group participate in the economy. To attract back funds that have already fled the country, guarantees must be given that both profits and capital can be taken out of the country under the same conditions open to any foreign investor. Currently generated funds will have to be treated in a similar manner unless strict exchange control is introduced. But if a restrictive exchange control policy is adopted, newly generated capital will be forced to look for profitable internal investments. The Government can greatly facilitate this process by suggesting, in detail, projects suitable for investment. This can be tied in with outlining investment opportunities for other foreign investors and is particularly needed because of the lack of ideas existing in the Asian community. If these relatively simple measures were carried out, Uganda could expect to gain annually a minimum of several million pounds for at least the next few years.

Appendix I
Gross Domestic Product at Factor Cost (£ Million)

Year	Monetary	Nonmonetary	Total
1954	92.8	36.0	128.8
1955	102.0	38.2	140.2
1956	102.8	38.8	141.6
1957	109.4	37.3	146.7
1958	105.9	40.5	146.4
1959	108.0	41.0	149.0
1960	110.8	41.3	152.1
1961	111.2	45.2	156.4
1962	107.9	48.7	156.6
1963 (est.)	128.7	47.3	176.0
1964 (est.)	145.9	48.5	194.4

SOURCES: 1. 1954–1959 GDP figures are from *The Real Growth of the Economy of Uganda 1954–1962*, Uganda Government pamphlet, April 1964, p. 29.
2. The remaining figures are from *Background to the Budget 1964–65*, Uganda Government pamphlet, May 1964, p. 1.

Appendix II
Gross Capital Formation, 1954 to 1963 (£ Million)

Year	Public Sector	Private Sector	Total	Percentage of the Monetary Economy (at Market Prices)
1954	8.3	10.2	18.6	18.9%
1955	9.7	13.5	23.2	21.3
1956	8.4	13.3	21.8	19.9
1957	8.9	11.5	20.4	17.5
1958	8.6	11.0	19.6	17.1
1959	8.3	8.8	17.1	14.6
1960*	8.2	10.8	19.0	15.8
1961*	6.9	10.4	17.3	14.2
1962*	6.3	10.2	16.5	13.8
1963 (est.)	6.4	13.0	19.4	13.6

* Revised
SOURCE: *Background to the Budget 1964–65, op. cit.*, p. 28.

Appendix III
Commercial Bank Deposits and Advances, 1959–1963

As at End of Month		Total Deposits (£ Million)	Total Advances (£ Million)	Advances, Deposits (%)	Net Overseas Balance (£ Million)
1959	June	18.1	9.4	52.0	+5.2
	December	16.8	13.1	77.9	+1.6
1960	June	15.1	13.0	85.9	+2.3
	December	13.3	14.1	106.1	+0.4
1961	June	15.8	14.3	90.2	+1.6
	December	15.7	15.1	96.3	+0.7
1962	June	17.6	16.4	93.3	−1.2
	December	17.9	17.6	98.7	−0.8
1963	June	20.2	20.6	102.1	−0.4
	December	19.7	23.1	117.3	−3.8

SOURCE: *Background to the Budget 1964–65, op. cit.,* p. 31.

11

SOME PROBLEMS IN THE REGIONAL ALLOCATION OF INDUSTRY

James Stoner

Background: The East African Common Market

The East African Common Market area has been composed of Kenya, Uganda, and Tanganyika (now Tanzania) since 1927, when Tanganyika joined the customs union formed by Kenya and Uganda ten years earlier. Strains on this common market became rather severe in the mid-fifties when Kenya experienced an economic boom, partially based upon the expansion of its trade with Uganda and Tanganyika. The appointment during this period of territorial ministers who were oriented more toward their individual territories than toward East Africa as a whole also introduced divisive forces.

The independence of Tanganyika (1961) and then of Uganda (1962) led to a temporary easing of the overt tensions over the sharing of the benefits of the Common Market among the individual countries, as awareness of the economic conflicts was overshadowed by high expectations of swift strides toward a more comprehensive and integrated economic federation.

At the same time, the arrival of Tanganyika's and Uganda's independence and the approach of Kenya's (1963) brought with it increased activities and programs by the individual governments. These activities presented additional opportunities for conflict in the economic sphere. The attempts by each country to attract new industry (sometimes in covert and sometimes in overt competition with the other members of the Common Market), the negotiation and signing of new trade agreements by Tanganyika on virtually a unilateral basis, and each country's realization that its program for accelerated economic development could well lead it into future balance-of-payments difficulties[1] intensified the centrifugal forces already acting upon the Common Market.

The failure of the attempts to make concrete progress toward an East African Federation added to the economic and other frustrations that led Mwalimu Julius K. Nyerere, in April 1964, to raise the specter of Tanganyika's erecting tariff barriers against Kenya and Uganda and establishing import quotas on their products in order to equalize the imbalance of Tanganyika's trade with them.

Rightly or wrongly, many Ugandan and Tanganyikan leaders, both in politics and the civil service, are convinced that Kenya has benefited disproportionately from the existence of the Common Market. In particular, there is a feeling that Kenya has attracted far more new manufacturing ventures, sometimes at the expense of the other two countries, than would have been possible without the Common Market. Because of the high priority accorded to industrialization by the East African leaders, the competition for new industries is a source of strong divisive pressures.

Sources of Governmental Conflicts over the Location of New Industry

Three areas in which conflicts have arisen among the East African countries in their pursuit of industrialization are as follows:

1. Competition among the countries for potential investors who are considering establishing industries that could be viable in a variety of locations, and that do not require more than one country's market to reach an economic level of pro-

---

[1] Tanganyika and Uganda have favorable trade balances with the rest of the world but unfavorable balances with Kenya. Kenya is in just the opposite position. Many Tanganyikans and Ugandans feel that much of Kenya's development and perhaps even some fiscal profligacy have been financed at Tanganyika's and Uganda's "expense."

duction. Examples of this type of conflict, which has often been satisfactorily resolved by multiple-plant locations or separate company operations, include the production of textiles, beer, and cigarettes.

2. Competition among the countries for potential investors who are considering establishing industries that require protected access to the market of more than one of the countries. (With the growth of direct governmental involvement in industrial investment, the competition in some cases is shifting its emphasis from the courting of individual investors toward attempts first to negotiate intergovernmental agreements on the location of the industry in question and then to find an investor who will join the Government or some quasi-governmental instrumentality in establishing the industry.) Examples of this type of conflict include the protracted and, until recently, unsuccessful attempts of all of the countries to establish a large-scale radio assembly plant and a bicycle-manufacturing factory; the Kenya-Uganda conflict over the establishment of a pulp and paper-making factory;[2] and Tanganyika's inability over a three-year period to conclude the necessary interterritorial agreements that would make feasible a factory for the production of automotive vehicle tires (even though in September 1961 the location of the factory and the name of the company to produce the tires was announced).[3]

3. Conflicts that arise when one country seeks to establish an additional factory in an industry in which other countries have more than adequate productive capacity for the entire East African market. Establishment of the industry in the "have-not" country may require closing the "have-not" country's frontiers to the products of that industry originating in the other countries. Examples of this type of conflict are: the decision of the Tanganyikan Government to establish a cement factory in Dar es Salaam, even though the Kenyan and Ugandan cement factories have more than ade-

[2] See Joseph S. Nye, Jr., "East African Economic Integration," *The Journal of Modern African Studies*, Vol. I, No. 4 (December 1963), p. 475. Mr. Nye's article has been used throughout this paper as a general reference.

[3] The April 1964 "Kampala Agreement," referred to later, included provisions for the location of factories to produce bicycles, radios, and tires.

quate capacity to supply the entire East African market; the similar decision to establish an oil refinery in Dar es Salaam even though Kenya's refining capacity is sufficient for all of Tanganyika's potential requirements, as well as Uganda's; and the apparent decision of the Kenyan Government to move toward self-sufficiency in sugar production, despite the fact that Kenya currently imports the majority of its sugar requirements from Uganda, which has substantial production in excess of its own needs. This move by Kenya allegedly involved a Kenyan Government ultimatum to the major Ugandan sugar interest to establish a factory in Kenya or face the loss of his Kenya market.

Of these three causes of conflict the first is probably the least serious, although it can lead to the individual countries bidding against each other in the form of concessions offered to potential investors. Too great a level of success by Kenya in this competition for investors has led to pressures by Tanganyikan (and, to a lesser extent, Ugandan) politicians for the forced allocation of industry. Such political pressures almost certainly played a major part in the East African Tobacco Company's early decision not to centralize all of its production in one country and in the recent agreement by the company to ensure that production in each country is equal to that country's consumption. Except to the extent that the East African governments may, through such bidding, be "paying" more in the form of concessions for new industries than they would be if the bidding could be prevented and to the extent that the bidding process delays the investment decision, the economic "losses" of this type of competition are not particularly serious. In general, such industries are located in a manner reasonably consistent with comparative advantage and largely where the investors prefer to locate them.

The third cause of conflict, basically the pressure on the "have-nots" to "catch up," can develop into a serious disruptive influence, if the idea of sealing off each country's frontiers to products of the other Market members continues to be extended. The situation may tend to be partially self-correcting, because the traditional prestige industries for which this pressure is greatest are relatively few in number — most notably: hydroelectric schemes, oil refineries, cement factories, and steel mills. However, to the extent that any successful manufacturing enterprise tends to become a prestige industry in the eyes of a "have-not," the pressure to close frontiers may tend to grow rather than to diminish.

The second cause of conflict, the competition among countries for the establishment of new industries that require the market of more than one country, appears to be the area where the benefits of intergovernmental cooperation are clearest and where a relatively small investment in institutional adjustment and reorientation can bear fairly substantial fruits, both in terms of reduced intergovernmental conflict and increased or accelerated industrial development for each of the East African partners.

The Industrial Stalemate

Each East African government interprets one of its major goals to be inducing foreign investors to establish local production units to supply products currently being imported. The current pressures, naturally enough, lead each government to press very actively for the establishment of industries within its own frontiers and to pay relatively little heed to similar attempts by its neighbors — except when two countries are seeking the same industry or wooing the same investor.

As suggested earlier, for industries that are viable in the context of a single country (case 1) these pressures may result in a company being lured from one country to another or being granted greater concessions than are truly needed, or possibly they may cause some delay in the initiation of a project, as the company plays off one country against another. It is doubtful, however, that many new projects of this scale are indefinitely postponed because of the inter-country competition.

The situation is very different where industrial projects that require protected access to the whole East African market are concerned. In this context it is useful to identify two types of potential investors: the foreign manufacturer who is currently selling his product in the local market (the "established marketer") and the potential manufacturer whose product has not been successfully introduced to the market.

The "established marketer" will in general prefer to maintain the *status quo* as long as possible, producing in his current facilities and exporting his products to the East African countries. For a variety of valid economic reasons, it is not unusual for an established marketer to calculate that it is more to his own economic advantage to continue exporting to East Africa, even over a very substantial tariff barrier, than to incur the risks and costs of establishing a factory within the tariff wall. When pressed to undertake local manufacturing, companies in this category frequently have responded that the individual country market is too small, but that a viable operation might be possible if protected access to the entire East African market could be assured (possibly with a somewhat higher external tariff). Although it is somewhat inconsistent with their market position, these established marketers tend to insist that they cannot risk setting up a local plant, unless they are assured that no other company will be allowed to establish a factory until their own facility has become well established in the market. The argument is that some other company will set up an operation in one of the other East African countries under similar — or possibly even better — terms and neither plant will be able to reach a profitable level of operation. Because the established marketers, in general, would prefer to sell to East Africa rather than to manufacture there, the present lack of a system to grant the requested guarantees suits them very well.

The foreign company not established in the market may have a stronger incentive to manufacture in East Africa because local manufacture probably presents the cheapest, and possibly the only effective, way to break into the market. Such a company rightly fears that if it sets up a factory in one country, one of the established marketers will seek to set up a similar plant in another country. Even with some delay in coming into the market, but presumably operating under essentially the same tariff treatment, the established marketer is likely to have sufficient strength in the market place to drive out the other manufacturer, whose product will be new and relatively unknown. At present, the maximum assurance that one market member can provide to a potential investor is that no competing plant will be permitted to start up within its territorial limits and that competing goods will be effectively excluded by high tariffs or other means. Where an industry requires protected access to the whole East African market, these guarantees are clearly inadequate.

In cases where nonestablished companies have displayed a strong interest in opening a factory in one of the countries and the government of that country has approached the other two countries seeking interterritorial agreements that will facilitate the plant's establishment, it is not uncommon for one or more of the established marketers to advance very attractive counterproposals to one or both of the other two countries. The established marketer's proposals will usually call for less tariff protection and possibly even no manufacturing monopoly. This maneuver will frequently result in an indefinite delay as the governments attempt to come to some form of agreement over who will be allowed to produce the product in question. As the delay continues, the chance of the nonestablished company losing interest naturally grows. When it finally withdraws its proposal because of the inability of the initial country to grant the exclusive manufacturing privileges that the investor feels he requires, the established marketer will, in many cases, announce that changes in the market situation or the local political situation or his own company's financial situation or the delay he has experienced in getting agreement from the East African governments has caused him to postpone final action on the project. However, his interest in manufacturing in East Africa "still remains very high, and he is having a very thorough and complete study carried out by his technical experts in preparation for setting up a factory in the near future."

The natural result of this situation is a stalemate, with nonestablished companies being afraid or unable to set up operations, with the established companies exporting to East Africa, and with country A blaming countries B and C for refusing to agree to give (gratis) a monopoly for manufacture of the product in A. Until this "vicious circle" is broken, many opportunities to attract new industries will be wasted.

A Proposal

A fairly small change in the orientation and intent of an existing East African interterritorial organization, the Industrial Licensing Council, might yield a very substantial improvement in the situation just outlined.

The Industrial Licensing Council is composed of the Permanent Secretaries of Commerce and Industry of each country, the Financial and Legal Secretaries of the East African Common Services Organization, one person appointed by EACSO, and two designated by each country. The Council has the power to specify what products may be manufactured in East Africa and which organization will be permitted to produce them. The mechanism for doing so is to add the product to the list of "scheduled articles." The Licensing Council may then grant the privilege of manufacturing such a product through the issue of an "industrial license."

The original intention of the founders of the Council included the use of its licensing powers to direct industries to locations consistent with an over-all East African plan. However, by the time the Council came into operation, this intent had been dropped, and the operations of the Council have in practice been severely restricted. Probably the principal reason for the limited nature of the Council's activities has been the refusal of both Tanganyika and Uganda to support the addition of new industries to the schedule. The majority of the Council's activities have been concentrated on dealing with applications for textile-manufacturing licenses, the remainder of the Council's time being devoted to a short list of other products of relatively small importance as industrial ventures.

In 1961, a British Economic and Fiscal Commission (the Raisman Commission) noted that the licensing procedure "has not achieved the object for which it was established, and now serves very little useful purpose in relation to industrial development in East Africa as a whole."[4] The three subsequent World Bank reports on the individual countries have concurred with this view and have recommended the abolition of the industrial-licensing system. But in 1962 and 1963 Tanganyika mitigated its opposition to licensing and showed signs of a desire to move toward a more dynamic concept of the role of the Licensing Council.

Rather than abolishing the licensing system, I would recommend that the Council be given the mandate to facilitate the establishment of local industry by granting to the individual East African countries the privilege in turn to grant limited-term manufacturing monopolies for East Africa as a whole for specific industries or products. The Council could also serve as a means for facilitating

4 *East Africa, Report of the Economic and Fiscal Commission* (London: H.M.S.O., 1961, Cmnd. 1279), p. 29.

the simultaneous adjustments of the individual countries' tariff structures to encourage the establishment of such industries. The Council currently has the power to act in such a manner; no new legislation would be required.

The procedure would in principle be fairly simple. At the suggestion of one of the members, the Council would deal with the following questions:

1. Should industry X be placed upon the list of "scheduled" industries?
2. If so, for manufacture in which East African country should an industrial license be made available?
3. What uniform tariff and other customs adjustments (if any) should be made so as to increase the attractiveness of the manufacturing opportunity to potential investors?
4. For what length of time should the Council guarantee that no further licenses will be issued?

All decisions of the Council would have to be unanimous.

If such a new orientation of the Licensing Council were acceptable to the individual countries, the following procedure would be appropriate. Each country representative would present the Council with a shopping list of industries that he felt he could attract to his country if he could offer a limited-term manufacturing monopoly. Inevitably, there would be substantial overlap among the lists and a good deal of very tough bargaining. Perhaps, at the end of the session, country A's representative would return home with a list of industries (products) for which the Industrial Licensing Council would agree to issue a manufacturing license within a specified length of time to whichever company is designated by A. (Perhaps some performance standards would have to be set up for the company in cases where the product is of more than average importance to the various countries and imports are to be very severely restricted). Country A would be granted a certain length of time to specify the company to carry out the production, and the company would have to be in production within a specified period. Such a list is unlikely to be a very large one at the end of any single session, because the representatives would be unwise to yield industries to other countries without obtaining tangible concessions in return and because it would, in turn, be unwise to obtain concessions that could not be digested (i.e., projects brought into production) within reasonable time limits.

In order to facilitate the adoption of uniform interterritorial tariff and customs adjustments for scheduled industries that require them, the inclusion on the Council of the Permanent Secretaries of Finance in each of the countries merits consideration. Since the industrial-licensing meetings would essentially be bargaining sessions, increasing the number of members of the Council beyond the present twelve would be undesirable. Consequently, if the Permanent Secretaries of Finance are made Council members, some existing membership category should be excised. In fact, it might be better to limit the Council to two or three members from each country, with each country having one vote. The members might be the Permanent Secretaries of Finance and of Commerce and Industry and possibly one other member from each country (perhaps the head of the largest development corporation in each country).

These suggested powers and procedures for the Industrial Licensing Council would be specifically aimed at increasing the number of type two industries (those requiring more than a single country's market) established in East Africa as a whole. The emphasis would not be on forcefully allocating among the countries factories that would be established in East Africa anyway, but on increasing the number of new factories being set up.

The new orientation of the Licensing Council would not remove the basic conflict over the location of industry (each country would still desire as many factories as possible), but it would give the countries a specific institutionalized mechanism for dealing with the conflict. The opportunity for an established marketer to play one country against another in order to prevent a new factory from being set up by some other company would be greatly reduced, because a definite mechanism for calling his bluff would be available. In fact, a forward-looking approach to the licensing procedure would be for one country to bargain with the other countries for an industry without having specifically committed itself to any potential manufacturer. With a definite license in hand, the country would then be in a position to approach the established marketers with the choice of producing locally or losing much or all of their market in East Africa for a substantial and possibly indefinite period of time. When faced with this alternative, the established marketer is likely to find local production more attractive.

One of the additional fringe benefits of this new procedure should be the increased ability of the Ministries of Commerce and Industry to focus the attention of their staffs on projects of important size and scope. The exercise of deciding which industries should be sought most actively in the bargaining session and the subsequent necessity of meeting a deadline for their establishment, when the limited-term manufacturing monopolies are in hand, would assist the top officials in the Ministries of Commerce and Industry to allocate their time to important projects and to avoid becoming tied up with lower-priority items.

The veto power of each country would protect it from being deprived of an industry that would normally be established without an East African manufacturing monopoly. If country A is certain that an industry under discussion would, if not interfered with, be established in country A, the simple step of refusing to allow the industry to be scheduled would prevent the Licensing Council from distorting the normal workings of economic forces.

Postscript

At the time that this study was being prepared, only fragmentary information was available to the author on the so-called "Kampala Agreement" of April 1964. Although the exact nature of the discussions attended by the Ministers of Finance and of Commerce and Industry of the three countries is still somewhat clouded, it does appear that the Kampala meeting was called at Tanganyika's insistence and arose from Tanganyika's dissatisfaction with the current pattern of industrial growth in East Africa and with the imbalance of trade among the countries. According to a rather guarded statement in the *Tanganyika and Zanzibar Trade Journal* of July–September 1964, the Kampala Agreement provided that Tanganyika would be granted the exclusive right to assemble and manufacture motor vehicle tires and tubes, Landrovers, and radios, and was granted an option to put forward a proposal for assembling lorries and trucks. Uganda was granted exclusive assembly and manufacturing rights to bicycles and nitrogenous fertilizers, and

Kenya was accorded exclusive rights for the production of electric light bulbs. The Agreement included other provisions aimed at redressing the current imbalance of trade among the countries, such as measures for encouraging the reallocation of production by companies with factories in more than one country in order to decrease Tanganyika's interterritorial trade deficit.

Unfortunately, the Agreement appears to have been only a stop-gap measure designed to effect a temporary easing of the pressures arising from the most salient areas of conflict. It has not established a well-defined mechanism for dealing with new problems as they arise. If a more stable instrument for dealing with these conflicts is not developed, it is only reasonable to assume that crises similar to the one that compelled the Kampala meeting will reoccur.

PART III

FOREIGN AID

Michael Roemer's essay on foreign aid and the development plan has that aura of authenticity which is the product of operational experience. In his capacity as a Planning Officer in the Kenya Treasury, Roemer helped prepare and negotiate applications for external aid and also assisted in the preparation of the Six-Year Development Plan. The essay, by sketching the tendencies and criteria of a number of the major aid sources, by proposing a mode of development-plan project analysis with a view to securing foreign aid, and by suggesting ways to package the less pulchritudinous candidates for assistance, is a useful primer for aid administrators in all developing countries.

223

12

FOREIGN AID AND THE
DEVELOPMENT PLAN [1]

Michael Roemer

When the countries of East Africa shed their dependent status, the problem of financing economic development assumed new dimensions. Before independence, virtually the entire development budget or plan was supported by Britain; in fact, the proposed level of support was the determining factor in drawing up plans for development. At the same time, there was great flexibility in using United Kingdom grants and loans. In part, this was because, until recently, they were not tied to United Kingdom exports; and even after this policy changed, the tie was never comprehensive. Of equal importance in terms of flexibility was the fact that Colonial Development and Welfare grants were identified with specific projects only in the very broadest (and often vaguest) sense, while Exchequer loans were not tied to projects at all and could be used as general support for the development budget.

Since independence, this picture has changed in two significant ways. First, the independent countries have undertaken economic planning on a more comprehensive basis, under which British economic assistance is no longer the paramount parameter, though of

[1] This article is based on a paper presented at the University of East Africa's Foreign Aid Conference held in November 1964 at the University College, Dar es Salaam, Tanzania. Proceedings of the Conference are available at the Government Press, P.O. Box 9124, Dar es Salaam.

course it remains an important one. Second, new restrictions have been placed on the use of United Kingdom funds, most notably that they be used more completely than in the past to finance imports from Britain and that they be used for projects more strictly defined than in the past. In view of the increasing rigidity of the tie between British aid and export promotion, the augmented project orientation of that aid, and the national demand for accelerated economic development, the newly independent countries face both a relative shortage of development finance from their traditional source and reduced flexibility in using what is available.

These conditions force them to look for additional sources of overseas development finance. The World Bank and International Development Association, the United States Agency for International Development, West Germany's *Kreditanstalt fur Wiederaufbau*, and a variety of United Nations programs all become not merely the marginal sources of aid they were before independence but vital props for the development plan. And the long-discussed possibilities of aid from the Communist countries must leave the stage of speculation and be considered urgently and realistically. All this places a far greater burden on the department in government responsible for external aid. Financing development demands more knowledge, new techniques, and a high level of diplomatic finesse.

The purpose of this study is to define some of the problems facing the administrator responsible for negotiating external aid in a new independent country and to point to some possible solutions. The context is East Africa and, more specifically, Kenya, for that is the limit of the author's experience in dealing with external aid. But conversations with other practitioners of the novel twentieth-century art of procuring foreign economic assistance indicate that Kenya's problems are far from unique.

Aid Sources and Criteria

The United Kingdom

The first job of the aid administrator is to identify the various sources of aid available to him and to understand the widely differing criteria and terms under which the potential lenders and donors operate. Among the bilateral sources, the most important one for East Africa remains the United Kingdom, which is expected to support over 60 per cent of Kenya's development expenditure during the 1964/65 financial year. Commonwealth Assistance loans are likely to remain not only the most plentiful source of funds but the most flexible as well. Although, as mentioned before, they are to be used principally to finance imports from the United Kingdom, in certain circumstances they can also be applied against local costs. The line will almost certainly be drawn, however, against using these loans to finance imports from countries other than Britain. Commonwealth Assistance loans will not be given as budgetary support, but may be given for projects with fairly broad and loose definitions. While the interest will vary, generally it will fall in the region of $5\frac{1}{2}$ per cent–6 per cent. Repayment is over twenty-five years, including a five-year moratorium.

Another possible British source, particularly for projects with large equipment elements, is the Export Credit Guarantee Department, which is authorized to guarantee loans for the purchase of British equipment; these loans may exceed ten years and will also bear interest in the neighborhood of $5\frac{1}{2}$ per cent to 6 per cent.

The Commonwealth Development Corporation is a third British source, and one which has been extremely active in East Africa. Using funds borrowed from the Treasury, the C.D.C. makes loans for periods as long as twenty years at interest rates at present near 7 per cent; under certain conditions it will also invest through share participation. The Corporation has participated in a wide variety of projects and ventures in East Africa, from housing and municipal water supplies to tea growing and mining. As a development company, its approach is more commercial than are those of other bilateral agencies. The stress is on both profitability — that is, realizable direct benefits — and separate accountability for the undertaking involved. Although loans are often made to non- or quasi-governmental agencies, they usually must be covered by government guarantees.

The United States

For some years, the United States Agency for International Development has taken an active interest in East Africa. Probably the most demanding feature of its loans is that they are in some way tied to the purchase of United States goods. This need not be a direct tie. In fact, A.I.D. has been willing in a few cases to support up to 50 per cent of the local costs of a project; but it now insists that such expenditure be matched by the equivalent value of imports from the United States, whether these are purchased by the government or the private sector. There is no doubt that one major A.I.D. criterion for project selection is the proportion of American import costs to total cost. On large projects, if contractors are involved, they too will probably have to be American. While this may often result in higher expenditure, it may be offset by the willingness of A.I.D. to finance up to 80 per cent of project costs, a higher proportion than for most other agencies.

The loan terms of A.I.D. for East Africa have been generous; they are now at 2 per cent with a ten-year moratorium followed by a thirty-year repayment period. These terms, however, are subject to change each year. The agency prefers to concentrate its loans in a few sectors that it and the recipient government consider to have high priority for development. It also requires more complete documentation than any other lender, usually according to fairly strict standards. This does not always prove to be the burden it could be, as A.I.D. is often prepared to make grants to enable governments to hire consultants, who perform feasibility studies and whose reports serve as formal loan applications. It does mean, though, that a year and often two are required to move from the preliminary application to the completion of a loan agreement.

Western Europe

Of the Western European countries, France and Germany have been the most active aid givers. The French, of course, concentrate on their former colonies and are, for the present, unimportant in East Africa. On the other hand, West Germany has been active in Kenya, Uganda, and Tanganyika. The German aid agency is named *Kreditanstalt fur Wiederaufbau* (K.F.W.), which means Bank for Reconstruction. Although the size and terms of its credits and the rules and policy under which they are given appear to be subject to fairly close ministerial surveillance, K.F.W. still has considerable discretion as to terms and other program features. The Bank has displayed a highly creditable flexibility in its policies. For example, although the aid is for projects only, a given loan can be divided in several ways. Possibly a more important example is the fact that although, theoretically, the loans are intended to cover import content, they are not tied to German imports. In addition, justification for foreign exchange content can be expressed in the broadest of terms, and certification of imports is not a part of the claims procedure. The K.F.W. cannot support 100 per cent of any project, but the proportion of support is open to negotiation. If, as has been the case in Kenya, the level of support is the subject of a side letter and is not in the agreement, it can be varied during the course of project implementation.[2] The typical loan to Kenya is for fifteen years (including a five-year moratorium), and the interest rates vary from $3\frac{1}{4}$ per cent to $5\frac{1}{4}$ per cent, depending on the project being supported.

Several other Western European and certain Commonwealth governments show signs of joining the list of donor nations in East Africa. Although one of these may be able to offer large amounts of credit, most of them will provide comparatively small sums. Their chief contribution may be to finance selected projects in which the major donors show little interest, either because the projects are small or because they do not satisfy certain criteria. Thus, their aid may play a role similar to that of volunteer donors, such as the Freedom from Hunger Campaign or the Oxford Committee for Famine Relief, which have been able to provide helpful, if limited, amounts of assistance.

Communist Bloc Aid

Despite a paucity of operating experience with it, some mention should be made of bilateral aid from the Communist countries. For the most part these donors provide aid in kind, including both technical assistance and equipment. Although this can create many problems, such as the operation and maintenance of equipment that is new to a country, it can also be very effective on particularly large undertakings (witness Soviet aid to Egypt on the Aswan Dam). The Soviet Union has shown a tendency to provide assistance on projects, such as hospitals, which Western aid sources are

---

[2] Of course, it is generically true that the more detail that can be kept out of the agreement proper and relegated to a side letter, the more flexible the lender can be and the easier, from the recipient's standpoint, will be administration.

reluctant to support. Recently, a Chinese offer of a cash grant, apparently untied to any project, has been publicized; this would clearly be a welcome departure from the provision of aid in kind. In addition to the behemoths, several of the Eastern European members of the Bloc seem prepared to offer assistance in various forms. These offers still require considerable exploration.

International Institutions

The most important multilateral source of financial aid is the International Bank for Reconstruction and Development (I.B.R.D.) and its soft-money affiliate, the International Development Association (I.D.A.). The I.B.R.D. combines a good knowledge of and sympathy for the problems of underdeveloped countries with the sober, analytical concern for project viability of a banker. Although it is true that the I.B.R.D. often lends money for projects that, because of the risks involved, would not attract private capital, it is also true that the Bank has never suffered a default. Bank interest rates vary, depending on the market rates at which the I.B.R.D. itself borrows, but are usually in the range of 5 per cent to 6 per cent. Repayment periods also vary, ranging from ten to as many as thirty years, with grace periods as high as five years or occasionally even more.

Projects for which I.B.R.D. finance is sought come under extremely close scrutiny, and no aspect seems too remote for investigation. Bank officials look very closely at the organizational arrangements surrounding the project and at the provisions made to operate and maintain the project after its completion. A preference is shown for self-contained undertakings that can be accounted for separately; if the project earns direct revenues and is supervised by a separate organization (as opposed to a government ministry), so much the better. Power projects or rail and harbor development are good examples. These criteria are not unyielding. They have not ruled out road projects, which usually do not earn direct revenue; nor did they preclude a loan made to Kenya in 1960 in general support of the Swynnerton Plan for agricultural development. The import content of a project is an important selection criterion, for that is the only element the I.B.R.D. can support. In purchasing for projects financed by the Bank, international open tender procedures must be used. As a result, project costs can be kept to a minimum commensurate with the desired quality of materials and equipment. In claiming reimbursement, fairly exacting standards of documentation are required. And the appraisal of a project goes on even after it is accepted, in the form of end-use inspections that determine the success of project implementation.

The International Development Association was established in 1960 to provide money on easy terms ($\frac{3}{4}$ per cent, ten-year moratorium followed by a forty-year repayment period) to countries whose external debt servicing has become a major burden on their foreign exchange resources. The management of I.D.A. is the same as the I.B.R.D.'s, and the Association applies the same criteria and high standards of scrutiny to applications. In fact, the only basis upon which an application can be made to I.D.A., instead of the I.B.R.D., is the credit-worthiness of the applying government; any project that I.D.A. accepts could, in theory, be accepted by the Bank as well, were the country in a more propitious loan-servicing position. The choice between an I.D.A. credit and an I.B.R.D. loan is entirely the Bank's. If the ultimate user of the credit is a nongovernmental organization such as an agricultural credit institution, the money must be re-lent by the government at terms closely approximating those of the original loan. This procedure results in a small profit for the government that it can use as it wishes. Since the I.D.A. is not restricted to supporting the import content of a project, it may be able to provide a much higher level of support than the Bank. This also means that it might consider certain projects that the I.B.R.D. could not because of low import content. The I.D.A. has shown an interest in education recently, particularly in East Africa, and this may turn out to be one of its most important contributions to development in this area.

One United Nations institution, though primarily associated with technical assistance, also is important in the financial-aid field. This is the United Nations Special Fund and in particular its pre-investment surveys. The Fund carries out extensive and consequently costly investigations into major projects that could, if properly documented, attract external aid. Such investigations are usually beyond the means of the country involved, either technically or financially, and the Fund, therefore, is able to play an important role in development financing.

Analyzing the Development Plan

In the ideal procedure for purposes of academic discussion, the aid administrator is presented with a tentative development plan and given the task of finding enough finance to fill the gap between locally available funds (such as government revenues or stock issues) and the target level of government development expenditure. Probably this seldom happens in practice, because, to begin with, knowledge of the available external assistance often influences, as it should, the content of the development plan. Moreover, because of the time involved in negotiating aid, the government must begin the process long before the plan is available. It is useful, however, to understand the ideal procedure, because it involves considerations that apply even when development planning and aid negotiating proceed simultaneously.

Categorizing Projects

The attractors. From the standpoint of the aid administrator, the development plan breaks down into three broad categories of projects: the attractors, the possibilities, and the improbabilities. The attractors are those projects which satisfy the criteria of almost any aid agency. These are, first of all, visible and self-contained projects that lend themselves to separate accounting and organizational arrangements. In addition, without extensive investigation, it is apparent that they offer large and immediate economic benefits. Such projects usually involve major construction, and the period of construction or development is easily distinguishable from the period of operation. They have high import content, which not only provides a fillip for donor-country exports, but also makes for simple disbursement procedures using equipment invoices. Hydroelectric projects probably fit these standards better than any others, but road projects, railway networks, harbor development, and telecommunications networks also tend to fall into this category. Even some irrigation schemes, water supply projects, and industrial plants may qualify.

Although such projects form an important part of any development plan, they probably cannot attract sufficient overseas finance to cover the gap between projected plan expenditure and locally available funds. In Kenya, for example, aid attractors account for about 30 per cent of planned government expenditure over the 1964–1970 period (about 50 per cent if all public sector agencies are included). Local resources will not be sufficient to finance much more than 25 per cent of planned expenditures.

The possibilities. The most difficult and critical job of the aid administrator is to identify and find assistance for those development plan projects which can be classed as possibilities for external aid. These projects almost always have high economic benefits and sometimes have at least moderate import content. But often they are not so easily separable and identifiable as the attractors. The attributes of this group can be best described through examples. Agricultural development projects, which involve extension service staff and credit, have a high priority in Kenya's development plan, yet these have import contents no higher than 25 per cent and are difficult to define as to development (versus operating) period, accountability, and direct benefits. Although education programs do consist of a series of construction projects, often with appreciable import contents, they also involve staff as a major element, and their economic benefits accrue over very long periods and are extremely difficult to quantify. Virtually all housing and health projects suffer from a substantial number of the same deficiencies as aid attractors. The tourist development program often lacks identifiability and coherence, scattered as it is among many small projects under the control of a variety of agencies, some in the private sector. In order to attract aid for these projects, the aid administrator must so organize them as to compensate for their major deficiencies as attractors. This task will be discussed in some detail later.

Improbabilities. The improbabilities are a group of projects largely having to do with internal security, defense, and administration. They include police and army buildings, prisons, administrative buildings, staff housing, and possibly broadcasting facilities. Their main purpose is to create the necessary stability and lay the essential groundwork for development, which most aid agencies tend to regard as the special responsibility of the developing country. However, A.I.D. has displayed considerable interest in the internal security field and may be regarded as a not unlikely donor through its public safety program and the Military Assistance Program, which is actually administered by the Defense Department and only coordinated by A.I.D. with other forms of assistance.

The Time Factor

Once the types of projects in a plan have been identified, two other considerations become important. First, attention must be paid to the time required to secure external finance — probably from nine months to two years, although in some cases claims against expenditure can be made retroactively. In one sense this should be a prior consideration, because the plan should be substantially completed far enough in advance of its starting date to allow considerable progress to be made on aid negotiations before that date. But there is a natural tendency to delay the completion of a plan until the last possible moment, and a concomitant tendency to try to rush a plan into operation as soon as it is completed. This means that the aid administrator is inevitably presented with one emergency job after another and is likely to have several running simultaneously. Alternatively, the aid negotiations may precede the completion of the plan, in which case the plan becomes more of a collection of projects that have been accepted for aid than a comprehensive document of priorities for development. In most cases, the aid administrator is beset by a combination of both tendencies. To the extent that projects without committed funds must be started early in the planning period, untied assistance will have to be allocated to them. This probably means that United Kingdom aid, which usually comes in the form of a block allocation to be applied to specific projects by agreement, or local funds will be used for the urgent projects. This may not be the optimum allocation of the resources available to a country, particularly if, with some time and thought, the project might have been made attractive to an agency for which alternative projects cannot be found, or if additional funds might have been attracted from some other and less flexible source of aid.

Local Financial Resource Requirements

Another consideration is the conserving of scarce local financial resources, the fund source that can be used with the greatest freedom and flexibility. One use for them has already been mentioned; the improbable aid projects. The more of these projects

in the development plan, the greater the strain on local development funds and the greater the demand for external aid to finance
the rest of the plan. A second use for locally available finance is
to provide matching funds for projects partially financed by external aid; a donor will almost never cover 100 per cent of a project.
It is clearly essential to conserve local funds for this purpose, particularly since many potential lenders insist on a substantial allocation of local funds as an indication of the priority attached to
the project by the government. To the extent that aid givers,
particularly the United Kingdom, provide untied grants or loans,
this stimulus to the demand for local funds is reduced. Furthermore, it is sometimes possible to match finance from more than
one aid agency to cover the whole of a single project. The Commonwealth Development Corporation, and *Kreditanstalt fur
Wiederaufbau* have been helpful in this respect, allowing their
loans to be used to cover the balance of a project partially financed
from another source.

Finally, local finance is needed as working capital, to cover costs
of projects before the government can actually draw aid funds
against them. This is particularly important if it has become reasonably certain that a loan under negotiation will eventually be
signed and assurances have been given that reimbursement can be
retroactive. Rather than delay the start of the project, local funds
can be used to get it underway.

Matching Aid Criteria to Plan Requirements

Selecting a Donor

Faced by the requirements of the development plan and armed
with his knowledge of the terms and criteria upon which foreign
aid is available, the aid administrator must attempt to arrange the
most effective match between projects and potential donors. In
the case of the aid attractors, the process is largely mechanical,
although it may nevertheless be quite time-consuming and exacting. It is essential to begin with sound, detailed plans, including
in some cases a complete feasibility study. As pointed out before,
this is the sort of activity that the United Nations Special Fund
will undertake. Obtaining Fund assistance is in itself a lengthy

task. The net result is that three years may elapse before a full report is received and the process of finding aid can begin. In the case of large, complex projects such as irrigation schemes, such a full-scale survey is probably inevitable and necessary. Fortunately, many projects in the attractor class require nothing so extensive. These can be planned quite satisfactorily by government engineers or, if the works organization is understaffed, by consultants hired for the purpose. Many aid agencies will reimburse for the cost of such planning.

In deciding on the source to approach, one major consideration is the type of equipment to be used. If, for example, the project involves road construction and the works organization regularly uses American road equipment and would be prepared to hire American contractors, A.I.D. may be an excellent source. Similarly, if the project requires the purchase of hydroelectric equipment and British companies can provide it at a reasonably competitive price, a loan guaranteed by the Export Guarantee Department may be the most appropriate source for financing a substantial part of the project. Another consideration is the kind of projects that the various agencies have financed in the past. The I.B.R.D. (and now I.D.A.) has financed road projects in East Africa and, being attuned to the requirements there, could probably handle a road application with a minimum of difficulty and delay. The Bank has also financed railway projects all over the world and is a natural source for the East African Railways and Harbors, which has, in fact, applied to the Bank for a loan to buy rolling stock. In general, it is a good idea to use the aid-attracting projects to draw funds from those agencies with the most exacting standards or which tie aid to equipment imports. The attractors can usually satisfy these agencies.

Packaging a Project

The ingenuity of the aid administrator is most strained when he tries to finance the aid possibilities. To make such projects attractive to the aid agencies, they must be designed to have as many attributes as possible of the aid attractors. This is more than just a matter of packaging for appearance. The features that make a project attractive to the donors go right to the core of successful project planning and management. The first step is to identify the project clearly and define its components, relating apparently disparate elements to form a more coherent project than had been conceived before.

This process will be undertaken for the livestock industry in East Africa. At present, each of the three countries has many different, often unrelated, projects to develop the industry, which has certainly not attracted aid from overseas on any important scale. The United Nations Special Fund has agreed to survey the industry and to evolve a comprehensive plan for its development. This plan will, in effect, define a major project, encompassing all the existing elements of livestock development in the region, and it is felt that this project is very likely to attract overseas aid. Similarly, it should be possible to construct a region-wide plan for the development of the tourist industry that would give interested donors something more tangible to focus on than the conglomeration of lodges, parks, and roads that now mark tourist development in each of the countries.

In order to define a project, its duration must be established. Many projects in agriculture and education, which involve large expenditures on staff, can continue indefinitely. If they are conceived in this way, they have little chance of attracting aid. In the case of agricultural extension, the project should last only until the staff has had time to teach the farmers enough to make the scheme or crop-planting program a success. Thereafter, staff costs should either be covered by a charge on the growers or be assumed as a recurrent expense by the government, which will enjoy increased revenues due to the higher taxable farm incomes resulting from the successful project. This is consistent with the principle adopted in private industry, under which certain operating costs are capitalized during the period of plant start-up. On this basis it may be possible to finance agriculture extension through external aid. The World Bank has, for example, financed extension staff in Kenya under the Swynnerton Plan.

Education projects involving the costs of employing expatriate teachers can be considered to end when expatriates are replaced by local teachers. In other words, the period of development is considered to last until the country is self-sufficient in a certain class of teaching manpower. If definite plans for achieving self-sufficiency are formulated, donors such as I.D.A. may include staff costs in education loans. It would probably enhance the application if the teachers involved were particularly scarce, as are local science and technical teachers, and if the expatriates to be covered by the loan were to participate in the training of local replacements.

The Implementing Agency

Once the project has been defined as to its components and duration, the organization responsible for its implementation must be determined. In many cases this may mean establishing an entirely new agency. Separate organizations have many advantages. First of all, in order to establish a new agency it becomes necessary to define its responsibilities, which means, in effect, to undertake the process of project definition discussed earlier. Second, separate accounts must be kept for the organization, with the result that lenders know exactly what they are supporting and reimbursement procedures are simplified. Third, the question of revenue for the organization inevitably arises, and this forces the government to consider ways of making the project self-supporting. This is a worth-while discipline, because it helps to identify the elements of subsidy in a project (for example, the provision of government-paid staff or infrastructure such as roads) and tends to limit the time during which such subsidies are allowed to continue. It also identifies the period during which recurrent expenditures, such as those for extension staff, can be considered a legitimate charge on development. This may also make such costs acceptable to the aid agencies. Fourth, a special organization gives the project a voice of its own, eliminating the danger that the overworked government machinery will in time consider the project less interesting and important, and hence will devote less effort to implementation. Finally, special organizations give all parties concerned with the project, including lenders and the government, a well-defined object for their suggestions, complaints, and supervision.

Kenya has successfully organized its development of a smallholder tea industry by establishing the Kenya Tea Development Authority, a statutory agency that has charge of the planting, collecting, and processing of tea grown on many farms distributed all over the country. The Authority has its own extension staff and operates a fleet of trucks to collect tea from small holdings and deliver it to factories managed for the Authority by private tea companies. All the costs of tea development, except road construction and maintenance, are charged to the Authority. By appropriate charges to tea growers benefiting from its services, the Authority is expected to pay its own way once the planted tea has reached maturity. Under this arrangement, the project has attracted finance from the C.D.C., I.D.A., and K.F.W. to cover its deficits during the development period. It is doubtful that Kenya could on any other basis have interested these lenders in tea development. Similarly, agricultural credit is often organized under a separate company to attract lenders, notably the I.B.R.D. Industrial and agricultural development companies serve much the same purpose, and these have been successful in attracting investments by the C.D.C. and other donors. Companies to develop housing estates and tourism may have potential for attracting new overseas finance to these fields.

The use of semiautonomous agencies should not be viewed as an unmixed blessing. If these proliferate, the government may find it very difficult to retain sufficient control over economic development. Coordination will certainly be more difficult, and duplication of function may result with consequent inefficiency in the administration of development. Separate organizations are not a panacea, and the fields in which they are to operate should be chosen with care. But properly utilized, the semiautonomous agency has a great potential for the implementation of sound development projects and the attraction of additional development aid.

It is evident from the considerations discussed here that the aid administrator, in preparing a project for application to an overseas agency, is directly concerned with the basic elements of sound project-planning. They illustrate that the effective aid administrator must play an imaginative role in project formulation as well as in donor identification. And the measure of his success will be the ability of his government to compete successfully with the scores of other countries seeking aid from the world's limited supply of development funds.

INDEX